THE LIFE AND ADVENTURES OF A QUAKER AMONG THE INDIANS

By Thomas C. Battey

Missionaries and teachers to the Indians played a unique and valuable role on the Western frontier. They were men of peace. And in spite of criticism for interfering with the Indian life style and for attempting to shape them in the image of the white man they often played important roles as mediators in the conflicts between white men and Indian. Frequently the success of their role as both peace-maker and spokesman for the Indian prevented unnecessary bloodshed and helped white authorities to better understand the Indian's point of view. Such a man was Thomas C. Battey – Vermont Quaker, teacher and Indian partisan.

In 1871 after years of teaching in Iowa, Battey accepted a position with the Wichita Agency in Oklahoma as teacher to the Caddo Indian children. He remained there for eight months then moved to the Kiowa Agency in the northern part of the state as field agent as well as teacher.

Known as Thomissey by the Indians he earned their profound respect and friendship such that he was able to travel widely among them always unarmed and frequently alone and never suffered harm. During the Modoc War he succeeded in convincing the Kiowa chiefs to accompany him to a meeting with peace commissioners from Washington. This led to a settlement that kept the entire area from erupting into another bloody and fatal war.

Battey lived with the Indians for three years. During this time he shared all the difficulties and hardships of camp life. He was an intelligent and perceptive observer and noted down many aspects of Kiowa custom and ritual. His journal and letters home form the basis for this narrative originally published in 1875. This volume is a reissue of the 1875 version and does not contain the chapter on the origins of the Modoc War removed from the original manuscript by the Board of the Society of Friends.

Recommended by the Office of Indian Affairs when first issued "as a truthful statement of the customs and habits of the Kiowa Indians" it remains an absorbing and invaluable first person account of Indian life in the 19th century.

Corner House Publishers

SOCIAL SCIENCE REPRINTS

General Editor MAURICE FILLER

Kicking Bird, Kiowa Chief.

THE

LIFE AND ADVENTURES

OF A

QUAKER AMONG THE INDIANS.

BY

THOMAS C. BATTEY.

ILLUSTRATED.

CORNER HOUSE PUBLISHERS
WILLIAMSTOWN, MASSACHUSETTS 01267
1972

REPRINTED 1972

BY

CORNER HOUSE PUBLISHERS

Printed in the United States of America

PREFACE.

In presenting this book to the public, the author lays no claim to literary merit, neither does he intend to bring himself or his labors too prominently before the world. Should anything, however, herein written appear to have the "ring" of egotism, it has arisen from his incapacity to separate himself from many of the incidents narrated. This book has been prepared, in view of the amount of "sensational" literature with which our country is flooded, as a "little drop" among many which go to swell the insetting tide of less exciting, less imaginative, but more healthful, more instructive publications, destined, to some extent at least, to take the place of the former.

The author went not among the Indians as an adventurer, but as an instructor and civilizer; and his aim in this work is to give a truthful and impartial narration of the home life of the Indian, and to exemplify the efficacy of the principles of peace in the life of one, who, for a period extending to years, travelled extensively — many times entirely alone and always unarmed — among different tribes, regarded by the civilized world as savages, and in a land where it was not considered safe for white men to travel, even in companies, without being well equipped with revolvers, knives, and carbines.

Though sensible that he accomplished little while travelling among them as a kind of outside *conscience*, endeavoring to exert a restraining influence over their wild lives, until, broken in health and constitution, he was compelled to forsake the field of labor, yet as his position of instructor in a wild Indian camp gave him an opportunity possessed by few of becoming acquainted with the red man in his rude home, and of studying his nature on his own native plains, he may, perhaps, be held excusable, if not justified, in thus intruding "still another book" upon the reading public.

Thus pacifying his own conscience, the author sends this volume forth to win a position, whether of honor or dishonor, among the thousands which have entered the lists before it.

CONTENTS.

CHAPTER I. PAGE

First Journey to the Indian Country. 9

CHAPTER II.

Account of School among the Caddoes until the Return of the Agent. 27

CHAPTER III.

Extracts from Diary. — Caddo School until the Improvements in the Building. — Visit to Kiowa Boarding-School. — Scenery along the Route. — Guadelupe. — His Speech at Lawrence. — Captain Black Beaver. 35

CHAPTER IV.

Work on the House. — Wichita Grass Houses. — Caddo Houses. — Agent visits Kiowa Camp. — Death of Newahkasset. — Tonquewa Massacre. — Impressions respecting going to live with the Kiowas. — Boy sent out of the Chamber. — Legend of Medicine Bluffs. — Two small Boys quarrel. — Interview with the Mother of one of them. — Death of Nellie Block. — School Report. . . 52

CHAPTER V.

Journey to the Agencies. — Returned Captives. — Clinton Smith. — John Valentine Maxie. — Adolph Kohn. — Temple Friend. — Death of Ten Bears, a Comanche Chief. 76

CHAPTER VI.

First Trip to Kiowa Camp. — Apache Camp. — Dogs. — Return to Agent. — Martha Day, a Mexican Captive. — Return to Camp. — Kicking Bird. — Kiowa History. — Visit with the Agent to Indian Camps. — Kiowa Traditions of the Creation. — Future State. — Horseback. 93

CHAPTER VII.

Opening of the School in the Kiowa Camps. — Adventure with a middle-aged Warrior in my Tent. — Sickness among Children. — Bad Medicine. — Superstitions. — Council. — Removal to Cache Creek. — Osage War Dance. — Kiowa Feast. — Apache Medicine Dance. — Visit from the Pawnees. — Their Reception. — Pawnee War Dance. — Visit to Mount Scott. 115

CHAPTER VIII.

Agent Tatum. — His Administration and Labors. — Release of Mexican Captives. — Council with Kiowas and Comanches relative to Release of Prisoners. — Dismissal of Military Guard. — Death of Dangerous Eagle's Wife. — Sand Storm. — Tarantula. — Centipede. — Scorpion. — Rattlesnake. — Big Bow. — Raiding Party of Comanches stopped. — Visit to Wichita Agency. . 136

CHAPTER IX.

Council. — Thomas Wistar's Labors. — Mexican and Wife. — Change of Intentions respecting Release of Satanta. — Letter to the Agent. — Letter from Washington. — Arrival of Comanche Women and Children. — Captain McClermont. 154

CHAPTER X.

Journey to the Kiowa Camp. — Building of Medicine House. — Situation of Camp. — Medicine Dance, &c. 166

CHAPTER XI.

Military System of the Kiowas. — Buffalo Hunt. — Dressing the Hides for Lodges and for Robes. — Dangers of the Buffalo Hunt. — Sickness. — Petroleum Spring. — Report. — Continue Sick. — Journey Home. 185

CHAPTER XII.

Satanta and Big Tree. — Council. — Demand for five raiding Comanches. — Comanches refuse Compliance. — Agree to join a Party of Soldiers and go into Texas. — Comanche Horses stolen by Whites from Texas. — Journey to Kiowa Camp. — Medicine. — Consternation in Camp. — Telegram renewing Demand for five Comanche Men. 196

CHAPTER XIII.

Agent's Message to the Kiowas. — Night on the Plain. — Lone Wolf's Camp. — Lone Wolf's Speech. — The Return of the Warriors. — Interview in Kicking Bird's Camp. — Kicking Bird's Speech. 215

CHAPTER XIV.

Visit to the Kickapoo Camp. — Camp among the Mountains. — Kickapoos. — Return to Kiowa Camp. — White Wolf. — Nephew of Kicking Bird shot at by White Men. — Texan Desperadoes. — Breakfast with an old Kiowa Warrior. — Mules stolen by Comanches and recovered by Kicking Bird. — Death of Stumbling Bear's Grandson. — Lone Wolf's Son killed in Mexico. . 232

CHAPTER XV.

Religious Feelings. — An Instance of the Overruling of Providence. — Singular Weather. — Captain Black Beaver's Speech. — Visit to the Wichita Agency. — Stereoscopic Views in Kiowa Camp. — Murder of a Surveyor. — Trading for Ammunition. — Sulphur Spring. 246

CHAPTER XVI.

Visit of the Executive Committee. — Council at the Wichita Agency. — Thomas Wistar's Speech. — J. E. Rhoads' Speech. — Other Speeches. — Similar Council at the Cheyenne Agency, and at that of the Kiowas and Comanches. — Start for Caddo. — Adventure at the Washita, and Return. 263

CHAPTER XVII.

Journey to Kiowa Camp. — Night at White Wolf's Camp. — Comanches steal Kicking Bird's Horses. — Tour with three Kiowa Braves. — Killing Buffalo. — Breaking the Wild Horse. — Mountains. — Soil. — Mesquite Timber. — Return to Camp. — Comanches. — Wild Bees. 275

CHAPTER XVIII.

Kicking Bird's Interview with the Agent in his private Office. — Woman's Heart's Stormy Visit. — Kiowa Council. — Kicking Bird dejected. — Interview with Kicking Bird at the Trading-House. — The Matron and Seamstress leave the School, &c. . . 290

CHAPTER XIX.

The Comanche Medicine Man. — Depredation on Agency Stock. — Discouragement of the Kiowas. — Interview with Kicking Bird. — Pen-ha-teth-kah's and Quirtsquip's Band return. — They report other Comanches and Cheyennes on the War-Path. 302

CHAPTER XX.

Leave the Work on Account of poor Health. — Capture of the Supply Train, and Murder of the Men. — Adobe Walls. — Kiowas not engaged in these Depredations. — Register their Names. — Meeting with the Caddoes. — Attempt of Cheyennes on the Wichita Herds. — Murder of the Wood-Cutter at Fort Sill. — Lone Wolf and his Band become hostile. — Conclusion. 309

APPENDIX.

Social Life and Relations of the Indians. 319

ILLUSTRATIONS.

I. KICKING BIRD, Kiowa Chief (Frontispiece).

II. HORSEBACK, Comanche Chief.

III. BIG BOW, Kiowa Chief.

IV. KIOWA BRAVE and WIFE, Lone Wolf's Daughter.

V. SATANTA, Kiowa Chief.

VI. BIG TREE, Kiowa Chief.

VII. KIOWA WOMAN, Big Tree's Sister.

VIII. KIOWA GIRLS.

These portraits are engraved from actual photographs, taken from life, by Wm. S. Soule, who spent some years among the Indians as a photographer, and is prepared to fill orders for photographs of Indian celebrities, at No. 363 Washington Street, Boston.

Office of Indian Affairs, Central Superintendency.

LAWRENCE, KANSAS, 8th Month, 16, 1875.

THIS book is recommended to the public as a truthful statement of the customs and habits of the Kiowa Indians; the information of the writer having been obtained by an actual experience, during a residence of eighteen months, or thereabouts, with them, moving as they moved, and camping whenever and wherever they camped.

His services and beneficial influence over these savages, formerly of the most warlike and dangerous, while appreciated by those having charge of Indian Affairs, can probably never be fully recompensed by the government.

Broken constitution and loss of health are his results. But these Indians have been made to understand that they have friends among their pale-faced brethren, anxious to do them good, and that their "Great Father," at Washington, is disposed to deal justly with them. And it is worthy of note that "Kicking Bird's" band of Kiowas (with whom THOMAS C. BATTEY labored) remained peaceable and loyal to the government during the Indian War of 1874, in the Indian Territory.

Very respectfully,

CYRUS BEEDE,

Chief Clerk.

INTRODUCTION.

An opening presenting, early in the spring of 1871, for engaging to an Indian agent, in the south-western part of Indian Territory, as teacher of an Indian school, I accepted it, and left home, early in the tenth month of that year, and taught a school among the Caddoes, on the False Washita River, for eight months. Of my labors there, my journeys to and from there, and my subsequent life among the wild Kiowas, the following brief narrative — compiled from a diary kept at the time — will, it is hoped, prove interesting. Though not written by a hunter or a frontiersman, and consequently devoid of wild and thrilling adventure, — which might engage the attention for a time, fire the mind with excitement, but leave nothing permanently instructive, — it may yet contain many incidents of general interest, and afford pleasant entertainment to the reader.

It was more with the view of instruction than excitement that these memorandums were made at the time, and which now induces their publication. A life of nearly three years among those people, — much of the time living among them in their lodges, moving as they moved, wandering in all their wanderings, and living upon their unwholesome food, — while it may be devoid of the exciting scenes, hair-breadth escapes, and daring deeds incident to frontier life, may yet afford food for thought, and incidents of instructive import.

I now offer to the public the narrative of my life among them, with such thoughts and reflections as arose from time to time, — though I was not able to accomplish much, or to see my desires fulfilled respecting them, — with a hope that it may have a tendency to remove at least some of the many prejudices against these wild tribes, and open the way in the hearts of others to labor in this field of Christian benevolence, to save from annihilation this interesting, but fast-perishing race.

LIFE AMONG THE INDIANS.

CHAPTER I.

FIRST JOURNEY TO THE INDIAN COUNTRY.

HAVING received intelligence of a party being about to leave Lawrence, Kansas, for the Cheyenne Agency, and it being an almost indispensable consideration to have company, especially in the latter part of the journey, where, for several hundred miles, there are no settlements, — the country being entirely an unsubdued wilderness, traversed by outlawed desperadoes and roving bands of Indians, — I left my home and family on the second day of the tenth month, 1871, in order to join them. On account of the direction of my line of travel, the connections were imperfect, and I was delayed fifteen hours before reaching Lawrence, causing me to miss joining the party at that place. Pushing forward, I overtook it at Emporia, where arrangements were made for the long journey, by wagon train, for the agencies. We left that place on the 6th, J. J. Hoag being wagon-master and superintendent of the train.

Before leaving this place, we were reminded of our proximity to the borders of civilization, and the character of the region we should now have to traverse, by the breaking open and robbing of the post office, from which six hundred dollars in money, besides the registered letters, were abstracted.

A German laborer also, who, according to frontier custom, scorning to seek lodging in a house, lay down by the coal-house near the Junction depot for a night's repose, was attacked by two men, who knocked him on the head with a revolver, and demanded his money. He, being rather thick-headed, was not stunned by the blow, and, springing up suddenly, threw both of his assailants to the ground, thereby freeing himself from them, when, perceiving one of them in the attitude of shooting, he ran towards a light, which proved to be at the house where our party was quartered. His head was badly gashed and bruised.

The journey from Emporia to Newton, some eighty miles, was accomplished in three days. The first sixty or sixty-five miles we followed up the valley of the Cottonwood, a fine stream of water flowing through a beautiful valley of rich, arable land, bounded at first by rolling prairies, afterwards, as we advanced towards the head of the stream, by bluffs containing immense quantities of magnesian limestone of an excellent quality for building purposes. Several small towns are springing up in this valley, through which the Santa Fe Railroad is laid, and is now in running order to Newton.

The latter part of the way was over high prairies, or plains, of thin, poor soil, incapable of enduring either wet weather or drought, being of a dense, heavy clay; yet the occasional cabins of the homesteaders, though few and far between, gave indications of the approaching tide of civilized life.

On these prairies I saw the first drove of Texas cattle, consisting of about five hundred head, had my first experience of camp-life and sleeping on the lap of Mother Earth, with no other canopy than that afforded by the starry vault above, unless at times we may have found the leafy crown of some spreading tree, under which to unfold our blankets for a night's repose. It was here, also, that I obtained my first taste of buffalo beef, having procured some from a hunter.

We arrived at Newton on the morning of the 9th, where our train was increased by two wagons and two men, making it to consist of five wagons and ten persons, all told.

Newton is a town of about three hundred houses, and has sprung up in the incredibly short time of five months. Eight months before this there was no human habitation within about thirty miles of it. Being the present terminus of the Atchison, Topeka, and Santa Fe Railroad, it is the point of shipment from whence the Texas cattle are sent east. Immense trains, loaded with cattle, leave daily for different eastern points: the stock-yards are necessarily extensive, and the business carried on heavy. Being situated on the very outskirts of civilization, it naturally becomes the nucleus to which the most vile and desperate characters — outlaws, gamblers, and desperadoes, horse thieves, and murderers — are gathered; as a consequence, crime, drunkenness, and its attendant evils are common, and are not concealed. Almost every night has its row, and murders are of frequent occurrence.

A woman who lives here, and whose husband works in the lumber-yard where we were loading some wagons, told us that they had lived here but two months, and in that time there had been twelve murders committed in the town; several other persons had been carried away from gambling and drinking saloons with broken heads and other wounds, of whose death or recovery she had not heard. In going to the post office I scarcely saw a man who had not a bowie-knife and at least one revolver dangling from his waist, while the most horrid oaths and imprecations, even from the lips of women, constantly assailed my ears as I walked in the street.

Being obliged to remain here over night, we went out, and made our camp about a half mile from the town, and established a night-watch, in order, if possible, to prevent our horses and mules from taking too abrupt a leave before we were in readiness. Camp was visited no less than three times during the night by prowling marauders, who, being promptly challenged, made some excuse for their visit, and withdrew.

Wichita, where we arrived on the morning of the 11th, and where we recruited our provisions for crossing the plains, is situated on the east bank of the Arkansas River, in a broad valley of exceedingly rich soil, where good water is easily obtained by digging, and bids fair to be a place of considerable importance, being surrounded by an excellent country, which only awaits the tide of immigration to become one of the most productive parts of the west. But few homesteaders' claims as yet are taken in this lovely valley. This place is named from the Wichita Indians, who, with a portion of the Caddoes, remained loyal to the government during the late rebellion, and were driven from their homes in the south-west by the more civilized Indians, many of whom, having become possessed of negro slaves, sympathized with the Confederate States, and made war upon those who remained loyal. The latter fled to this place, and, making their camp here, remained until after the close of the war, when they returned to their country, in the south-western part of Indian Territory.

Wichita is nearly as large as Newton, about thirty miles from it, and eighteen months of age. It does not appear to have as extensive a business, on account of not being located on any railroad line, though there is a branch line in progress of construction from Newton, which, when completed, will be likely to remove most of the cattle shipping to this place.

From Wichita to Caldwell — near the boundary line between Kansas and Indian Territory — the country is a rolling prairie, crossed by numerous streams of water, and containing much good, deep soil, interspersed with considerable that I should consider thin, poor, and washy. Between these places we encountered a severe sand-storm, which compelled us to seek the shelter of some timber skirting Slate Creek. This storm was succeeded by rain the next day, so that we were again obliged to lie by under the lee of some sand-hills on the Chisaspia. We met, in three droves, about three thousand four hundred head of Texas cattle, and finally camped on Fall Creek, about a mile from the south line of Kansas, on the 14th, about sundown, nearly fifty-five miles from Wichita.

Early in the morning of the 15th we crossed Bluff Creek, and entered the Territory. From the bluffs overlooking the creek from the south, an extensive view is obtained of the valley to the north-west and west, exhibiting many miles of beautiful undulating country. Here I took my last look at Kansas.

This forenoon we passed several small towns of prairie-dogs, and saw several antelopes at a distance. Chow — a young Arapahoe, who formed one of our party — said he could see buffalo; but my poor eyes could not see them.

After dinner I sat down to write in my diary, and, consequently, fell some distance behind, when, from the shouting and motioning of some of the party, I conceived that there might be some danger ahead, and hurried up nearly as fast as possible, it being up a slope. I was somewhat out of breath when I came up with the hindermost wagon, just in time to clamber upon it before entering a drove of Texas cattle, consisting of about two thousand head. I had not thought of their being undomesticated, and that it was dangerous for footmen to fall in their way, which really is the case. We soon after met with another drove, consisting of twelve hundred head. About two o'clock we entered upon a community of prairie-dogs, miles in extent. These animals belong to the marmot family, are herbivorous and burrowing. They are about one foot in length, of a yellowish-brown or pale fawn color, and full of life and activity. The dirt thrown out of their burrows forms considerable mounds around the entrance to them, and, occurring at tolerably regular intervals, has suggested the name of towns. A small owl burrows with them, as does also the large yellow rattlesnake. I cannot say whether this latter is a welcome guest in their burrows, or tolerated as a necessary nuisance, from their inability to expel him from their habitations; but, from the fact of his maw sometimes containing a young dog, I am inclined to the latter opinion, while the snake undoubtedly enjoys a kind of complaisant satisfaction in the riotous living thus unwillingly yielded him by his four-footed friends. The owl, however, I am inclined to think, lives on friendly terms with the dog, and may act the part of a scavenger, ridding the burrows of whatever may be offensive. These dogs appear to be all the time in motion, — running, frolicking, barking, jumping, and plunging head first into their holes. I was much interested with the little fellows.

We did not get past this community until nearly night. In the mean time we saw several buffaloes, at the distance of half a mile or more; they being the first I had ever seen in a wild state, of course awakened no small degree of interest. Chow left, a little before going into camp, in pursuit of buffalo, shot one twice, but it growing dark, he did not get it.

The next morning, after crossing the Salt Fork of the Arkansas, we found ourselves in the midst of thousands of these animals. Those near by appeared to be moved with a desire to get farther from us, and were running, not, as one might suppose, whichever way fear may have led, but following, in immense herds, some chosen leader, in a heavy, rolling flight, unlike the movements of any other animal; not apparently rapid, and yet not occupying much time in putting a safe distance between them and the objects of their fear, when they, as well as those more remote, betook themselves to quiet grazing, or rolling in their wallows.

Such a congregated mass of animal life I had never before witnessed, and the scene was not only striking and novel, but bewildering and exciting. Far as the vision extended over the wide-spreading expanse of the plains, these shaggy-headed, huge-bodied, clumsy, and uncouth-looking quadrupeds were running, rolling, or grazing, in all the freedom of their native wildness, in such immense herds as to defy computation.

Miles beyond miles were covered with them, while, upon close observation, the long level line of the distant horizon proved to be a moving mass of life. In the course of the morning we met, in two droves, about three thousand two hundred head of Texas cattle. These droves, large as they were, could be comprehended, — seen over, around, and beyond, — while the immense herds of buffalo appeared to be limitless, both in extent and number. The noise of their tread, and the low, moaning sound of their breathing, and perhaps bellowing, — though I could not satisfy myself as to the latter, — sounded like distant thunder. It is true that near by there were spaces of prairie of some extent unoccupied by them; but, in looking off at a distance, they appeared to cover the plains.

Our men obtained several shots at antelopes and buffaloes, but without success, until stopping for dinner, a cow and calf were grazing but a short distance from the place where we halted. One of our men, by following the bed of the creek, and keeping a high bank between himself and the cow, crept up close enough to shoot the calf. The cow not taking to flight, as was expected, but continuing to stand on the defensive, was also shot; and by cutting out the hams, tenderloins, and tongues, we had a supply of good meat. The calf was apparently four or five months old, and measured four feet and four inches in girth. Soon after.

Chow, who had gone out early in the morning in order to replenish our larder from some of the immense herds around us, came in loaded with choice pieces, such as tongue, tenderloin, &c., having killed four buffaloes.

These plains are not level; at the same time the slopes are long, so that large tracts of country come within the scope of vision at a time, and the visible horizon is mostly an unbroken plain.

The 17th we left camp just as the sun was throwing his first rays upon us. One of our party, having started out some time before in order to shoot game, had shot a large, fierce-looking buffalo so as to break his back. When we came up we found him in a perfect rage of terror and anger, though he could not raise his hinder parts from the ground. His will was good to have shown us that he was not to be approached with impunity, but that from some cause, no doubt mysterious to himself, his physical organization refused obedience to his will. The wild flashing of his eye, gleaming with rage and terror, the ominous shake of his enormous head, with his furious efforts to raise himself upon his feet, admonished us that our safety depended more upon his inability to harm us, than any disposition of his wild, untamed spirit. Chow would go up to him, seize him by the horns, and laugh at his calamity, as though he could understand him; telling him his medicine was strong, but not quite equal to his present need, and now too late to make more.

Several bullets were shot through his lungs, aimed at

his heart, while he still maintained his position upon his fore feet. Chow continued to talk to him about his strong medicine, pulling his head around by the horns, while he made efforts to plunge upon him, and teach him a lesson on the propriety of catching a wild buffalo bull by the horns. At length the Indian put an end to the scene by shooting him through the heart, upon which he settled over, and yielded up his life. He measured seven feet and two inches in girth. Another was soon killed, and their tongues cut out, while the carcasses were left on the ground, food for the coyotes and buzzards, of which there are great numbers on these plains. We passed several other buffalo carcasses, which had been left in the same manner, — killed by some one just that he might say he had killed a buffalo; and thus are they, year by year, growing fewer and fewer, through this means, in connection with the immense slaughter by the Indians, and it is not improbable that before many more revolving seasons they will be numbered with the extinct races of the past.

Before noon, in passing a ridge, as we came by the head of a deep ravine, or cañon, a herd of some twenty antelopes came running over the ridge, and, circling around our wagons, came close to us, stood and looked at us for a short time, with an air of awakened curiosity, then very gracefully took to flight over the ridges, and disappeared from view. They are very beautiful animals, resembling the deer, but smaller. They are equally graceful in form and movement, and more pleasing in color, having considerable white on their flanks, sides, and haunches.

One peculiar characteristic of the antelope, notwithstanding his proverbial fleetness, renders him an easy prey to the hunter. He seems possessed of an uncontrollable curiosity, which leads him to approach and examine any strange object which may attract his attention. The hunter, availing himself of his knowledge of this trait, partially discovers himself to him, and suddenly drops into the grass, or a buffalo wallow, out of sight. The curiosity of the antelope is awakened, and he commences an approach, not in a direct line towards the object, but in diminishing circles around it, until, coming within short range, he falls a prey to the hunter.

Soon after, on a long slope, we passed an immense herd of buffaloes lying at their ease, and composedly chewing the cud in the sun: the sight was pleasing, — hundreds, if not thousands, of these lordly brutes gently ruminating, in quiet and peaceful enjoyment, on their own native pastures.

We were not out of sight of buffalo until nearly night, when we came to a piece of low, shrubby timber, perhaps from twelve to fifteen or twenty feet in height, called "Black Jacks," near which we encamped, and were much annoyed by wolves, which continued prowling and howling about our camp throughout the night.

After this we saw but two more buffaloes, the plains

became broken, and the soil somewhat better, especially between the Cimeron, or Red Fork of the Arkansas, and the Kingfisher, but was more broken and of poorer soil nearer the Cheyenne Agency.

The Cimeron, though a long stream, rising in the mountains of Colorado, flowing so far through a country where the annual rainfall is light, is but a small stream comparatively, except when swollen by the melting of the snows among the mountains near its source. At the time of its spring rise it is nearly half a mile wide, and becomes a formidable obstacle in the way of travel, not only on account of the water, but the sandy character of its banks and bed. But now, though the sand was quite an obstruction, I walked across it almost dry-shod. The water is not only impregnated with salt and alkali, but also with iron.

Our party killed several wild turkeys and geese; one of the latter measured five feet and ten inches in the spread of its wings. We arrived at the Cheyenne Agency about the middle of the afternoon of the 19th, having been fourteen days on the road from Emporia, in which we had travelled about two hundred and eighty miles.

The Cheyenne Agency is situated on the north side of the North Fork of the Canadian River, west of the ninety-eighth meridian of west longitude, in the midst of a broad and beautiful bottom. But few Indians were at the Agency, they having mostly gone out on the fall buffalo hunt. The agent, B. Darlington, was putting up a large mission school-house, for the benefit of the Cheyennes and Arapahoes. These Indians have but recently been removed to the Territory from their former homes in Colorado, from whence they had been driven by the tide of immigration, which immediately followed the discovery of gold and silver in the vicinity of Pike's Peak, and their lands were thus wrested from them without their consent. This leading to the committal of some outrages, terms of a treaty were agreed upon, by which a reservation was set apart for them on both sides of the Arkansas River, in the state of Kansas. This treaty was never ratified by Congress, and they for several years were left without any land they could call their own. Being thus deprived of their lands, they committed some depredations upon the settlers, which resulted in the treacherous massacre of Sand Creek, and their ultimate removal to the Territory, where they at present reside, living mostly at peace, though not satisfied with their removal from Kansas and Colorado.

Perhaps this Sand Creek massacre should receive more than the passing notice I had intended giving it; and I will just state here, that in the summer of 1864, some depredations and robberies were committed by the Cheyennes and Arapahoes upon settlements in Colorado, their former home, from which they had been driven, and for which they had not been compensated. In consequence of these outrages, the Cheyenne village of Cedar Bluffs was attacked by United States troops, and between twenty and thirty Indians killed, and as many more wounded. Petty depredations were continued until fall, when the Indians, becoming tired of hostilities, desired peace, and applied to Major Wynkoop, commander at Fort Lyon, to negotiate a treaty. He ordered the Indians to assemble about Fort Lyon, under his assurance of safety and protection. They accordingly assembled, about five hundred men, women, and children, under the charge of a chief who had all along opposed hostilities with the whites. While here, in a defenceless condition, under promise of protection from a commissioned officer of the United States army, Colonel Chivington, at the head of a company of United States troops, was permitted to surround, and slaughter without mercy, the whole band. This inaugurated an Indian war, which, as has been stated, withdrew eight thousand troops from those engaged in suppressing the rebellion, cost the government about thirty millions of dollars, at the small loss to the Indians of not over twenty men killed.

After remaining over night at this Agency, which really seemed like an oasis in a desert, I started on, with an ox train, to complete my journey to the Wichita Agency, the point of my destination. In the afternoon met with Jonathan Richards, the agent for the Wichitas, who was on his way to Lawrence, on business connected with his Agency. After a few minutes' conversation with him, I journeyed on, crossed the main Canadian, which is a large stream, not far from three fourths of a mile in width, but at this time so reduced as to be but a few steps across. The same remarks will apply to this river that were made respecting the Cimeron. Encamped for the night near George Washington's, a Caddoe chief. The morning of the 21st, after breakfasting and getting the cattle yoked, our wagon-master, in order to help over the sand-hills which lie between this point and the Agency, concluded to take five yoke of oxen into his teams, which Washington had promised to send to the agent. They had been worked, but having been for some time idle, true to the instincts of the undomesticated Texas cattle, they had become nearly as wild as ever, and had to be caught with the lasso by a Mexican employed on the place. This was very dexterously done, but after being caught the difficulty was far from being ended. Some of the more docile ones submitted readily to the yoke, while those that were more wild would plunge at the men, charging with all the strength and spirit of their wild natures; but, by keeping the rope with which they had been lassoed wound around trees, they were brought up before reaching the objects of their fury, causing the strong ropes to crack again, while they themselves would be thrown clear over their heads, upon their sides or backs, by the violence of the charge. Though thus brought up, and thwarted in their object, the charge was again and again renewed; but they were always arrested in time to prevent a full appreciation of the sharpness of their enormous horns.

This exciting business detained us for several hours, so that we did not get started until nearly noon, and, it becoming wet in the afternoon, we made but little progress, and went into camp early.

Our train consisted of eight wagons, fastened two together, making four teams; the foremost wagon of each two is called the *lead*, and the hindmost the *trail*, wagon. Every team in this train consisted of five yoke of oxen except one, and that of six. Our course lay through a very hilly and brushy country, belonging to the Wichita and Caddoe reservation.

On the 22d, after deliberately considering the subject, — the tedious slowness of the train, the shocking profanity of the drivers, notwithstanding their kindness to me, — I made up my mind to leave them, and pursue my journey on foot and alone, it being about twenty-three miles to the Agency. Accordingly I tied up my blankets, left them, with my victuals box and satchel, in the wagon I had occupied, and leaving the train to come leisurely on, proceeded on my solitary journey. The day becoming fine, and feeling well and hearty, I made good progress, over shrubby sand-hills, through valleys rich and beautiful, though not very plentifully supplied with water, arriving at the Agency a little after two o'clock P. M.

The Wichita Agency is situated on the bench land, or second bottom, north of the Washita River, at the foot of high, rocky bluffs, in one of the richest and most beautiful valleys of the south-west. Thus was this long and tedious journey finally accomplished, with feelings of thankfulness, though I had no friend to welcome my arrival. All with whom I met were entire strangers ; yet it was pleasant once more to find myself among a civilized people, however few or remotely situated from the rest of the civilized world. The third day after my arrival, the train I had left arrived with my luggage.

CHAPTER II.

ACCOUNT OF SCHOOL AMONG THE CADDOES UNTIL THE RETURN OF THE AGENT.

On my arrival at the Agency I found a small school had been in operation three weeks, under the care of A. J Standing, with from six to eight Indian children in attendance. A small room over the commissary, in the same building in which the school was taught, being set apart for my use, I occupied a few days in cleaning it out, fitting it up for a sleeping apartment, putting up a rude bedstead, visiting the school in order to make myself familiar with the scholars, before taking charge of them, in accordance with instructions left by the agent on departing. I took charge of the school on the 31st of the tenth month, 1871, six scholars in attendance, and continued it as a day school until the 10th of the eleventh month following, with but little variation, — some days more scholars than others, but at no time exceeding nine. Most of these, living at the distance of four or five miles, remained at the school-house through the week, sleeping on the ground, by the side of a log or fence, or anything that would afford a wind-break.

A Cherokee woman, who lived in the yard, cooked two meals a day for them.

At the end of this time, the weather becoming inclement, I felt that there was a necessity for immediate arrangements being made for the better accommodation of the children, or the school would have to close, as it could not be expected of the pupils, either that they could come from home every day, or continue to lodge, as they had been doing, in the open air. There being several rooms in the commissary, one of which was occupied as the school-room, others containing stores and annuity goods, I conceived the idea of changing the place of some of these things, and fitting up the building so as to board and lodge the scholars. But the agent being absent, and not having had an opportunity of conferring with him and ascertaining his views and plans, I could not know whether he would approve of the project, or would be able to carry out the design if he should approve it. I conferred with A. J. Standing, who heartily entered into my views, and we together consulted with W. H. H. Howard, the acting agent, who left us at liberty to adopt any measure which we thought would conduce to the advancement of the school, provided we would take all responsibility of the undertaking upon ourselves; and I accordingly dismissed the scholars with instructions that they should not return until the fourth evening, when I should have made arrangements for them to sleep and eat in the house — but two school days being thus lost. We then went to work and removed upwards of twenty tons of flour from a room adjoining the school-room: the acting agent had tables and benches made, and it was fitted for a dining-room. Another room adjoining this we appropriated for a kitchen, and the Cherokee woman was installed as cook. One small room up stairs was fitted for a sleeping apartment for the girls, and a larger one for the boys. Bed-ticks were made and filled with hay for the girls' apartment, while the beds for the boys were made by spiking scantling to the floor, for the head and foot, filling in between them with hay, and covering with wrapping blankets, — a thin sleazy blanket used to protect annuity goods during transportation; these latter were secured in their places by nailing them to the scantlings. A quantity of annuity blankets completed the beds. Gunny sacks were crammed into the openings, to prevent the too free ingress of the wind: dishes, knives, forks, spoons, and combs, were procured, the blackboard slated, and we were in readiness against the time set for the return of the scholars. A. J. Standing and myself, having done most of the work, had been kept very busy.

Some of the scholars came back, on the evening of the 14th, prepared for the opening of the school, in its new capacity the next day.

In thus fitting up a portion of the old commissary and opening a boarding-school, during the absence of the agent, without an opportunity of conferring with him on the subject, I felt that I had assumed a responsibility which might expose me to censure, if nothing more; but as I had deliberately weighed the subject, and felt no condemnation, I was satisfied as to its expediency, trusting that it might be, as the event has proved, the beginning of a great benefit to this people.

I doubt whether I should have undertaken it alone; but finding a hearty co-operator in the person of A. J. Standing, who entered into the work and plans with energy and zeal, not only as an assistant, but offering valuable suggestions in the arrangements, justice to him demands that I should honorably ascribe to him the merit he deserves, and my appreciation of the faithfulness with which he entered into the spirit of the work, and performed the different duties which fell to his share in its accomplishment.

The school was opened as a boarding-school, with eleven scholars, on the 15th of the eleventh month (November), 1871, and gradually increased in numbers until no more could be accommodated in the building. It had been previously supplied with sets of school charts, illustrated with the figures of animals and other objects; also a number of slates, writing-books, readers, &c. We could make no use of the latter for some time, at least to advantage, and there were no maps to be had in the country. Though I might be regarded as an old teacher, yet here among these wild children, of a strange language, with no one to interpret, I felt myself to be indeed a novice, and had many things to learn, many plans to adopt, which are seldom put in practice among civilized scholars, who understand the language of the teacher, and to some extent know, from home instruction, the nature, use, and advantage of schools before entering them.

Here, however, the teacher must get down to the very foundation of knowledge, begin at the very beginning, and work his way up through the double process of teaching the spoken as well as the written language, — adapting his system of instruction to their crude comprehensions, making use of the things they know to teach them the things they do not know.

Although I do not profess that I adopted the best system of instruction that could be devised, yet, as it proved eminently successful, I will give a brief synopsis of the course pursued.

The school was divided into classes of from four to eight, and each session was opened with some concert exercise, such as repeating the names of the numerical figures, previously made upon the blackboard. Afterwards, when these had been learned, the multiplication table made a good exercise. Then, having drawn upon the blackboard the picture of some animal with which they were familiar, I would place its English name in Roman characters over it. Upon their first seeing it, they would give its Caddo name, which I would put under it. Then, while one class was exercising at the reading charts, all the other scholars were employed in drawing pictures of this animal, and printing its names upon their slates, — thus keeping them busy; also learning the English names of animals, as well as acquiring the use of the pencil. After exercising each class at the charts as long as it was thought best, they were taught to count in English on the fingers or counting-frame.

During the fore part of the term, I occupied myself, between school hours, in constructing and painting a set of "outline maps," which employed my spare time for nearly two months. When completed, I commenced making pictures, on the blackboard, of animals not found in America, and exciting their curiosity as to what they were, and the reason they had never seen them, viz., that they lived in a country on the other side of the "great water," of which they had heard their old men talk. Then, introducing the map of the world, I explained to them what it represented and its different parts, pointing out the country in which we live, the ocean, or "great water," the country that particular animal represented on the blackboard inhabits, and proceeded to explain the different divisions of land and water, as delineated on the map. I gave them an idea of the magnitude of the different countries and oceans, &c., from the distance they could travel in a day, and the number of days it would take to go across. Their interest was thus awakened in the study of geography, and they made rapid progress in acquiring geographical knowledge, as well as that of the English language, of numbers, and of the different kinds of animals inhabiting the different parts of the earth. They manifested an interest in the knowledge they were acquiring, which I had seldom seen equalled among civilized pupils, except in individual cases.

After the school had been in operation as a boarding-school one month, the agent returned, and heartily approved of the enterprise.

But the school having been commenced during his absence, and before measures had been perfected for the organization and maintenance of it, — the large amount of work engaging his attention, after his return, in getting the affairs of the Agency in smooth running order, — the impatience of the Indians, because everything could not be done at once which they wanted done, — not having any idea that time is essential to the accomplishment of work, — the mill, the scales, buildings for other purposes, and many things immediately needed, while the school was in actual progress, conduced to divert the mind of the agent into other directions, however unintentionally, so that it did not receive that attention which its importance demanded, and was continued for some months under many and very great disadvantages. Improvements were commenced, however, after the pressure of other things had been removed, which conduced much to the comfort and efficiency of the undertaking.

On the return of the agent, Polly, the Cherokee woman, who had honorably and faithfully discharged her duties, as matron and cook, to the best of her limited knowledge, was removed, and a white family, in which were two grown-up daughters, besides the mother, were installed in her place.

The change was agreeable, and could we have been furnished with lights, to have enabled us to have made profitable use of the long winter evenings, and to exercise that care over our wild pupils which their uncultivated habits demanded, the school would have been abundantly more profitable and beneficial in its influence.

CHAPTER III.

EXTRACTS FROM DIARY. — CADDO SCHOOL UNTIL THE IMPROVEMENTS IN THE BUILDING. — VISIT TO KIOWA BOARDING-SCHOOL. — SCENERY ALONG THE ROUTE. — GUADELUPE. — HIS SPEECH AT LAWRENCE. — CAPTAIN BLACK BEAVER.

As some incidents connected with my stay at this Agency, and subsequent removal to that of the Kiowas, may be interesting, I will now transcribe from my diary, going back to the time of the commencement of my school.

11*th Month*, 2*d*, 1871. — Had a long and interesting conversation with Captain Coffee and Little Captain, acting chiefs of Guadelupe's (pronounced *wah-loo-pe*) band of Caddoes during his absence, — he having gone to Lawrence with the agent. I wrote my name on a slate, and told them, through Caddo George as interpreter, "That is my name — stands for me;" they looked at it — laughed — looked again — turned it bottom upward — looked at it from all directions, and in all positions — but evidently could not see anything in it which they could construe into any representation of me, or any other man. I saw they did not comprehend it, and took the slate, drew a profile picture with a short, sharp turn-up nose, hair combed back, somewhat curly, and wearing a straight collar. They readily saw that *that* might represent me. I then wrote my name under it, and succeeded, as I thought, in making them understand that the picture represented me, and the writing my name — the word used to represent me. I then made the picture of a lion, and showed it to them. They did not know what it was. I wrote, in Roman letters, "Lion" under it, as its name, which was read letter by letter, pronounced, and explained to George, and by him to the others.

I next drew a buffalo, and placed under it the word "Buffalo," as its name; not the animal itself, or its representation, but its name — the word people used when they talked about it to one another; as George is the *name* of a man; not the man himself, but the word which people use in speaking of him: I finally fancied that they understood my meaning, as they are in no wise deficient in sense. By thus opening to their comprehension the nature and use of writing and the object of schools, an interest was awakened in their minds, which was afterwards manifested by their sending their children to be instructed in the rudiments of school learning.

23*d* — Snow this morning. As the house is very open, not banked up, and we have no stove for the dining-room, and only a small sheet-iron tent stove for the school-room, it is impossible to keep comfortable, especially our half-clad scholars, — there being but three boys who have pantaloons; the thighs of the others are naked, besides being otherwise thinly clad. Of course they must suffer in such weather. Snow enough fell to mark out fox and geese upon this morning, and some pains were taken to show the children how to play this game. I have found that to awaken an interest in some civilized sports, different from their customary games, is one step towards awakening an interest in the school and its lessons. In this they resemble our own children: remove outside sports and the playground from our common schools, and we should find their interest in them materially weakened. I have accordingly taken part with them in their sports, endeavoring to introduce suitable ones for the playground,

In the middle of the forenoon, a flock of wild turkeys passed near the school-house, upon which the wild instincts of our scholars were manifested by a general stampede; and an exciting foot-race, bows and arrows in hand, was at once entered upon, in which, as might be expected, the turkeys were the winners. The scene was somewhat entertaining and enlivening, and I could not decide which were the greater curiosity, — the wild turkeys running and skulking among the brush, or the wild boys and girls who were chasing them. But I was abundantly more successful in collecting these untamed children into school again, than they were in catching the turkeys.

These boys are quite expert in the use of the bow and arrows, being furnished with them nearly as soon as they can run alone. Boys six or eight years of age will not only kill a bird no larger than my thumb, at the distance of several yards, but, as I have seen, actually cut off its head with the arrow.

12th Month, 2d. — As I am so much of a novice, and have had so little experience in an Indian school, I have felt very anxious to visit one, or have conversation with some one who has been longer engaged in the work, in order to endeavor to gather some ideas that would be of advantage to me in conducting this school; and a team being about to go to the Kiowa Agency, I placed the school in the charge of A. J. Standing, in order to visit the school there, there being but one school day before I shall expect to return.

We made good progress, and passed some objects of singular interest to the lover of natural scenery, among which might be mentioned Cedar Springs, Harker Mountain, and Medicine Bluffs. The first of these is a beautiful spring of clear, sweet water, at the foot of a precipice of red sandstone, forming a deep ravine fringed with cedars and other trees. The road crosses at the top of the rock, a few feet below the general level of the surrounding country, while the water springs out at the base. The second is a spur of the Wichita Mountains running out from near Mount Scott to where our road passed. It is a mound consisting of bare rocks piled up in all manner of forms, having a few shrubby trees at the base, but not extending to over one third of its height, which is from two hundred to five hundred feet above the plains. The last named place is nearly a perpendicular mass of rock, situated near Fort Sill, on Medicine Bluff Creek. But the grand objects of interest in the whole journey are Mounts Scott and Sheridan, rising in majestic grandeur above the surrounding mountains. These mountains have a very remarkable appearance, rising, in immense masses of rock, from the midst of vast plains. We passed within about eight miles of Mount Scott, and perhaps twelve or thirteen of Mount Sheridan. On arriving at the Agency, I proceeded at once to the boarding-school for Indian children, conducted by Josiah Butler and wife.

The next morning was a beautiful one, but before noon the wind arose, and the air was filled with clouds of dust; the weather became cold, the wind turned to the north, and a furious snow-storm followed, which, however, passed away, and it became clear in the evening. Notwithstanding the day of the week, the scholars were convened, after the usual Sabbath school, and read in my presence; also specimens of their writing, both in their copy-books and on slates, were exhibited, all of which showed marked progress for the length of time they have been receiving instruction.

On the 4th returned to the Washita, and the two

following days was in school beforenoons only, while in the afternoons I went around to some of the Caddo villages, endeavoring to induce them to send more children to school, but succeeded in getting two girls only.

18*th.* — The agent, having returned, visited the school to-day, and appeared to be well pleased with its organization, and the progress the scholars were making. He informed them, through an interpreter, that he had in his absence visited several schools, but that he had been in none the scholars of which appeared to be making more commendable progress than they were.

28*th.* — Though the scholars learn fast, they do not comprehend the nature or use of schools, and I have great difficulty in making them understand that they should keep still, without talking or laughing aloud. They do not appear to know anything about whispering, but talk freely. I had expected this, but when they have been to school as much as some of them have to me, I looked for more improvement in this respect; but not having yet any interpreter, it is very difficult to explain to their understandings what I want or expect of them. I have requested the agent to send his interpreter to my assistance, for half a day or so; but he does not yet come, and I am obliged to get along as I best can without. Again; at home they have no lights in the evenings but the fire, and provide but little fuel; their houses being open, they go to bed early, each wrapped in his blanket, and then talk, sing, laugh, get up, go out of doors, come back, punch up the fire, wrap up again, lie down, talk, — and so the night passes, until they talk or sing themselves to sleep; then they sleep very late in the morning. Hence, while I have no difficulty in keeping them up until nine o'clock, I have quite a time in getting them to lie still enough to go to sleep till midnight or after. An immense stock of patience is requisite, and as my supply is small, I have to make the best use of what I have, and endeavor to have it frequently replenished. I sometimes think that the nights are more trying than the days, and require more self-command; tired, sleepy, and worn out, as it were, and yet cannot go to sleep until all these wild children are so far wearied out that they can keep awake no longer, and quietude at last prevails.

29th. — This morning six of our children ran away; whereupon I mounted a pony, pursued after them, and succeeded in bringing back three of them, after a chase of nearly two miles. I would have brought back two more, but my pony would not go any farther; and they, seeing the dilemma I was in, — as they were in sight, — ran and hid in the woods. However, when they got home, the head man of their village made them saddle a pony, and brought them back by noon. The other boy went across the river, and I did not go after him. The reason of the elopement I knew not at the time, but subsequently learned that they were afraid of chastisement in consequence of breaking a light of glass, by throwing a ball through the window accidentally. After ascertaining the cause of their running away, we arrived at a better understanding. I explained to them that I did not punish scholars for accidents they could not avoid. Had rather a pleasant school to-day, after all.

1*st Month*, 1*st*, 1872. — In the afternoon, Dr. A. Tomlinson had a meeting with the Indians in the schoolroom, after which, while busying myself here and there with the school children, I noticed an old Indian in the dining-room, of a full, open countenance, wrapped in a buffalo robe, after the wild Indian style, watching me. As that was no new occurrence, however, I thought nothing of it, until he spoke to me by the interpreter. I went to him, and he said, "My friend, I can see your heart." This salutation, coming from a wild Comanche, somewhat startled me, particularly as at the time I was much depressed, feeling that there was no good thing there. After a little pause he continued, "Tell him I see his heart; it good — full of love; he love Indian; I can never hurt man when I see heart like his — full of love — I love him."

This speech greatly surprised me, as I had previously said nothing to him. This Indian is a very large man, a Comanche chief by the name of Pi-ouh. I could but believe that his heart was touched by a power above his own, and that in him I should find a friend who might be of use to me in the ordering of future events.

3*d*. — This morning school was visited by Guadelupe, principal chief of the Caddoes, who made a long speech to the children, in which he told them that all white children go to school; that they do not talk and laugh out loud—*they* tried hard to learn; and he wanted them to be like the white children—mind all their teachers tell them, and try hard to learn. He also told them that at night they went to bed to sleep, not to play, and they should go to sleep at once; not talk and play, so as to keep all in the house awake. I had also an opportunity, for the first time, of talking to them through an interpreter. Guadelupe is about starting for the Staked Plains, to endeavor to induce the wild Comanches of that region to come in, settle down, and "take steps in the white man's road." It is said that he has great influence among those Indians. He has but just recovered from a severe attack of sickness, since his return from Lawrence, whither he had gone with the agent. The object of his going to Lawrence, as well as his feelings in regard to his people's becoming civilized, are so fully set forth in a speech made at a meeting of the Associated Executive Committee, that I shall feel myself excusable for introducing it entire, as, like most Indian speeches, it has the advantage of being short.

Guadelupe said, "I don't want to say much; I only want to say a little to the superintendent. I have come from a long way off. I came not for anything bad; but I came to find a good way for my people. We want you to try hard to help us into that good way. We do not want to be like some other tribes, who delight in killing and destroying; but we want to learn how to build houses, raise corn, and provide for our wives and children, that they may live and be happy. My young men are staying from the chase until I return home, where they will welcome me, and listen to the words I may have for them. I know they will be ready to do their part in building houses and farms, and trying to be good. Many of the wild Indians also will visit me to hear my words, and see my place; if I have a good house and farm, comfortable clothes, and a happy family, it will have a great influence on them, to turn them into the white man's path to peace and civilization.

"Many of the wild Indians are afraid to plant corn, from a superstition that they will all sicken and die. I will try hard to show them that it will make them live, and be happy and good. I desire much that white intruders may be kept away from us, as their influence is not good. They bring in whiskey by night, get our people drunk, and raise many rows, making our people very bad. Drinking whiskey is a very bad thing. I used to drink; I drank until I lost all my cattle, and ponies, and everything. I drink no more. The white man frequently asks me to drink. No, I will not drink; it makes me bad.

"When I get home I will call all my people, with other wild Indians, and speak to them of the good things I have seen. Will the superintendent speak good words to me, and give me good advice to take to my people?"

These are not the words of Guadelupe alone; they

are the words of his tribe spoken through him — a tribe who, at this day, cannot call one foot of land their own; who have been three times driven from their homes, and have lost all their property as often; have been almost compelled to remain in an uncivilized state, and are surrounded by wild and lawless tribes, who look upon them as intruders upon their hereditary rights. Should it so be that this tribe should be exterminated by their wild neighbors, or driven back into a savage state, from which they are but just emerging, it would be from the fact that they "do not want to be like the wild tribes, who delight in killing and destroying," and the want of that help which is here asked for; since there can be no doubt but that if they would join with the wild tribes in their depredations, they would no longer be looked upon as intruders. These words would stand recorded in the annals of time as a stigma upon Christianity, if this call for help, coming from a whole people, is permitted to pass unheeded, by a professedly Christian government. When an apostle dreamed that he saw a man of Macedonia stand and call, "Come over and help us," he received it as the voice of God, and obeyed it accordingly. Guadelupe, in very deed personating his tribe, has called aloud to the Christian world, "Try hard to help us into that good way. We do not want to be like those wild tribes who delight in killing and destroying." Should not these words be received as a call from the Supreme Father of all in behalf of his poor, benighted children? Surely, if we cannot, as the Scriptures assert, think a good thought without the aid of the Holy Spirit, what short of the same Spirit ever put these words into the mind of this untutored Indian? Shall this appeal to the world of professing Christians be made in vain?

27th. — Assisted in issuing rations until nearly four o'clock, then went out on the hills north-west of the Agency, extending my walk nearly four miles. Made a sketch of the Twin Rocks — a couple of rocks of stratified red sandstone, perhaps twelve feet in height, with overhanging tops much larger than their bases, and of a very peculiar form: the body of the rocks is red, while the tops, being covered with lichen, are of a pale-green color. Another rock in a deep hollow, one fourth of a mile from the former, of the same kind, rises, as a crooked pillar, some eighteen or twenty feet in height, of which I also made a sketch. These rocks are about three miles from the Agency, in the midst of a rolling, shrubby prairie.

31st. — After the return of the agent, A. J. Standing, who had assisted me a part of the time, was removed from the school altogether. But it having latterly so increased as to require more attention, he was again restored, and to-day has taken charge of some of the classes, which is certainly a very great advantage, as I had been compelled to neglect some of the branches, especially the writing.

2d Month, 2d. — This evening, after the scholars had gone home, a poor, crippled Indian was brought into the school-room, to remain for the night. His thigh-bone was broken, about eighteen months since, by the stumbling of his horse while running buffalo. Never having been properly attended to, — the flesh badly lacerated, although it at first began to heal, — it eventually grew worse; the flesh rotted from the bones; so that now he is in a most deplorable and suffering condition, and little hope of his ever being in any better.

This man lay upon the floor of our school-room for a full week before he was removed, being accommodated with a bed and blankets taken from those supplied to the scholars, which were no more than enough to make them comfortable, while the room was so crowded as to have no space to spare, and every jar or noise causing him very much pain and annoyance.

13*th.* — School greatly increased, numbering, on my register, thirty-seven. This increase shows the estimation the Indians place upon our efforts for the education of their children.

17*th.* — From some cause I have not felt entirely satisfied with my present position, or that it was my proper place to remain in this school; yet, in looking the subject over, I can see no other way than to remain here; but a secret feeling that I am not where I should be, continues with me almost constantly. I spoke to the agent about it, who proposed my going with him to select a site for a school-house for the Wichitas and Wakoes, proposing to put me into the school, when in readiness to commence. This day we rode out to select a location for the same, found a very suitable place, situated upon a slight eminence, about five miles from the Agency and one mile from the Wichita and Wakoe village. A beautiful spring of good water issues from the ground, about one half a mile from the selected site, the stream from which flows near to it. This place, though not on high ground, overlooks a most beautiful valley, through which Sugar Creek flows into the Washita, embracing many square miles of beautiful and rich country. Though the soil, as everywhere in this country, is of a dark-red color, judging from the exuberant growth of vegetation, it must be deep and fertile.

18*th.* — Kicking Bird, — one of the most celebrated of the Kiowa chiefs, — his wife, Guadelupe, Captain Coffee, and Little Captain, took dinner with us at the school. After noon, I went with some others over the river to Jake's village; found one of the school children sick, but brought four home with us. Passed the farm of Captain Black Beaver, a Delaware Indian, whose residence is about three fourths of a mile from the school, but on the opposite side of the river. He is a full Indian, has travelled very extensively in what is now Wyoming, Montana, Idaho, Oregon, Washington, California, Nevada, Utah, Colorado, New Mexico, and Mexico. In the latter country he was captain in the United States army, having enlisted, as he himself informed me, in order to see how white people fought with "them big guns," — he having seen cannons somewhere in his travels, and could not make up his mind how they were handled. In conversation with him at one time, he told me of having visited, on two different occasions, among the mountains of Arizona, the remnant of a white race, who lived in a walled town, or rather a town built on a kind of peninsula, being nearly surrounded by a cañon, or impassable ravine, so that there was but one way of approach, and that by a narrow neck of land, across which they had built a wall, which effectually excluded the wild tribes by which they were surrounded. Here they lived, shut out from the rest of the world, by agricultural and horticultural pursuits, raising peaches and other fruits. He describes them as living entirely at peace, being kind and hospitable to strangers, whom they admit into their town. The second time he visited them, they recognized him and his party while at a distance, and a deputation carrying fruits were sent out to offer them the hospitalities of their town. I think I have seen a similar account in print.

Since leaving the Indian country I have endeavored to ascertain whether any explorers or travellers in Arizona or Nevada had described this or a similar people, and find that William J. Howard, a Santa Fe jeweller, in a visit to the Zuñians, a branch of the Pueblos, "among the mountains, far from any white settlers or Mexicans, found four white Indians, with blue eyes and flaxen hair." "The other Zuñians make these whites perform all the manual labor, refusing to associate or intermarry with them." See A. D. Richardson's work, entitled "Beyond the Mississippi," pages 253 and 254.

In the same work, pages 585 and 586, I find that General William J. Palmer, in the summer of 1868, visited the Zuñi Indians, of whom it is said, "The Zuñis preserve the old Aztec faith pure and simple." "They raise fruit, corn, and sheep, in abundance. . . . Palmer saw one of their white Indians. He had red hair, blue eyes, and a complexion fair even for a white man." "He showed none of that preternatural paleness of the eyes, feebleness, and appearance of being a freak of nature generally observed in Albinos, but seemed to be a strong normal man. From generation to generation these white Zuñians have white children."

Richardson further describes the Pueblos as a "race of half-civilized Indians, who live in towns, and claim to be unmixed descendants of the ancient Aztecs. They never intermarry with whites, and their women — almost the solitary exception to Indian tribes in general — are reputed inflexibly chaste." — *Beyond the Mississippi*, page 264.

In a report upon the Indian tribes, made to the War Department by Lieutenant A. W. Whipple, Thomas Ewbank, Esq., and Professor William W. Turner, published in 1855, after a description of the ancient town of Zuñi and the Zuñian Indians, I find the following paragraph: —

"It is to be regretted that we obtained no portrait of the white Indians of Zuñi; but the small-pox being prevalent among them, it was deemed imprudent to visit their houses. Some of them, however, were seen, having light or auburn hair, fair complexions, and blue eyes. It is remarkable that the first Indian from Zuñi seen by Father de Niça, in 1539, is described as a white man of fair complexion." — See *Report*, page 31.

It appears in the published journal of the exploring expedition, under command of Lieutenant A. W. Whipple, that the expedition was at Zuñi on the 23d of November, 1853. — *Journal of Expedition*, page 68.

Pueblo Zuñi is among the Zuñi Mountains, in the western part of New Mexico, west of Albuquerque is an ancient city, and contains about two thousand inhabitants, and has been known to the Spaniards for over three hundred years, during which time it has not materially changed in its appearance.

Captain Black Beaver * has a large farm under cultivation, and lives in a very comfortable manner, having good, substantial frontier buildings. He commenced life as a wild Indian trapper, until, becoming familiar with almost all the unexplored regions of the west, and being a remarkably truthful and reliable man, he was much sought after as a guide, and accompanied several expeditions in that capacity. His life has been one of bold adventure, fraught with many interesting incidents, which, if properly written out, would form an interesting and entertaining volume.

* This Captain Black Beaver was guide to Captain Marcy in his explorations in the west, also to Audubon the naturalist.

CHAPTER IV

WORK ON THE HOUSE. — WICHITA GRASS HOUSES. — CADDO HOUSES. — AGENT VISITS KIOWA CAMP. — DEATH OF NEWAHKASSET. — TONQUEWA MASSACRE. — IMPRESSIONS RESPECTING GOING TO LIVE WITH THE KIOWAS. — BOY SENT OUT OF THE CHAMBER. — LEGEND OF MEDICINE BLUFFS. — TWO SMALL BOYS QUARREL. — INTERVIEW WITH THE MOTHER OF ONE OF THEM. — DEATH OF NELLIE BLOCK. — SCHOOL REPORT.

2d Month, 22d, 23d, and 24th.— The carpenters having commenced work improving the chambers of this building, the school was dismissed and the scholars sent home on the 23d. A. J. Standing and myself set to work tearing up the sleeping mats from the floor, and cleaning up generally. The chambers being partitioned off, rude bedsteads and bed-ticks made, we worked hard in getting the ticks and bolsters filled with good clean oat-straw, and bunks put up, which we got accomplished late in the evening. Our sleeping apartments now look more like civilized life than heretofore, and the scholars can sleep in beds, instead of being huddled down together on the floor.

25th. — After our meeting for worship, which had been continued, on the first day of the week, since the establishment of the Agency, I rode over to the Keechi and Wakoe villages, in company with agents Richards, Tatum, and some others, to see their grass houses, which are built in a circular form by erecting poles bound together at the top, and thatched with long, coarse grass. Openings about two and a half feet wide and four in height, being left upon opposite sides, serve for doors, windows, and ventilators. Platforms are made quite around the lodge, except at the openings, about two and a half feet high, by erecting perpendicular stakes from the ground to the poles, forming the main frame-work of the lodge. Cross-pieces are tied from these stakes to the outside or frame-poles, at the height mentioned; poles are laid upon these, and covered with willow rods woven together with bark or buckskin strings. These serve, by being covered with buffalo robes, blankets, &c., for beds, and extend around the lodge on both sides, from doorway to doorway. In front of these, in some of the lodges, were stools, made by cutting off logs about ten inches in diameter, square and smooth, then dressing a portion of it away so as to form a leg, which was driven into the ground sufficiently deep to hold it firmly, while the top is from twelve to fifteen inches high. The fireplace is in the centre of the lodge, and consists of a round hole dug a few inches in depth and something over two feet across. The lodge complete looks from without like a large well-formed haystack.

These grass houses are only used as summer residences, being too airy for winter use, and are from twenty to thirty feet in diameter. Lodges made from the skins of the buffalo, properly prepared and put up, being much warmer, as excluding the wind more effectually, are used to live in during the winter.

The Caddoes build their houses on the same general plan, being circular or oval in form, having two opposite openings, and a similar platform extending around the sides. The sides, however, differ from the Wichita houses by being made of small stakes, set in the ground close together, and about seven feet high, slightly drawn in at the top. These are chinked and pointed up with mud and grass, and a slight frame-work is placed above to support the thatching; no opening, in many instances, being left for the egress of smoke, which must escape through the thatch, after filling all the upper part of the house, darkening and rendering the domicile extremely uncomfortable.

3d Month, 2d.— This morning our agent started, in company with J. D. Hoag and Cyrus Beede, for the Kiowa camps, one hundred miles or more up the Washita, in order to see Big Bow, a degraded Kiowa chief,— that is, one whom, on account of his bad conduct, agent Tatum no longer recognizes as chief. Their object I know not farther than by supposition. He is a notorious raider, in the practice of killing people, and committing depredations on the whites, whenever opportunity presents. Such opportunities he makes quite frequently, and told our agent, in my hearing, that he intended to continue his present mode of life while his friend Satanta remains in the Texas prison. He further said he expected to go on the war-path when the grass was sufficiently grown to fatten his horses.

I suppose the object of the visit is to induce him to relinquish his present designs, and perhaps to go to Washington. Guadelupe, with some of his young men, accompanied them as guides.

5th. — It does not seem like spring; there having been no frost to come out of the ground, it is settled like summer; no mud; the ground was mellow, and ready for spring work three weeks ago. This is a most beautiful country, and I think the ague would be mostly, if not entirely, avoided by settling on the high lands: as in other prairie countries, there is no scarcity of timber or water. The soil is rich, and the climate such that the finest fruits of the temperate zone might be raised in exuberant abundance, provided there is sufficient rain-fall during the summer.

Very different is the soil from any I saw in Kansas, unless it might be in the Arkansas valley, and very different also from that of the high plains we crossed in the Territory. These affiliated bands surely have a choice reservation. O that they were sufficiently civilized to improve it as it might be, and as it some day will be! I never, in any country, saw such a growth of vegetation as in this valley of the Washita.

9th. — The agent and company arrived, last evening,

from the Kiowa camps, having had quite a satisfactory interview with the chiefs of that tribe, and had been gone a week this morning. They were treated with the utmost kindness. Lone Wolf and his wife removed everything from their lodge, and gave them possession of it during their stay, which was two nights and one day, then escorted them the whole distance back to the Agency. From their description the country over which they travelled is greatly diversified with mountains, hills, valleys, cañons, and plains.

While at the camp some of their young men advocated making captives of them, in order to procure the discharge of Satanta; but the chiefs were opposed to any such measure, as being a breach of hospitality, and would not permit it to be attempted. Guadelupe made a speech to them in the council, in which he told them that when he was a young man, he was foolish like them, — went on the war-path, — took scalps, — which the Kiowas knew to their sorrow, — but had now entered upon another and better road, was travelling in it, and would not leave it to go back to their old ways.

The buffalo, deer, and antelope would soon be gone, and he wanted to learn how to raise cattle and corn, that he might have something to eat when the buffalo could no more be found; — with much more to the same effect, adding that he wanted to see all the Indians entering upon the same road; for it is a better way to travel than their old ways.

Guadelupe speaks in a serious, calm, and cool manner,

and his words sink deeply into the hearts of his Indian hearers; hence his great influence among them.

Last night died Ne-wah-kass-ett, chief of the Wichitas. He had been sick a long time, was some better for a week past, and yesterday came to the agent's, about four miles. In the evening he was taken worse; the medicine-woman was called in, and administered medicine, but he continued to get worse, and died before morning. Early this morning Keechi, the brother of the dead chief, took his rifle, and entering the lodge of the medicine-woman, without saying a word, deliberately shot her dead, for having administered bad medicine. In all probability the woman had done the best she knew, and deserved a reward instead of death. When the circumstance became known in the village, the house or lodge in which she lived was torn down, and, with all her effects, piled upon her dead body and burned; after which Keechi came to the Agency covered with blood, having cut his arms and breast in mourning for his chief, whom he will, unless prevented by the agent, succeed in the chieftainship. This circumstance illustrates the powerful hold of superstition upon the minds of this benighted people, often, as in this case, leading them into deeds of violence and blood.

13*th.* — This morning, Little Captain came into the school, wanting to talk to the scholars. He told them that Guadelupe was going away, and asked him to come and talk to them, as he had not time to do so himself. "He told me to tell you that he wanted you to try hard and learn to read and write; if you do not see the need of it now, it will be good for you by and by. Try hard, and not play; be good children; do not quarrel and fight with each other, but try hard to learn, and not be wild Indians." One of the scholars, who had lately entered the school, and understood both the Caddo and English languages, interpreted his speech to me, and I made a few remarks to him, expressive of my gladness that he, Guadelupe, and others of their head men, took so much pains to help us along in our work, by coming in and giving our children good talk. It helped us much, by letting us know that their hearts were alive to the subject, and it made the children better by knowing that their chiefs and principal men were anxious for them to come to school, behave well, and try to learn. I hoped they would continue to feel interested, come and see us often, as we were always glad to see them.

27th. — A few rods from the school-house, while walking about to-day, I found a human skull lying upon the ground, probably that of an Indian, who had been killed on some occasion, and perhaps scalped by an enemy, which has been no uncommon occurrence in this land.

Some six years since, a portion of a tribe residing in Texas, called Tonqueways, who are reported by all the Indians of this country as being cannibals, had been in the Shawnee country, and killed and eaten a couple of Shawnees; after which, as they were returning to Texas, they encamped about five or six miles from this place, near the trail-road to Fort Sill, being in number about three hundred. The Shawnees, having collected a force composed of Shawnees, Creeks, and Delawares, pursued and overtook them there. Taking them by surprise, they slew over one half of them, losing in the conflict some of their own men, so that nearly two hundred human beings perished on that occasion. The allied force took care of their own dead, while those of the Tonqueways, who were thoroughly routed, were left on the ground, to be consumed by wolves and buzzards. Two or three years afterwards most of their bones were gathered up and buried; but some still remain to mark this scene of former barbarities. One of our scholars, a Creek, had a brother engaged in this sanguinary conflict.

30th. — This morning, on awakening, a thought presented itself to my mind in such a manner as to affect me deeply through the day. It was as though I had distinctly heard the question audibly addressed to me, "What if thou shouldst have to go and sojourn in the Kiowa camps?" The thought was entirely new to me, and coming in the manner it did, it affected me to tears, looking as I have, and still do, upon the Kiowas as the most fierce and desperately bloodthirsty tribe of Indian Territory. I could not dismiss the subject from my mind through the day, so as to be clear of it for more than a few moments at a time. The intensity of my feelings was in no degree diminished when, in the evening, Kicking Bird and his wife came to me with an interpreter, and informed me that they had come to ask me to be a father to their little girl. I told them that if they would bring her here, and leave her with me, I would be a father to her, and treat her as I would one of my own children. They talked together a little, and then Kicking Bird said, "We cannot leave her; we have lost five children; she is all we have; we cannot leave her here; but we want you to be a father to her, as you are to these children here." I said, "Do you mean that you want me to come to your camp and live with you, that I may be her father?" Kicking Bird replied, "Yes, that would be good — what we want. If you will come I will be your friend, and nobody shall do you any harm; my people will be your brothers." I replied to him that I could not leave these children yet, and I would have to think of it a great deal before deciding to come. To this he said, "You think, and when you make up your mind to come, let me know, and my wife and I will come and get you, and you shall live with me in my lodge, and be a father to the Kiowa children, as you are to the Caddoes."

This interview had not the effect to lighten the burden already on my mind; scarcely daring to doubt but that it would be my duty, at no distant time, to give up to go among that fierce and bloodthirsty tribe.

4th Month, 4th. — Last evening I told the boys, on their going to bed, that I intended to stop their unnecessary running about in the night, if I had to send some of them down stairs to sleep in the school-room; whereupon A. J. Standing said, "The first boy we catch running about for play we shall send down stairs to sleep." But we had no sooner got into bed than they had a candle lighted, and some of them were running about as lively as though they were bent on testing the matter, and ascertaining whether we were in earnest in what we had said to them.

I quietly got up, went to their sleeping-room door, and opening it suddenly, distinguished the flying form of one boy, and all was dark in an instant. I produced a light, went to the bed of the boy I had recognized, and found him apparently fast asleep. However, I was not long in arousing him, when he snatched up his clothes, and ran down stairs. I followed him. He jerked the bar from the door and opened it suddenly, in order to make his escape to his village — a proceeding I had anticipated, and was consequently on hand in time to frustrate that design. I barred the door again, and while he was dressing, opened the school-room door; but he being determined on going home, I had to be on the alert to prevent him from giving me the slip, and making good his escape.

I ordered him into the school-room, after making him understand that if he would go to his bed, and lie there until morning, he could go up stairs; otherwise, he must go into the school-room. He resolutely determined that he would do neither, and being nearly grown, strong, and active, I soon found that his going into the school-room was depending upon my physical ability to put him there. Accordingly I took hold of him, and, notwithstanding his efforts at resistance, succeeded in forcing him into the room, gathered up some blankets, and threw them to him. He made himself a bed, and lay down. I locked the door, and taking some other precautions to prevent his escape, and satisfying myself that he understood me, I left him till morning, when I found him as pliable as need be, having learned that my firmness was not to be trifled with. He has been a better boy to-day than for some weeks past.

6th. — Went to the Kiowa Agency on horseback, and had rather a pleasant trip, though it is a long, solitary road of thirty-five miles; and having no company, I could but feel a little lonesome. Reached the Agency about the middle of the afternoon.

8th. — Returned to the Wichita Agency, passing Medicine Bluffs and Harker Mountain. The old Indian legend of Medicine Bluffs may be briefly related as follows: —

Many years since, a noted medicine-man of the Comanche tribe, in company with some of his personal friends, in their travels rode up the slope of the hill, when this frightful precipice of two hundred or two hundred and fifty feet appeared before them, stopping them in their course. But the medicine-man was not to be stopped, neither turned aside. Uttering some words of Indian magic, he rode his horse over the precipice; but, to the astonishment of his friends, instead of being dashed to pieces at the bottom, he was gently borne across the chasm to the opposite bank of the stream, where, finding himself alone, he turned his horse to look for his friends, whom he beheld at the top of the bluff, afraid to follow and too proud to go around. To relieve them from their unpleasant position, he rode back to the bottom, crossed the creek, and rode directly up to the perpendicular wall of rock, which rent at his approach, dividing the bluff into two parts by forming a chasm through the cliff several feet in width, through and up which he rode, rejoining his companions at the top, who then followed him down through the pass thus made, now known as the Medicine-man's Pass. This pass is an inclined passage, twelve or fifteen feet wide, extending through the cliff to the top.

Notwithstanding my insensibility to good in meeting, yesterday, I might mention that to-day, in riding along on this solitary road, I was refreshed and tendered by the overshadowing presence of Divine Goodness, in which my soul was poured out like water before the mighty Rock of Ages, in which state my dear and most precious family were remembered, in earnest breathings for their preservation, as well as my own, in this time of heartfelt separation.

The prospect was afresh opened to my view of yielding to offer myself to go among the wild and roving Kiowas, and I was favored to see that a whole surrender is required; that heretofore I had clung, with the arm of earthly love to my precious wife and children, but that the time was near in which I must forsake all, make all that I hold dear upon earth, as a "whole burnt offering," relinquish the thought of being joined by them in this land, and even of hearing from them with any degree of reliability. My very soul was solemnized within me, and I could but cry, "O Most High and Holy One, whose right it is to rule and to reign in the hearts of the children of men, enable me to say, in the depths of true and consecrated sincerity, 'Not my will, but thine, be done.'"

May these lofty hills, these beautiful valleys, and these wide-spreading plains, which have been for ages silent witnesses of atrocious deeds of blood, re-echo with high and living praise, from now blaspheming tongues, to thee, the Almighty Creator and Preserver of all things, and the Redeemer of a fallen race from sin and the wages of it.

May the darkness of superstition, which now hangs as a thick cloud over the inhabitants of this land, be dispelled by the bright-shining rays of the Sun of Righteousness, that these poor, deluded creatures may see themselves in the true light, and learn to "know thee, the only true God, and Jesus Christ, whom thou hast sent," which is, indeed, life eternal.

10*th and* 11*th*. — Cut out ten pairs of pantaloons for the boys: thus I find my slight knowledge of tailoring, previously acquired, to be of advantage in preparing clothing for these children, where no tailors are.

22*d*. — Hands are at work arranging things more comfortably at the house and surroundings. Most of the putrefying matter about the buildings has been removed. A gate is placed so as to obviate the necessity of the work-cattle being driven through the play-yard, and a fence is being run across, so that the wild cattle may be corralled without passing through the school-grounds, and last seventh day the cattle were issued to the Indians from the old butcher-pen, situated a mile or more down and across the river from the school, instead of issuing in the school-yard, as heretofore.

28th. — After our meeting to-day, went with the agent to see a sick Indian. He is a very old man, perhaps eighty years of age. We found him lying, with only a blanket thrown over his naked body, in the open sun, on a platform made by driving stakes into the ground, laying poles across, and then tying willow rods together with strips of bark or raw hide. We got him into the house, administered some medicine, and then went to Guadelupe's, who is about to start to the Kiowa camps, at the request of Superintendent Hoag.

5th Month, 9th. — This morning, while a couple of our small boys were at play, one of them became suddenly angry, and seizing a sharp-cornered club, dealt the other a hard blow on the head, inflicting a severe scalp-wound.

The blow, very fortunately, fell upon a thick portion of the skull, or he might have been killed. I sewed up the wound, dressed it with camphor and sugar, and put him to bed. The other boy was locked up in the chamber, and kept there all day, food and water being carried to him.

In the course of the day, Captain Black Beaver came in and talked to the scholars in the school-room, then went into the chamber and talked to our little prisoner.

He told him how badly it made him feel when he heard what he had done. "That his teachers feel badly, the agent feels badly, his chief, and all his friends, when they hear what he had done; and more than that, his Father in heaven was displeased. He sees us all the time, He knows all the time — all we do, all we think. He does not like to see his children get angry — quarrel, and hurt each other. You ought to be very sorry. Your teachers do right to lock you up, so you think how bad you [have] been, and not do so any more. You ought to live like brothers, and love each other; then you feel good, make your teachers, your chief, and your friends feel glad, and God will make you happy." A Christian sermon from an Indian.

Early in the evening the mother of our prisoner came in, and in a loud, excited, angry voice demanded her son, in order to take him home. I informed her, in a calm but firm voice, that she could not take him away, but if she wished to see him, I would let her into the room; but she must first promise not to attempt to take him away, as I had sent for his chief (Guadelupe). She agreeing to the terms, I took her into the room where he was lying upon his bed. She soon had him up, and made for the door, having hold of the boy. The door being open, she was about to pass out with him, upon which I took hold of him and she of me; whereupon I closed the door and locked it. She spoke a few words to her daughter, who was outside the door, who immediately ran down stairs, mounted the old woman's pony, and went to their village, I supposed for some of her older brothers. I soon got her out of the room, and went down stairs. The agent and interpreter having been sent for, I explained the case to the old woman, and wished to hear what she had to say. She said, "The boy did right, as the other boys all plague her boy till he get mad." I replied that I know that sometimes other boys plague him, sometimes he plagues other boys; she knew Indians all love to joke one another, but they ought not to get angry at fun. The other boy only threw a green plum at her boy, and then he struck him with a club. She instituted inquiry of the scholars, who told her that was all; the other boy threw a plum at him, which hit him on the forehead. Whereupon she talked largely of the maliciousness of throwing a plum and hitting her boy's forehead; he ought to get mad and do something. I wished her to think of the difference between being hit with a small plum, which she knew could hurt no one, and being struck a forcible blow with that club — holding it up to view. She then said that white people and Indians were different, and walked in different roads; that their way was, when they get into quarrels, to draw their clubs, tomahawks, or pistols. To which I replied, She knew that was not the good way; to which she for the first time assented, and I continued, that I was wanting to bring them into a better way than they had been following.

The white man's road is, when any one gets angry and hurts another, to shut him up where he could hurt no one else. That if the thing were turned about, and her boy had been the one hurt, and I had shut the other one up, where he could have a bed to lie upon, his meals and drink carried to him, she would have thought that I had not punished him with sufficient severity; she only looked at one side; I had to look all round, so as to see both sides, and take such measures as would prevent the recurrence of any more such acts. If I allowed such things to pass unnoticed, the practice might become frequent; perhaps some one be killed; it might be her boy; but I expected to keep him a prisoner until his chief came, not only for his good, but for the good of the school, that other boys might know what to expect. I then told her that I had expected to have him come down to the evening exercises; but as she was here, and had once attempted to take him away, contrary to orders, she must promise to let him remain, and not try to get him away. To which she replied, she *would* get him away if she could, if he came down. I told her if that was her intention, he should not come down; and I wanted her to remember that it was she that was keeping him up stairs confined in a dark room alone, as I should have had him come down, had she not been here, or had given me her word that she would not try to slip away with him; and closed the interview. The old woman remained all night. During the evening exercises, another son of the old woman came outside, and slyly made an effort to get him and his clothes out of the chamber window. But the exercises closing, that design was frustrated, and not again attempted. The next morning, after his mother had gone away, the boy was brought down to the school; but at noon an older brother, who was watching an opportunity to steal him away, accomplished his design and took him home. It was to prevent this that I had sent for Guadelupe, who came to the agent, but not to the school; so I had no opportunity of talking with him, in order to get him, if he approved of the course I had pursued, — which he told the agent he did, — to forbid their stealing him away; as it would injure the usefulness of the school, if not entirely destroy all discipline in it, if women and young men may come and steal the children away, whenever they are brought under correction. In a few days the boy was sent back to school; but being determined that this practice should be nipped in the bud, I got Captain Black Beaver to go with me to see Guadelupe, who came back with us to the school, in order to have the benefit of an interpreter. I had a long talk with him, relative to the different bearings of the circumstance, and the effect upon the school if parents or others are permitted to steal their children away when they are corrected; telling him I had come a long way to try to teach their children a better way than they had been following. They knew that I would not hurt their children, that when they get out of the way, and I undertake to bring them back into the right road again, — try to cause them to leave off their bad ways, — if their parents or friends steal them away, it makes my hands hang down. I can do nothing. I cannot prevent their watching around, and stealing their children when I do not know it; and if that is the way they expect to do, the school had better stop, for I could do nothing towards controlling the scholars.

He said, when he found out, on Monday, that the boy was not sent back to school, he went to his mother and brother, told them they had done wrong in taking him from school, that they must send him back at once, and not take him away any more, without the consent of the teacher. Thus had he, without my knowledge, taken steps to prevent the continuation of such occurrences, showing his confidence and interest in the school.

6th Month, *4th*. — Little Nellie Block died this morning, after a lingering illness of some months. She was an interesting and beautiful little girl, of Creek and Caddo descent, and one of the sweetest tempered children it has been my lot to have the care of. I took the school children to see her, and to attend the burial this afternoon. Her remains were buried upon the top of the hill, back of the agent's residence. Most of her clothes, a coverlet or two, were placed in the coffin; and when it was let down into the grave, her mother threw in at the head a bundle of clothes which had been tied up by themselves and kept out of the coffin. Had some talk to-day with Agent Tatum relative to my going among the Kiowas. A way appears to be slowly opening for this work.

12*th.* — My last forenoon in school. Captain Black Beaver having a team going to Wichita, Kansas, in company with a wagon train which is to leave to-morrow, and there being but two more days of school before vacation, A. J. Standing being willing to undertake to close the quarter, I made arrangements for going home.

Started on my homeward journey on the morning of the 13th. Arrived at Wichita on the morning of the 20th, having made a very quick trip across the plains, during which we passed about twenty-eight thousand head of Texas cattle; two ox trains, one of thirty-five wagons, the other of forty-five; also one mule train, consisting of four wagons, all laden with supplies for the Agencies and Fort Sill. But not a buffalo or antelope was seen on the journey. The waters, especially of the Canadian, were high, but not so as to detain us.

Took the cars early in the morning of the 21st; stopped a short time at the superintendent's office at Lawrence, and arrived at Cedar Rapids about one o'clock in the morning of the 23d. It being the first day of the week, and no train leaving, I made arrangements for forwarding my luggage, and walked home, about eighteen miles, arriving a little past seven in the morning, finding my family well, and thankful for the favor of a peaceful return.

ADDENDUM TO CHAPTER IV.

The following report of the state and progress of the school was written out and signed before my leaving, ready for presenting to the agent at the conclusion of the school: —

SCHOOL REPORT.

To J. Richards, United States Indian Agent.

Respected Friend: A day school was opened by A. J. Standing, 9th month, 23d, 1871, and continued by him until I took charge of it, the 31st of the 10th month following, but little having been previously done towards the school education of these Indians, only one of the scholars knowing the letters of the alphabet at the commencement of his school. I found it small, but satisfactorily and favorably progressing, and continued it as a day school until 11th month, 10th, when, the weather becoming inclement, it became necessary to provide immediate accommodations for lodging the scholars from a distance, who had hitherto slept in the open air. Accordingly, with the assistance of A. J. Standing, the necessary arrangements for a temporary boarding-school were made.

The school was opened as a boarding-school 11th month, 15th, with eleven names on the list, which have since increased to thirty-eight: the average attendance for the first half of the term was sixteen and a half; for the last half, twenty-six and a half; the greatest average any one week was thirty-one and one fourth.

The ages of the scholars range from five years to twenty; they are mostly of the Caddo and Delaware tribes, with a few Creeks. Nearly all have shown aptness, ability, and a commendable zeal in their studies; two thirds of them now, at the close of the school, reading fluently in books, — using the 1st, 2d, and 3d Readers, — the remainder on charts. Twelve have made commendable progress in writing, their copy-books being models of care and neatness. Several show considerable talent and interest in drawing, and romanizing letters, which have formed an important part of our school exercises. Geography and the multiplication table have been used as concert exercises. In acquiring the former the scholars have shown remarkable aptness, having now a general acquaintance with the maps of the world, North and South America, and the United States; also a knowledge of the races of men, and the more remarkable animals, inhabiting the different parts of the world. Several show good ability for mental work, readily counting by 2s, 3s, 4s, 5s, and 6s, and have made some progress in written arithmetic. Spelling appears to be peculiarly difficult, owing, no doubt, to their ignorance of the formation of written language, — by far the greatest progress being made by those who had previously acquired some knowledge of the English language.

The general demeanor and moral behavior of the school are much to their credit, there seldom happening anything to mar the perfect harmony of the school. Until the latter part of the term, owing to lingual difficulties, it was impossible to impart much religious instruction. We have now in the school, as a scholar, a good interpreter, through whom we have endeavored to impart some of the truths of Christianity, which have been listened to with marked attention, and we believe the seed falls on good ground. Owing, however, to the practice of dismissing the scholars on 6th day evenings, we have been unable to organize any 1st day exercise for their instruction, which we regret.

The parents and guardians oı children show commendable interest in the school, both by visiting it and taking measures to secure the regular return of their children. The chiefs and head men of the tribes generally appear alive to the necessity of education, and have rendered valuable assistance, by their occasional visits to the school, and addresses to the scholars.

One marked feature in the school is the small attendance of girls as compared with that of the boys; the prevailing idea appears to be that the boys ought to be educated, while it matters little about the girls; those, however, who have attended have manifested no lack of ability or aptness in learning, though, evidently from the effects of home training, they are more inclined to stand in the background; not coming forward with that promptness which characterizes the boys. The health of the school has been pretty good in the main, though in spring there were a few cases of ague, and one or two cases of pneumonia in the winter. One death has recently occurred among the scholars, and there are two cases of sickness at the present time.

Respectfully submitted,

THOMAS C. BATTEY, *Principal.*
A. J. STANDING, *Teacher.*

CHAPTER V.

JOURNEY TO THE AGENCIES. — RETURNED CAPTIVES. — CLINTON SMITH. — JOHN VALENTINE MAXIE. — ADOLPH KOHN. — TEMPLE FRIEND. — DEATH OF TEN BEARS, A COMANCHE CHIEF.

In accordance with an apprehension of duty, as explained in the preceding pages, I stopped at the superintendent's office, while on my way home, for the purpose of consulting him, and the agent of the executive committee, respecting establishing myself in the Kiowa camps. The Kiowas were a wild, depredating tribe, who had hitherto resisted all attempts to bring them into friendly relations with the government, or to a knowledge of civilized life, still continuing to commit depredations upon the white settlements, stealing horses and mules, murdering men and women, and carrying their children into captivity. The superintendent and general agent, by whom the necessary arrangements would have to be made, approved of the concern, but could see no opening by which it could be accomplished at present, and I continued my journey towards home.

The succeeding summer, the Kiowas, with parties

Horseback (Ter-re-o-quoit), Commanche Chief

from other tribes whom they could induce to join them, murdered not less than forty white persons, stole several hundred horses and mules, and took three white children captives, so that the agent, in discouragement, wrote to me that, from present appearances, he did not think it would be prudent for me to go among the Kiowas the coming winter, and proposed that I should go to one of the bands of the Comanches, instead of the Kiowas, at the same time expressing his desire to see me at the Agency.

Notwithstanding this discouraging view, my mind was still secretly drawn to the Kiowas, and without knowing how the thing would work out, I felt best satisfied to make my way to the Kiowa and Comanche Agency, given up in mind to work a while among the Comanches, if way did not immediately open for my going with the Kiowas.

Accordingly, on the first day of the 10th month, 1872, I parted with my very dear wife and children, and started on my intended journey to the Kiowa Agency, via Lawrence in Kansas, where I arrived about midnight of the 2d of the month. Here I was detained until afternoon on the 4th, on account of the absence of the superintendent. I was much discouraged, upon his return, in finding that no arrangements had been made for the furtherance of my concern, and that there would likely be none for some time to come, or at least until the return of the Indian delegation from Washington. I, however, felt best satisfied to proceed on my journey, and took the cars that evening for Wichita, arriving there on the 5th, late in the evening. This being as far as I could go by rail, and no mule or ox train being about to start in the direction I was desirous of going for some time, I joined a couple of young men, who were going to cross the plains on horseback, to the point whither I was intending, they having ponies sufficient to carry me and a part of my luggage. Making arrangements for the transfer of my trunk by the first ox train, we started on our journey of two hundred and forty miles, about eleven o'clock, on the 8th.

Evening, put up at a ranche kept by a man from Pennsylvania, who, though very genteel in his manners. and appearing disposed to accommodate travellers to the best of his ability, retails liquors by the dram, permits card-playing, gambling, &c. His ranche, like most others, is built of logs, and roofed with dirt, on which is quite a growth of grass and weeds. Two large herds of Texas cattle are being pastured here, and are enclosed in the corral near the ranche at night. The Texan herders were drinking and playing cards until late in the night, and as one small room serves for kitchen, dining-room, sitting-room, bed-room, store, saloon, and corn-crib, there was not much space between my bed on the floor and the gambling-table where these degraded beings were keeping up their wild orgies, — swearing, drinking, smoking, and shuffling their cards. I wished I had made my bed out of doors, on the ground; however, knowing why I was there, I was favored to withdraw my mind from these unfavorable surroundings, and feeling a degree of comfortable quiet, soon dropped to sleep.

9th. — This morning, much of the time we witnessed a phenomenon of optical illusion much spoken of by travellers. About ten o'clock, a short distance ahead of us appeared to be a lake, adorned with beautiful islands, which were covered with trees. The shore of this imaginary lake was fringed with trees swaying back and forth in the breeze, which gradually disappeared at our approach, while others, equally beautiful, would be formed, to greet our vision, farther on. These also disappearing as we drew near, continued an ever-varying scenery of land and water, though not a drop of water was actually visible upon the parched surface of the plains. At one time, on our right could be traced, for a great distance, a long, winding river, fringed with timber, the bank being plainly visible in that portion of its course which lay near us, flowing onward in front of us, and across our course towards our left, where it seemed to discharge its waters into a boundless ocean, the surface of which, near the shore, was studded with islands covered with waving trees.

Upon the shores of these, unceasing billows rolled and broke in white foaming surges, stretching away to the utmost extent of the vision. At the same time, farther round to our left, and apparently not over half a mile distant, appeared a beautiful grove, the tree-tops gracefully swaying in the breeze; but as we drew near, lake, river, ocean, islands, and groves, like the panorama of a dream, gave place to the unchanging and monotonous landscape of the plains.

12th. — Last night and the night before, the wolves and coyotes exercised their vocal attainments by discoursing the most diabolical music that human ears ever need to listen to, no doubt to their own satisfaction, as they stopped of their own accord.

It is certainly not very entertaining, while with weary, aching limbs enveloped only in a blanket, stretched upon the bosom of mother earth, courting "tired nature's sweet restorer," to be thus serenaded, throughout the long hours of night, by these hungry and bloodthirsty animals, who are only prevented from bestowing closer marks of attention by their cowardly instincts.

At this moment, while I am seated at the door of the ranche — where we have put up for the night — writing, a pack of fifteen or twenty gray wolves are hovering about in plain sight, waiting for the darkness of night to give them the desired opportunity of trying their murderous teeth upon some unfortunate straggler from a Texas drove. These they often pursue for many miles, tearing out pieces of living flesh with their steel-like jaws, as they scour the plains in headlong flight, until the poor animal, worried out and exhausted by the loss of blood and muscle, as well as his own furious efforts to escape his merciless tomentors, yielding to the imperiousness of fate, falls heavily in their midst, and is torn limb from limb ere life is yet extinct, amid the horrid snarls and growls of his blood-seeking foes.

There are, besides the coyotes, three varieties of wolves that I have seen in this country — the black or brown wolf, the gray wolf, and the white or mountain wolf. The latter, though larger, is not nearly so numerous. The gray wolf may be said to be the wolf of the country, and is a fierce but cowardly animal. I have frequently seen a dozen or more in a pack, but have not known of their attacking man, though they are more bold in the winter, when the ground is for some time covered with snow, and they are pressed with hunger.

The coyote is more slim, more of a gray, and less red than his more northern namesake, and is very abundant,

15*th*.—After having crossed the Cimeron, North Fork, and Main Canadian Rivers, — the latter, when I crossed it last spring, being nearly half a mile wide, deep for fording, and swift; is now, owing to its long course through the parched plains, a mere brook, which a child could easily step across, — we this day arrived at the Wichita Agency.

Proceeding directly to the school-house, I opened the school-room door without knocking, and stepping in, stood in front of the school. The room instantly rang with joyful acclamations.

Though the scholars kept their seats, they could not

resist the impulse to shout my name over and over again. The teacher at first rose up in astonishment; but seeing me in my present condition, travel-soiled as I was, he comprehended the whole cause of the uproar, and not having before seen me in such a plight, could not refrain from laughter himself. After shaking hands all around, I retired to the room I had formerly occupied, to improve the appearance of the outer man by the renovating application of soap, water, and razor, and exchanging my travel-soiled garments for those more befitting a civilized being.

Before this was more than half accomplished, school broke for the day, and "Thomis!" was the cry, and up stairs was the rush, filling the stairway, hall, and room, insomuch that I had much ado, by telling them that I would soon be down, to induce them to leave me by myself. Indeed, it seems pleasant to get among these wild but really affectionate children once more.

17*th.* — After lying over one day at the Wichita Agency, I this day came on to that of the Kiowas.

24*th.* — Several of the school children being very sick with pleuro-pneumonia, and no nurse at the school, I was detailed to take care of the sick children.

Found one of the boys in a very suffering as well as dangerous condition; the others comparatively easy, but needing careful nursing.

To-day, Horseback, a Comanche chief, brought in and delivered up to the agent two white captive boys, whose stories, condensed, might be given as follows: —

CLINTON SMITH.

One year and a half since, he and a younger brother were taking care of cattle or sheep but a short distance from their father's house, near San Antonio, in Texas, when they were seized by a small party of Arizona Apaches, and carried away captives. A few days subsequently, Clinton was sold to a band of Quahada Comanches, by whom he has been held in captivity up to the present time. He is a boy about thirteen years of age, and talks fluently in the Comanche language. His father had been making all the exertion in his power for the recovery of his children, — had visited the Agency, and written on different occasions, but all had been unavailing until the present autumn. So many outrages, murders, &c., having been perpetrated on the frontiers of Texas, by the wild bands of Indians, including the Kiowas and Quahada Comanches, that government determined upon their chastisement, and sent Colonel McKenzie, with some troops, into that region. He fell upon an encampment of the Quahadas, killed several of the men, and took about one hundred and twenty of their women and children into Texas as captives; afterwards, discovering a camp from which the Indians had all fled, he destroyed their lodges — reported to have been upwards of one hundred.

Hence, finding themselves in a narrow place, cut off from the rations and annuities by their agent, driven from the haunts of the buffalo by the military, and winter approaching, they have but one alternative; that is, to agree upon terms by which they can secure their rations and annuities, and, if possible, the liberation of their women and children.

Horseback, though in no wise implicated in the affair, has been among the Quahadas, and persuaded them to give up these boys, and to come in and make peace with the agent; but they, being in mourning for their dead, as well as for their women and children, will not come in at present.

Clinton informs that there are other white boys in captivity among them, but as they were continually watched, they could not speak to each other in English, and he could tell nothing more about them.

This boy was clothed and placed in school, upon his restoration, and kept there until a suitable opportunity occurred, after some weeks, of sending him to his friends.

John Valentine Maxie

is a boy about nine years of age, was brought in with Clinton Smith by Horseback, and delivered to the agent. He had been some years with the Quahada Comanches, had forgotten his name and language, and could remember nothing but the scene of his capture. His account of this, as elicited by the interpreter, was, that his father was killed at the wood-pile, his mother, together with a babe in her arms, were killed, while himself and a little sister were carried away; but his sister, being unable to walk, was killed that night. He also was clothed and placed in the Agency school. Notices of their restoration were published in the Texas papers, and after about two months the father of this boy came to see him, and found indeed his own son. The real story of his capture, as I learned from his father, was substantially as follows:—

Some three years since, he (the father) was suddenly called to go several miles from home, in the early evening, leaving his father, wife, children, and a neighbor's wife and child, at his home. It appears that his departure was noticed by some Indians lurking near, who soon made an attack upon the old man (grandfather to the boy), who was chopping wood at the door, the children being at play near him. He was killed at once, and the neighbor's child was also killed, upon his attempting to run. The women in the house, hearing the noise and screams of the children, ran to the door, when the mother of our little captive, with a babe in her arms, was shot, and falling in the door, was drawn in by the other woman, and the door closed. The Indians, then, after shooting an arrow through his leg, so that he could not run, seized this boy and his sister, and fled with them. The woman was not killed; but the ball, after passing through the head of her babe, severed the artery in her arm, from which she came near bleeding to death, but is still living, to receive, as from the dead, this her only surviving child. Strange as it may appear, after the child had seen his father, though all attempts to bring incidents to his memory by which he might be identified, had proved unavailing, it seemed as though a new light had suddenly broken upon him, and not only his name, but several incidents of his early life, were unsealed to his memory, proving his identity beyond a question.

This boy was in the encampment which was surprised by Colonel McKenzie, and with great presence of mind mounted a pony, fled to another camp, gave them notice of the approach of the soldiers, and thus prevented their surprise.

28*th.* — Kicking Bird and seven other Kiowa chiefs came in and delivered several stolen mules to the agent. Upon the subject of my going among them being explained to them, they all gave an unqualified word of approbation, offering to do all they could for me. Kicking Bird himself said he would take care of me, but his wife having recently died, he could not do as he had said he would do, and he thought I had better not go out to their camp until the chiefs return from Washington. They claim that they intend now to settle down, and not "do bad any more," but travel in the road that Washington makes for them, and until their chiefs come back to teach them Washington's road, they will travel the one their agent makes. Several of the chiefs came round and shook hands with us, saying it felt good to take their agent by the hand again. He told them they might always take him by the hand, by doing right; it was by doing bad, — killing people, stealing mules, horses, and children, — that prevented their taking his hand. They had killed more than forty persons, stolen a great many mules and horses, this past summer; he had withdrawn his hand, but when they do right he will give it to them again.

11*th Month*, 14*th*. — Since my last entry, when not otherwise engaged, I have been constructing, painting, and varnishing, a set of outline maps, for the use of my school, if I live to get one in operation at the Kiowa camps. I have made eight maps, viz., one hemispherical map of the world, North America, South America, Europe, Asia, Africa, United States, and Indian Territory. This afternoon Horseback brought in and delivered up to the agent two more white captive boys, who were duly washed, shorn, and clothed. Their hair hung in mats, which it was impossible to comb out, and was, of course, alive with vermin. They were thinly clad, and were suffering much with cold. After being washed, shorn, and clothed, their appearance was much improved, they looking like smart, intelligent boys.

ADOLPH KOHN,

one of the boys mentioned above, is a German; says he is eleven years of age, speaks German, English, Spanish, and Comanche. He says he has a father, mother, and nine brothers and sisters. He was captured some three years since, near San Antonio, Texas, while taking care of sheep. A few days after, his captors — three Arizona Apaches — traded him to a band of

Quahada Comanches, with whom he remained up to the time of his delivery. His treatment undoubtedly has been similar to that of other captives; that is, he has been compelled to herd ponies and mules, and perform the drudgery for the camp generally.

On one occasion, a sick child, of which he had the care, died, and he was severely whipped. He is now very much elated with the idea of his deliverance, and the prospect of being again restored to his family and friends. Adolph was placed in school, and kept there for some weeks, when, a suitable opportunity presenting, he and Clinton Smith were sent home to their friends.

Temple Friend,

brought in by Horseback with Adolph Kohn, though appearing to be a very intelligent boy, having been taken young, had forgotten the English language, remembering only the scene of his capture, — his mother having been killed while his father — whose given name he remembers to have been John — and a sister older than himself were away from home. There seemed to be no clew by which this boy could be identified; and the whole household at the agent's were becoming much attached to him, when an old gray-headed man, — L. S. Friend, — a Methodist minister, who had for many years acted as a missionary on the frontiers of Texas, arrived from Kansas, where he now resides, having seen a notice in the papers of the delivery of two unknown boys at this Agency, and also received a letter from the agent to the same effect, came to see if he could recognize in one of them his long-lost grandson.

He had spent much money, and had travelled over fifteen thousand miles in his unwearied search; and now his efforts were crowned with success. The old man gently put his arm around the boy, and drew him towards him. The tears started in his eyes, as he slowly uttered the words "Temple Friend." The boy started as if from sleep, looked at the old man, and having learned a few words in English, replied, "Yes." The old man then pronounced the name of his sister, "Florence Friend." The boy, with a look of unutterable amazement, replied, as before, "Yes."

We learned from the grandfather that Temple is thirteen years of age, was captured in Texas, and has been with the Indians five years.

His mother (step-mother), though transfixed by an arrow through both arms and breasts, having the cords of her hands or wrists severed, and having been scalped in two places, still lives to rejoice over the return of this her long-lost son, "who was dead and is alive again, was lost and is found."

17*th.* — At our meeting for worship to-day, I was favored to feel a living desire to accompany my spirit for the growth in grace of such as may have experienced that birth in which they can grow in grace, and that those who may not yet have come to it may be brought forth in the newness of that life which is eternal; particularly these poor deluded, benighted, and superstitious heathen children. It often causes deep emotions to arise in my soul, when surrounded by these affectionate children, to contemplate the fearful state of darkness in which they are groping their way, accompanied many times by fervent, and I trust living, desires for their enlightenment, through the knowledge of the precious truths of the gospel, together with a willingness to labor, in my weak capacity, for that cause and purpose. O the fearful ignorance and superstition, the heathen darkness of this land!

23*d*. — This day died Ten Bears, head chief of the Yamperethka band of Comanches. He arrived with the Washington delegation, on the 21st instant, very weak and much exhausted, having been sick several days, — his lungs in a very bad condition. A bed was soon made for him in the office, and I was detailed as his nurse; but, being very old — probably upwards of eighty years — and very much exhausted from his long journey, he soon passed away. This morning he gave a picture of A. H. Love, President of the Peace Society, to the agent, and told the agent that he wanted his people to quit raiding in Texas. With the exception of his son, who arrived about two hours before his death, his people had all left him.

Indeed, this appears to be the prevailing custom among the wild Indians: when a person becomes old and feeble, so as to become in their estimation burdensome, they are neglected; and when sickness and death come upon them, they are sometimes abandoned to die alone; hence a life of barbarity, if not ended by violence, usually ends in cold neglect, without comfort, without sympathy, and without hope.

Yet when death has actually closed the scene, the relatives affect great grief, cut themselves with knives, and make bitter wailings, often burying the household goods, wearing apparel, &c., with the deceased, and even burning the lodges in which they died.

Thus passed away, in old age, the head chief of the Yamperethkas; a man raised in heathen darkness, living and dying in close proximity to Christianity without the outward knowledge of Christ, or the benign spirit of the gospel; who probably never learned, and perhaps never heard, the name of the blessed Saviour of men, except from profane lips. For several years past he has been friendly to the whites, has now ended his days among them, and a white man ministered to his latest wants on earth.

In respect to old and infirm persons being forsaken by their people, I have known several instances among the Comanches and Wichitas, but not among the Kiowas or Apaches. And on more than one occasion has such forsaken person found their way to the Agency, and been duly taken care of. On some occasions, after being thus abandoned, — "thrown away," as they term it, — old men have made "medicine" of preparation, and then taken their own lives with their own hands.

This "throwing away" old, infirm, or sick people, does not appear to arise from any loss of affection, but from a superstitious fear of the evil spirits that have taken possession of the individual.

CHAPTER VI.

FIRST TRIP TO KIOWA CAMP. — APACHE CAMP. — DOGS. — RETURN TO AGENT. — MARTHA DAY, A MEXICAN CAPTIVE. — RETURN TO CAMP. — KICKING BIRD. — KIOWA HISTORY. — VISIT WITH THE AGENT TO INDIAN CAMPS. — KIOWA TRADITIONS OF THE CREATION. — FUTURE STATE. — HORSEBACK.

12th Month, 1st; 1st Day of the Week. — Kicking Bird having come in last evening, attended our meeting with us to-day, after which the agent furnishing me with a mule to ride, with some rations, I set out with him (Kicking Bird) and Dangerous Eagle for his camp.

We rode fast from about four o'clock until eight in the evening, when we arrived at the Apache camp, having been duly notified by the dogs that we were approaching some place.

After making our way through the midst of hundreds of dogs, every one of which appeared to exert his vocal and explosive powers to the utmost, filling the air with perhaps the most horrid din of snaps, snarls, yelps, growls, and howls, that my ears ever became acquainted with, we found a convenient place for lariating our ponies and mule. This is done by simply fastening the animal by a long rope or lariat, so as to allow him to graze, while he is at the same time secure from straying away. We then proceeded to the lodge of Pacer, the head chief of the Apaches, being escorted by most if not all the dogs in the community, still continuing their deafening clamor, and crowding upon us to that degree that we had to keep them off with clubs, — Dangerous Eagle having generously provided me with one for that purpose. Arriving at the lodge, arrangements for our supper were soon entered upon by the two wives of our host, himself stalking about in his blanket, destitute of shirt, leggings, or moccasons.

The lodge, like nearly all belonging to the wild Indians, was built in the form of a conical tent, made by stretching several tanned buffalo skins, strongly sewed together, over poles set in a circle, crossing at the top in the centre, and fastened by thongs. The tent, being raised and spread, is fastened down by pegs at the bottom. The entrance is a small hole opening towards the east, and covered by a piece of thick skin so tanned as to be somewhat stiff, and ornamented with paint. This is fastened, by buckskin strings, on whichever side the wind may happen to be, so as to form a self-closing door. The opening is not over three or four feet high, and does not extend to the ground, barely admitting a large man. Indeed, it was with some difficulty that I got through with my overcoat on, the side pockets stuffed with comforter and gloves.

The internal arrangements are very simple. A round hole is dug in the centre for the fire, three sides are occupied by the beds, while the side in which is the entrance is used as kitchen, pantry, and general store-room. The beds are elevated above the ground, perhaps from four to six inches, and serve for seats and lounges in the daytime, or when not used for sleeping purposes. They are made by laying small willow rods across a couple of poles, and covering them with buffalo skins prepared especially for the purpose, blankets, and ordinary robes, making, but for the vermin, a comfortable bed.

A large kettle was boiling over the fire, the contents of which were stirred from time to time with the broad rib of a buffalo, while another large kettle was sitting by the fire, in which our coffee was boiling. In due time supper was announced, consisting of boiled beef from the large kettle over the fire, coffee, and very good biscuits, or short-cakes, baked in an old-fashioned bake-kettle, or Dutch oven. After we had partaken all that was desirable, and pushed the dishes back, our host and his two wives finished what was left. A basin of water was then passed around to drink, and to wash our fingers, which is usually done by filling the mouth with water, and spurting it upon the hands, afterwards wiping them upon a dirty cloth provided for the purpose, and passed around to all who have partaken of the meal.

Supper being ended, we withdrew to another lodge,

where most of the principal men of the encampment were in waiting to extend the hospitalities of the pipe, which was continued until a late hour. Conversation being in an unknown tongue (to me), I was not peculiarly edified therewith; but the fumes of the pipe, as it circulated from mouth to mouth, filled the lodge with the most unendurable fragrance of tobacco and kinnekenick. The smoke would subside for a time as the pipe became exhausted. This was but a momentary relief to me, as it was replenished, after short intervals, by the person occupying the honorable position of pipe-filler. He was amply equipped, with a piece of an old barrel head, upon which was piled up a quantity of tobacco and kinnekenick, well cut and thoroughly mixed. The consumption of this was the signal for the dispersion of the company, and we retired through the army of dogs, which kept up a continuous parting salute, as we passed along to the place where our mule and ponies were lariated. Here we spread our blankets upon the ground, and lay down to sleep, or to enjoy, for the rest of the night, the joint serenade of dogs and wolves. Some of the latter came so near that I could hear their footsteps on the dry grass, and one of our lariats was cut by them only a few steps from my bed, letting one of the ponies loose; but as the wolf is the acknowledged brother of the Indian, it may be presumable that they were only watching us; perhaps smelling me with a sniff of jealousy, as being no relative of theirs.

2d.—After taking breakfast with Pacer, we proceeded on our way, travelling from about ten in the morning until two in the afternoon, passing near several Comanche camps and many hundreds of their ponies. On arriving at Kicking Bird's camp we were not met with a running salute of dogs, but a host of children came out to met us, and to stare at the "white man" who was accompanying their chief. Our horses and luggage were taken care of by the women, while we repaired to the lodge of Zebile, Kicking Bird's brother. Here we remained, enveloped in the smoke of tobacco and kinnekenick, while Kicking Bird was informed of the affairs of his camp, and in turn had given his talk, explained the cause of the presence of the white man, when we partook of some supper, and retired to Topen's lodge to sleep. Topen is a fine-looking little girl, Kicking Bird's only child. She soon produced the little map of North America I had drawn and given her, which had been kept very nicely. Kicking Bird's encampment is situated upon a creek, six or eight miles above the remains of old Fort Cobb, in the midst of a dense growth of small timber, and consists of about forty lodges, all constructed upon the same general plan as the one described as Pacer's, with plenty of wood and water at hand.

6th.—After remaining in camp until yesterday afternoon, endeavoring to render myself familiar with all, and writing down many Kiowa words, in order to memorize them, we came on to the Agency, staying last night at the Apache camp, and arriving at the agent's about noon to-day. I might say that I have been treated with the greatest attention and kindness, though no doubt many of the Indians look upon my being among them with mistrust, fearing that my motives may be to their disadvantage.

MARTHA DAY,

a Mexican woman, who had been some two years in captivity among the Quahada Comanches, last night made her escape to the Agency, where she has been cared for, clothed, &c.

She yesterday informed Black Beard, her owner, that she intended to run away from him. He told her that she had better not make that attempt, as it would cost her her life; if the agent should not kill her, he would return her to him, as she was a Mexican, and he would kill her. Apparently in great distress of mind, she proposed to herd the mules, as she could not sleep. As it was rainy, and the proposition accorded so well with their propensities to laziness, it was fully assented to, and she took charge of the mules. These she soon left to take care of themselves, while she set out for the Agency. Eluding the guard, she entered the porch on her arrival, where she sat until morning. After the family had arisen, she came in, and was of course well taken care of. The Quahadas, armed with bows, arrows, and revolvers, watched every window and door to which they could gain access, in order to get a sight at her, but were foiled in all their attempts. In the evening she was put on the stage, in company with the father of Clinton Smith, and started on her home journey, rejoicing in fear, and yet manifesting a thankful heart. We have since been informed of her safe arrival at her home and among her friends. She was quite a good-looking young woman, intelligent, and appeared to have had some education before her capture by the Indians, and is now about eighteen years of age.

The following day the Quahadas were very inquisitive about her, wanting to know where she was, and to be paid for her; but all attempts in that direction were fruitless, the agent simply informing them that he had sent her where they would not see her. If they had brought her in and given her up, they would have received one of their prisoners whom McKenzie had captured; but now they would receive nothing.

8th and *9th.* — Returned with Kicking Bird to his camp, spending the night near the Apache camp, the lodge being so full that I spread my blankets upon the ground outside, and enjoyed a good night's sleep, though surrounded by hundreds of Indians, who, but a few months ago, would have rejoiced at such an opportunity for securing the scalp of a white man.

After leaving the Apache camp, where Kicking Bird, Trotting Wolf, and myself took breakfast, and, consequently, were far behind the other Kiowas, while riding along in company with these two chiefs, my mind became unusually overshadowed with Divine Goodness,

— with a precious feeling of calmness, — in which I was favored to approach the throne of mercy with an unusual sense of nearness thereto, which feeling continued while we travelled many miles.

In the evening Stumbling Bear, a Kiowa chief, informed me of a war, while General Hazen was their agent, in which he himself killed and scalped five men, and Kicking Bird seven. I suppose that it would be a difficult thing to find, in the whole tribe, a man, over whose head twenty years have passed, whose hands have not been imbrued in blood.

10*th.* — Since living in an Indian camp, I have often noticed a peculiar howling cry, for an hour or so, about daybreak, without knowing the cause of this dismal wail. It is the hour of lamentation, in which those who have recently lost relatives or friends by the hand of death, raise this cry of grief.

To-day there have been several outbreaks of this kind, in consequence of the dangerous sickness of several young children in the camp. Pleuro-pneumonia is of frequent occurrence among them, owing to their exposure, few if any among them wearing anything upon their feet or legs. Indeed, young men of twenty years of age and upwards are not unfrequently running about with no other covering than a single blanket, let the inclemency of the weather be what it may; and I have many times seen their middle-aged and old men go out to breakfast, away from their own lodge, with only a blanket about them, even in winter's cold. Yet, when prostrated with pleuro-pneumonia, the wife or mother, instead of endeavoring to assuage the sufferings of the patient by judicious nursing, or to arrest the progress of the disease by the application of remedial agents, has recourse to the tricks of jugglery, or other absurd and superstitious performances, and betakes herself to these detestable howlings, in which, as was the case to-day, so many of the women and children join, that the whole encampment resounds with the dolorous wail. This wail is so unlike any other earthly sound as to be utterly impossible to give an adequate idea of it on paper. It must be heard to be appreciated.

15*th*. — In company with the most of Kicking Bird's people, started for the Agency. During my stay in camp I have endeavored to render myself familiar with the children, mingling with them as much as possible out of doors, and, whenever opportunity offered, exhibited my charts. Several have learned their letters, and some young men form very well-shaped Roman letters with a pencil. I find that, day by day, they are becoming more and more familiar, and I think some of the prejudices of the older ones are giving way, so that when the time comes for me to erect my tent in the midst of their camp, many of their children will enter it with some degree of confidence, who could not have been prevailed upon to do so in the beginning of my acquaintance with them. On one occasion, the lodge in which I was sojourning was taken down, and the man and his wife left for some other place, leaving me without knowing where to go or what to do, as Kicking Bird was away at the time, so that I could talk with no one in the camp. However, ere very long, Zebile came to me, and by signs bade me enter his lodge. My goods were soon brought in, so that I felt quite at home.

I have made some progress in learning the Kiowa language, and was particularly struck with the simplicity of their modes of numbering, — being a decimal system even more simple than our own.

Encamped for the night near a Comanche camp, and on the morning of the 16th went into the Agency, finding that a box of books, charts, slates, &c., had arrived, during my absence, for my use, so that I shall be in readiness ere long, I trust, to open my school in camp.

Perhaps it would not be uninteresting to the reader to have a short account of Kicking Bird, whose name will often occur in these pages, as it has already done.

Kicking Bird is a chief of distinction, not only among his own tribe, but has great influence with other tribes, particularly the Apaches. He is not a full Kiowa, his grandfather being a Crow Indian, who was captured while young, and brought up among the Kiowas, married a Kiowa woman, and raised a family of children, one of whom became the father of Kicking Bird, who is distinguished for eloquence, bravery, military capacity, good sound practical sense, and his friendship to the whites.

He might be considered the first chief of the tribe: although no chief is amenable to another, still there are, at the present time, no less than twelve chiefs who look to him for counsel in all matters of importance. His long-continued attachment to the whites at one time so far brought him into disrepute with his tribe, that they charged his friendship to cowardice, called him a woman, and refused to listen to his counsels. Finding his influence in the tribe nearly gone, he raised a force, conducted a raid into Texas, and had a severe engagement with the white soldiers, where he conducted his men with such ability and coolness as to come off victorious, and win a testimony of respect from the commander of his enemy's forces. On his return home he again advocated peace with the whites, and has steadily continued to do so from that time to the present.

The tribe, thoroughly convinced of his bravery, no more attribute his desire for peace to cowardice, and listen to his eloquent arguments, — in most cases yielding to his counsels; so that he really stands at the head of all those Kiowas who are disposed to live peaceably, as Lone Wolf does at the head of those occupying a less friendly position.

Lone Wolf is several years older than Kicking Bird, not so far-seeing, more hasty and rash in his conclusions, as well as more treacherous and cunning, but with less depth of mind. He is the acknowledged leader of that portion of the tribe who are more inclinable to hostilities.

It appears, from what I have learned from Kicking Bird, that the Kiowas, many years since, lived far to the northward, where it was very cold most of the year,— far beyond the country of the Crows and Sioux. He states that when they lived there, they knew nothing of ponies, but used dogs to carry their burdens, to draw their lodge-poles, and remove all their fixtures from place to place. In process of time one of their men, in his travels, went far to the southward, and after some years of roaming, was taken prisoner by a band of Comanches. They took counsel to put him to death, but one of their head men prevailed upon the rest to spare him, on the plea that they had never before seen any one like him, or any of his people, and it might be that if they treated him well, he might befriend any of their men who might fall in with his tribe. He further counselled his people to send him home with honor. The counsel of this chief prevailed, and he was fitted out with a pony, saddle, and bridle, and sent home. On his return, his pony, saddle, and bridle were objects of general admiration and envy, paving the way for the reception of his glowing description of the fine country he had seen. He told them that in the country he had visited, the summer lasted nearly the whole year, and the plains were stocked, not only with game, but large herds of ponies such as he was riding.

Hearing the old man's glowing account, and seeing his enviable pony, the subject became the topic of national council, and it was finally nearly unanimously decided to follow the old man to the beautiful country he had seen. Accordingly upon the opening of the following spring, the whole tribe, with the exception of a few who could not be prevailed upon to receive the reports of the old man, commenced their migrations to the southward, leaving their dogs with their friends who remained in that country. They continued their migration, under the leadership of the old man, until, in process of time, they fell in with a party of Comanches, who made war upon them, but eventually becoming possessed of ponies, they followed their enemies to this land, where they have ever since resided.

1*st Month*, 6*th*, 1873.—Yesterday, Black Beard, a Quahada chief, brought in, and delivered up to the agent, three Mexican captive boys, whom they had held in captivity for two years past. These boys are apparently as much pleased with the prospect of their restoration to their friends, who reside near San Antonio, Texas, as any of the other captives; but not being able to converse with them, I could not learn their histories.

This day the agent, interpreter, myself, and two others, set out on our contemplated tour to the camps; but, getting a late start, it was dark when we arrived at the widow Chandler's, on the Little Washita River, whose husband is now a corpse in the house.

7*th*.—After the burial of J. Chandler, who has been the agent's interpreter for some years, we proceeded to Mahway's camp, by way of the Keechi Hills, a series of rocky mounds, rising abruptly from an undulating country, giving it a wild, romantic appearance. From the summit of the most prominent of these, which rises, perhaps, two hundred feet above the surrounding country, a beautiful view, for many miles, is obtained. We stopped a short time at Mahway's (Shaking-hand) camp, and then proceeded to the Wichita Agency. I put up at the school-house for the night.

9th. — After visiting Howeah's camp, on the Washita, we arrived, last evening, at Kicking Bird's camp, which is now situated on the north side of the Washita, off the reservation for the Kiowas and Comanches. Had a long council, which was continued this morning, in which nine Kiowa chiefs were present. They expressed their determination to cease raiding and depredating upon the whites, and wished to be at peace with other Indians, making a special request that some good white man should go with them, to meet the Utes in council, in order to make peace with them.

After the council was ended, with Kicking Bird for guide, we left for the other Kiowa camps. Crossed the prairies and entered the mountains ere night overtook us, and were compelled to encamp among them.

It was a beautiful evening, though cold, and we had built a roaring camp-fire, about which our little party were sitting, in the double enjoyment of its genial warmth, and the beauty of the wild scenes, lighted up by the silvery light of the moon. One of the party asked the chief what the Kiowas thought of the moon. He replied, "It is the Great White Man:" then, looking for a cluster of stars, which he did not succeed in pointing out to us, he stated it to have the outline of a man, and to be the Great Kiowa. He subsequently pointed out to me the Pleiades, with some of the surrounding stars, as this cluster.

The Great Kiowa, he said, was a very large man, and also very powerful. He was so large that he could cross the widest rivers at a single step. He made all this great country, with all its lakes and rivers, its mountains and plains; he also made all the animals, of every kind, that were found in it before the white people came, — such as the buffalo, the bear, the beaver, the deer, the antelope, and the wolf.

After having made all these, he travelled a long while to the westward, until he came to a very large, hollow tree, lying on the ground; walking up to this, he made three feints as if to strike it, and the fourth time he gave it a hard blow, upon which out marched a body of Kiowas, — full-grown men and women, — who ran from him as if in great alarm. He called them back to him, telling them that he was their father; that he made them; that they were his children. When they came back to him, he discovered that they were disfigured by having some of their members improperly placed upon their foreheads. Correcting this error in their formation, he sent them away; and again striking the log as before, another body of Kiowas came forth. These also consisted of grown men and women, and upon their fleeing from him, were called back, as the others had been; but finding them correctly formed, he sent them away. The third time the log was smitten as before, and this time children came forth with the men and women. Being displeased at this, he called them to him, and discovering indications that evil had been wrought by them while yet in the log, he became very angry, and told them that since they had done wrong before coming forth from the log, he should make no more Kiowas. He then gave every man a bow, and some arrows with stone heads, and every woman an instrument with a stone edge, for dressing the skins of animals. Instructing them in the use of the instruments he had given them, and further teaching the women how to make clothing and lodges from the skins of animals, after dressing them, he told them that he gave all this country to them, and all the animals it contained, that they might use their flesh for food, and their skins for clothing and lodges to live in.

Then, leaving them, he travelled far towards the rising sun, until he came to a great water. There he, for the first time, met with the Great White Man, who was well clothed, and riding a fine horse — himself being but poorly clad. They approached each other, and the Great Kiowa, claiming the country, informed the Great White Man that he made it, and had made a people to live in it; that the people he had made were his children; that he had given this country to them, and it was theirs. The Great White Man replied that he had done well; he himself had many children, who lived away across the great water, in a country he had made and given to them.

He further said that he had given them books; taught them how to make fine clothes, such as he himself wore; to build fine houses to live in; and how to make the ground produce such things as they wanted for their sustenance.

After this the Great Kiowa returned to his children, and told them of his interview with the Great White Man, and the words that passed between them; again told them that they were his children; that this country was theirs; that he had given it to them. The Great White Man had made a country for his children beyond the great water, and they ought to stay there; but, should they find their way to this country as their father had done, they must fight them as enemies, and never make peace with them; and though there might be a great many more of the white people than of them, they should never become extinct, but should continue to be a people forever. After this, the Great White Man and the Great Kiowa went up among the stars, to look at what they had done, and watch over their works. The Great White Man became the moon, and the Great Kiowa a cluster of stars.

Kicking Bird said that he thought the Great Kiowa did wrong in counselling his children to fight the white people, and never make peace with them, as this tradition is instilled into the minds of their children from their early infancy, and it is hard work to eradicate it from their minds so that they shall not continue to feel a secret enmity towards the white people. But since they receive their annuities, rations, and many other favors, from the hands of the whites, he can but feel grateful to them, as do also many of their old men; and had it not been for the instilling of this sentiment into their minds in their early years, they would long since have been friendly to the whites. He feelingly spoke of his deceased wife, calling her a good woman, mentioned her love and friendship to the white people, based upon the many kindnesses and favors received from the agent and others, concluding his discourse by saying that he had told his people that he had firmly resolved, that unless they went no more into Texas on their thievish and murderous raids, he should throw them away, take such as might still cling to him, and settle down with the whites at the Agency, and leave them to suffer the consequences of their choice.

In reply to the question, "What becomes of us when we die?" he answered that he did not know what became of white people, as they were not made by the same being that made the Indians. But when Kiowas die, the spirit travels a great way towards the sunset, and crossing a high mountain ridge, it comes at length to a wide water, which it has to cross. Upon arriving at the opposite shore, it is met by former loved friends, who have gone before to this happy land, and who now rejoice to meet it again. There the game is always fat and plenty, the grass is always green, the horses large, swift, and beautiful. The inhabitants are never sick, nor feel pain. Parting and tears are unknown — joy fills every heart. A high mountain stands near the boundaries of this land, and watchers are set upon it, who are continually looking along the road leading from this country, watching for the spirits of the dying and newly dead, — whether they die naturally, in battle, or by accident; and when they discover any coming along the road, they immediately call to the friends of the coming spirits, who go forth with rejoicings to meet them, and conduct them to the lodges they have prepared for them.

10*th.* — After having crossed several steep and rocky ridges, we descended to a wide and beautiful valley, bounded on the north and north-east by the mountain ridges we had just crossed, and on the south and south-west by the more elevated portions of the Wichita Mountains. In this valley a large part of the Kiowas, several bands of Comanches, and the Apaches have their camps.

The view of the Wichitas from the elevated dome of Mount Scott, in the south-east, to Mount Sheridan, in the south, in connection with the beautiful valley beyond which they arose, formed a scene of sublime grandeur not easily described.

After visiting the camps of Sun Boy and Lone Wolf, a portion of our party, myself for one, determined on visiting the summit of Mount Sheridan, which we immediately set about, and effected in a short time. It rises about eleven hundred feet above the surrounding plain. Ascending its sloping sides, covered with trees, we came to the nearly perpendicular walls of granite which form its summit.

These, at the south end of the mountain, rise about two hundred feet, while they are much higher at the north, — probably not less than four hundred feet. These rocks render the ascent laborious and difficult, but once surmounted, the magnificent grandeur of the scene crowns all. Hundreds of square miles of rich and beautiful prairies, valleys, hills, and plains, are spread out as a map at our feet, in all their wildness and solitude. The less lofty peaks of the Wichitas were scattered about us here and there, to the east, west, and south, — being a perfect wilderness of rocky summits. The mountain ridges we had crossed in the morning, and which cost us hours of toil, could scarcely be distinguished from the plains, so low and insignificant did they appear.

The more elevated head of Mount Scott stood out in the east, at the distance of six miles, as a giant among dwarfs, while, taking the whole view, in all the ever-varying richness of scenery incident to the proximity of mountains and plains, hills and valleys, the effect is striking and sublime.

On our return to the Agency late in the evening, we learned that four of the women captured by Colonel McKenzie, having been released at the solicitation of Horseback, on account of his procuring the release from captivity of the four white boys mentioned heretofore, had returned during our absence.

12th. — Horseback came in with a number of mules and horses to deliver up as stolen property, and proposed in his speech having a treaty made with the Texans. One of the returned women told the story of the battle, and of their capture and treatment by the soldiers. She said they had been universally well treated, had plenty of good food, and were not required to do anything, not even to bring water or provide wood at their camps.

Her remarks respecting the kind treatment received by them gave the agent an excellent opportunity of contrasting her statement of the universal kindness with which they were treated, with what they knew all white captives, especially females, received at their hands, — always being much abused, and often suffering death as the result of it.

Horseback acknowledged the truthfulness of the contrast, owning that he knew that the white man had a better heart than the red man, and he wanted to live in friendship with him.

Horseback is a chief of no ordinary capacity, having about two hundred people in his band. He is probably about fifty years of age, and though not a Quahada, yet possesses a very great influence with the chiefs of that band of Comanches. He, being sick at the time the Washington delegation left, had to remain at home, and has become active in his demonstration of friendship to the whites, probably more from policy than from any inherent good feeling towards them. However that may be, he has not only secured the delivery of the white children held in captivity by the Quahadas, but also from twelve to fifteen Mexicans, since the delegation left, and has now made out all the horses and mules stolen by the tribe. He, being a man of great determination, has exercised his firmness and resolution, this fall and winter, by visiting and bringing into the Agency, on peaceful relations, the Quahada band of the tribe, and is now anxious for a man to go to his camp as a teacher, being determined to leave the old road, and travel one that he is beginning to see will be more elevating to his people. His conduct, for a few months past, is highly commendable, and, if continued, will place him at the head of all the Comanche chiefs, though standing in the background hitherto.

CHAPTER VII.

OPENING OF THE SCHOOL IN THE KIOWA CAMPS. — ADVENTURE WITH A MIDDLE-AGED WARRIOR IN MY TENT. — SICKNESS AMONG CHILDREN. — BAD MEDICINE. — SUPERSTITIONS. — COUNCIL. — REMOVAL TO CACHE CREEK. — OSAGE WAR DANCE. — KIOWA FEAST. — APACHE MEDICINE DANCE. — VISIT FROM THE PAWNEES. — THEIR RECEPTION. — PAWNEE WAR DANCE. — VISIT TO MOUNT SCOTT.

1*st Month*, 23*d*. — I this day record the opening of a school in the Kiowa camp, on the Washita River.

Having got my tent, blackboard, maps, charts, &c., in readiness, I left the Agency last 2d day; a son of the agent and two of the employees accompanied me, to assist in setting up my tent. But not getting the right directions as to the road, we were two days in reaching camp and setting up the tent. They left me yesterday, and having some other preparations to make, I could not open school until this morning, when, with twenty-two scholars, it was opened in the presence of most of the chiefs, several women, and a number of young men. It being the first attempt at anything of the kind ever undertaken among the Kiowas, it is regarded as a novelty by them. After the withdrawal of the chiefs and old people, several young men remaining in my tent, a middle-aged man came in with an uplifted hand-axe, his face hideously painted with black lines, expressive of intense anger, advanced towards me with a most horrid oath in broken English, and, suiting his action to his words, was, in appearance, in the attitude of striking me with the edge of his weapon. Putting on as bold a front as I could command, I stepped up to him, seized him by his uplifted arm, and forcibly put him out of my tent, telling him I should permit no such talk or action in my lodge.

I had no thought of fear until after closing the session for the forenoon, when, on thinking it over, I was somewhat unnerved. I think it very probable that there may be several young, middle-aged, and even old men, who may view this movement as an aggression upon their ancient customs, and conceive the idea of frightening me from the field, without manifesting any open opposition to it; but meeting prompt action, I think it will not be repeated, though some other form of interrupting the school may be resorted to.

P. M. — So many spectators being present who know nothing about schools, I found it next to impossible to bring the scholars to anything like order. As soon as the children attempted to pronounce a word after me from the chart, the visitors would burst into a laugh, every one talking in a loud voice, so that it was utterly impossible to proceed. I finally gave up the attempt, telling them, "Kiowas heap talk — heap laugh — I would wait till all done, — then, when no more talk — no more laugh — children talk," — keeping the children for some time standing silently before the charts. After a long time, they understood my meaning, and became silent, when I proceeded with the reading. Thus my long-cherished design of opening a school in the camp of the Kiowas is accomplished. I feel it to be but the beginning of many trials, and much labor both of body and mind. May I be favored with strength and fortitude sufficient for the occasion, and may the undertaking prove a blessing to this people, is the ardent desire of my heart.

30th. — Since opening my school, I have continued it from day to day, first day excepted, up to this date, though the violent snow-storm of the 27th, during which about twelve inches of snow fell, and the succeeding cold weather, which was intensely cold, — the mercury at the Wichita Agéncy sinking to thirty-four degrees below zero, — very much interrupted the school. It was impossible to warm my tent so as to be comfortable, and yesterday morning, after suffering from cold through the night so that I could not sleep, I went to Kicking Bird's lodge, where a fire had been kept up all night, in order to get warm, and from the effects of the heat, though I kept at some distance from the fire, I so nearly fainted, that I could not sit up; but had school in the afternoon.

This morning Kicking Bird informed me that the

Caddoes had been talking to them about me, making their own superstitions so operate upon the ignorant Kiowas, that, unless it be counteracted, my school will not be likely to amount to much, for some time at least. They have told the Kiowas that I am a bad medicine-man, having made several of their children sick last winter by "blowing" them; that two of them died — one a young man, who had the consumption before coming to school to me, and lived two thirds of a year after I left. The fact of so many of the Kiowa children being sick at the present time with bad colds, has rendered their minds very susceptible to this superstitious idea. But, in my estimation, their being exposed bare-footed, bare-legged, bare-armed, bare-headed, bare-necked, and bare-breasted, to the inclemency of the furious storm, — getting their blankets wet, in which many of them sleep at night, as well as run about by day, and then the sudden change to intense cold, — is a sufficient reason for the present sickness; but they can see no other than that given by the Caddoes. I should not have inserted this circumstance, but to show what absurdities are so fully believed by them that instances are not uncommon, among all these wild people, of the suspected individual suffering death at their hands. Instance the medicine-woman, after the death of the Wichita chief, narrated heretofore. Other instances might be given, not only among the wild Indians, but even among the Caddoes, in which a son has killed his own father on account of these superstitious suspicions.

The chiefs and head men of the encampment are holding council to-day, I suppose, in order to come to a decision as to what to do with so dangerous a man as they have among them. What the result of their deliberations may be I know not. Their children are kept away from my tent, and a couple of young men, armed with bows, arrows, and revolvers, are remaining in and about it, watching me while I am writing these lines.

Notwithstanding the intensity of their feelings, Kicking Bird, his mother, and daughter Topen, O-del-pac-quo-i-see and his daughter Amatze, and another young man, took breakfast with me in my tent.

Now, the countenances of all I chance to see, as they will peep into my apartment from time to time, look troubled and gloomy. But let the case result as it may, I fully believe it will be in accordance with His designs, who has the ordering of all things, and without whose permission they cannot harm a hair of my head. Though I perfectly comprehend my situation, I am preserved free from anxiety as to the event. Should they determine upon carrying me back to the Agency, or even a more sure mode of getting rid of me, I am persuaded that it will not be from any ill will to me, or the cause in which I am engaged, but, in their estimation, in defence of the lives of their children.

About five o'clock the council broke up, and most of the chiefs and principal men of the camp came directly to my tent, filling the main or public apartment, bringing pipes and tobacco, and wearing cheerful, smiling countenances, every one advancing, taking me by the hand, and pleasantly uttering my name, then seating themselves about the apartment. Two of them, viz., Kicking Bird and Stumbling Bear, entered my private apartment, and seating themselves upon the bed, called me to them. Stumbling Bear then rehearsed to me the talk of the Caddoes, saying, "No good talk, — Thom-is-sy good man;" then told what chiefs had given "good talk" in their council, and immediately introduced conversation upon other subjects, but would still come back to the subject first spoken of, indicating the character of the council, and the depth of feeling manifested in it. In the mean time, the chiefs in the other apartment were silently smoking. Thus, through the watchful care of an overruling Providence, who has thus far made way for me, unworthy though I am of the least of his many favors, through many discouragements, and even at times where there has appeared to be no way, has this gathering storm broken away, at least so far as not to wear so threatening an aspect as the blackness of its rising may have indicated.

The snow being much drifted in the ravines upon the prairies, and our beef having been eaten, Kicking Bird had a mule killed, this evening, for our subsistence until we can get to the Agency for rations.

2d Month, 8th. — Arrangements having been made for the removal of our camps, yesterday, with Trotting Wolf for guide, the men whom the agent had sent out for the purpose with a team, took my tent and fixtures, and proceeded, in advance of the tribe, to the place of our next encampment, on the South Fork of Cache Creek, perhaps twenty-five miles from the Agency. After raising my tent, a part of the tribe arrived, and encamped near by. This morning the Agency men and team returned, and in the afternoon, Kicking Bird and his people came, and put up their lodges around and near my tent.

It is astonishing in what an incredibly short time the whole aspect of a portion of country may be changed by these people. At noon to-day, except a few lodges upon the opposite side of the creek, though higher up and scarcely visible, my tent was the only indication of the proximity of human beings. The whole beautiful valley of Cache Creek was a solitude, from the mountains to the Agency. Presently a long, dark line is seen coming over the ridge which bounds the valley on the north, and in less than an hour the solitary vale is teeming with life and activity, — both sides of the creek being dotted with human habitations for nearly a mile in extent, in which are living several hundred of these wild people, each chief surrounded by his own band. Their lodges are so simple, and so easily taken down and reconstructed, that one may be in a camp at breakfast, — everything moving along in the usual manner; presently the ponies and mules are driven in, and the whole village is transferred to their backs and is gone, leaving little to mark its former site.

Again, as in the experience of to-day, a wild and solitary place is selected for a camping-ground. In the morning it is a solitude, — perhaps not a human being within thirty miles; in the evening a village has sprung up, the routine of business, — dressing of buffalo robes, tanning of buckskin, collecting of fuel, &c., going on with all appearance of having been there for months. The same village, but upon a new site; all is changed, and yet nothing new; old things are not done away, — the same people — the same lodges, — all in the same positions relatively — all opening to the east; each chief again surrounded by his own people, and all, as heretofore, following unrestrained the leadings of their own desires.

18*th.* — The school very irregular; some days it is impossible to secure any attendance; others, from ten to fifteen go diligently through the school exercises; but it is very evident, since the sickness mentioned among the children, that there is a strong opposition to their being in my lodge. This morning, while several children were quietly sitting around, attentively engaged, an old man came in, and, in a very violent manner, took the slates and pencils from them, and drove them out of the tent, thus winding up the school for this morning rather abruptly. In the afternoon, as the children began to collect for school, some young men came in and drove them out; then asked for slates and pencils. I refused to let them have them, telling them, if they wanted to use slates and pencils, to come in quietly, and sit down, and they could have them. There was room enough, slates enough, and pencils enough, for them all; but when they come in and drive the children out of my tent, they may go away, as I shall do nothing for them. Afterwards, one of them, as if to find out whether I really meant what I said, on a younger boy's coming in, drove him out; whereupon, without many words, as I was fully satisfied that I had been understood, I took hold of him and put him out of the tent. It is my determination that children shall not be abused in or driven out of my tent by the young men, if it lies in my power to prevent it. Fully believing that a firm hand is as essential to success in the management of the Indian as a kind heart, both should be joined together, and well stocked with patience.

19*th.* — Though surrounded most of the day by these wild Kiowa children or wilder young men, I have not been wholly devoid of feeling.

In looking over the events and experiences of my past life, it appears as though it had been nearly a failure. I see but little accomplished of all that might and should have been done, not having lived day by day so near to the Fountain of life and strength as I should; weakness, and even death, has been my lot, and I have gone halting all my life.

Even here, though endeavoring to live one day at a time, to gather my bread day by day, seeking help, strength, and wisdom from the true Fount of every blessing, I see but little improvement, and must confess with one formerly, "The good that I would I do not; but the evil which I would not, that I do;" and that "when I would do good, evil is present with me." Yet, since I truly desire to, and in some measure do, "delight in the law of God after the inward man," I mostly feel calm and peaceful, though not in a sense of abounding, but rather of deep spiritual, though peaceful poverty. Hence I have no reason to complain, if in the wisdom of Him whom I desire to serve, He sees it to be best for me to keep me in the low places, neither abounding in fullness, nor yet wholly destitute of Divine favor, so that His will concerning me be perfected, whether I see the desire of my eyes as regards this people, yea or nay. I know that they are equally with their more favored brothers the objects of Divine regard and compassion; that "His arm is not shortened that it cannot save" even to the uttermost; that His grace is sufficient even for their redemption, by which they must be changed, if changed they ever are, from this savage, heathen life to that of Christian civilization.

After retiring for the night, I was awakened by a fearful combination of noises, — drumming, howling of dogs, yelling of men, laughter of women and children, — and, soon after, the voice of Trotting Wolf near my tent, shouting my name, and, addressing me in Kiowa, bade me "be quick, come and see." I got up, dressed, and followed him to a place (only a few rods from my tent) near which all this jargon of boisterous, though perhaps not entirely inharmonious sounds had proceeded, and, sitting down in the grass, awaited the result.

A large fire was burning, the light of which illumi-

Big Bow (Zip-koh Eta), Kiowa Chief.

nated objects for some distance around, about which, at convenient distances, seated in groups, were some hundreds of these people, old and young, forming a kind of disconnected circle. while by themselves, near the fire, were the braves of this portion of the tribe. Among these the drum was beating continually, while their clear voices arose at intervals in a weird kind of wild harmony.

A couple of braves, nearly naked, but painted and with feathers in their hair, having long lances ornamented with feathers of various colors, left the others and advanced towards the fire in a series of fantastic jumpings, jerking up of one foot, and a variety of indescribable gestures and bodily contortions. These turning about near the fire, a number of others in similar habiliments, with uplifted tomahawks, hatchets, war-clubs, and one old cavalry sword, rushed upon them with the same indescribable gesticulation and jerking step,—bowing, jumping, striking, dodging, and yelling. In this latter exercise the whole assembled multitude, with one exception, joined their vocal powers. Ever and anon a dark figure or object flitted across the arena, which in the dim uncertain light had more the appearance of a demon than a human being. Perhaps the demoniac forms sometimes seen in pictures were real scenes in savage life. These hideous objects flew past in all possible attitudes. Sometimes suddenly dropping in the grass, they would for a time disappear from view; then bounding high in air, arms and legs distended wide, with two or three fantastic bounds would vanish in the darkness, amid the yelping of the dogs.

The fire was kept up by one of the old men, who from time to time, as the performers returned to the group of braves, gathered dry grass to throw upon it during each performance, making a very bright light for a time, but which, declining in its brightness, gave opportunity for the rushing, jumping, running, flying kind of demoniac exercise with which each entertainment concluded.

This was a kind of Indian theatrical performance in which on the present occasion the Osage war dance was enacted by Kiowas.

20th. — While eating our breakfast this morning, Kicking Bird and myself received an invitation to breakfast with Feather Head, which, not to be disrespectful, was accepted; and while partaking of his hospitality, a messenger bearing a similar invitation came in from Trotting Wolf. This latter was designed as a kind of feast, to which all the principal men of the encampment were invited. The bill of fare consisted of wild plums stewed, boiled corn and pumpkins, bread and coffee. There were no women in the lodge, but as many men as could sit around it. After some time, Trotting Wolf's daughter reached a bowl, two saucers, and a spoon into the lodge, accompanied by the utterance of my name. They were set to one side, and a short piece of board was similarly thrust through the entrance. Afterwards three kettles containing the food, some tin cups, and a kettle of hot coffee were introduced, whereupon one of the chiefs filled one saucer with the plum sauce, and the other with the mixed compound of boiled corn and pumpkins. Pouring coffee into the bowl, and placing them, with a spoon and a piece of bread, upon the board, they were passed to me. Then commenced the feast by starting the kettle of plums with two spoons around the circle, which, by the way, did not swing around very rapidly, as it stopped some time in front of each two men on its way, and it was very observable that its contents were materially lessened on every occasion. However, it got round once successfully, when, finding there was nothing but kettle and spoons, it was set aside. The spoons were put into the next kettle circulated with it. This, from some cause, made two entire revolutions before being set aside. Then followed in order the bread and coffee; which being despatched, the empty kettles, bowls, and spoons were withdrawn from the lodge by the same hand that had introduced them, though its owner did not venture into the lodge.

After the meal was concluded, the pipe circulated around the lodge, filling it with rising wreaths of blue smoke, blown upward and downward, and puffed in all directions from mouth and nostrils. After the amount of tobacco and kinnekinick prepared upon the board had been thus converted into smoke and ashes, the company broke up, and it was no small relief to me to get a sniff of the fresh air outside the lodge.

21*st.* — Evening. Witnessed another of their dances, being a representation of the Wild Apache Medicine

Dance, or, as I would describe it, an Indian masquerade.

All the performers, except two young women, wore hideous masks, some with distorted noses, grotesquely painted, and fantastically dressed, with feathers attached to their legs, arms, backs, and head-dresses. The latter consisted of light wooden frames. Small bells were attached to their legs, which made a jingling sound, as they jumped around, to the music of many voices, and the beating of a drum — in a manner indicative of a thorough limberness of every joint in the body. The two young women were very prettily dressed in garments made of some dark blue material for backs and fronts; the sides were of a brilliant scarlet, and put in goring; a broad flap of the same material was sewed around and over the arm-holes, serving for sleeves. Over this, and about the shoulders, was an ornament the most highly prized of anything worn by the young women, as it is by them esteemed the most beautiful. It consists of a cape made of red strouding or scarlet list cloth, is nearly covered with a peculiar tooth from the elk, only two of which are ever found in one animal, and often they have none. They are not very plenty, and are highly prized in consequence. These produced a rattling noise during the dances.

There were three sets who took part in the dance, one of which represented old, decrepit people apparently bent with age, and half starved, dressed in buckskins and rags, bearing masks of some white material over the face, with noses out of all proportion, and ears standing out several inches from the head; one of the women carrying an infant similarly masked. The actors must have been highly gratified with the approbation manifested with their performance, as shout after shout of applause arose from the assembled multitude.

The dance ended about ten o'clock, and all became usually quiet. This dance represents the medicine the Apaches use to bring rain. They assert that, when it has been a long time dry, this dance is commenced and continued the whole night. The fourth succeeding night thereafter there will be thunder and rain, it being very strong medicine with the Apaches; but, of course, the medicine of the Kiowas is much stronger.

23d. — I was favored to have most of the day to myself, though an incident occurred which came near occasioning some loss not only to my enterprise, but also to the encampment. I had been in the way of taking up my ashes in the morning, and pouring them out upon the ground in one place, not foreseeing danger therefrom, though the prairie is not burned off. But this morning, while sitting alone in my tent, I heard the crackling of fire, and ran out quickly to see what it meant, when, to my consternation, the flames were rushing before a hard wind directly towards the tent, and were then but a few feet from it. In spite of my efforts, had not the Indians rushed to the rescue, it would have been consumed in a few minutes. Their blankets, vigorously applied, soon subdued the flames, which were higher than our heads, and burned the grass within a foot of my tent, and at one time rolled up its canvas sides in a very threatening manner. I learned that the great concern of the Indians on first perceiving the fire, knowing that it was medicine day with me (i. e., the first day of the week), and that I was sitting alone in my tent, was that I would know nothing of it until my escape would become impracticable, and that I would be burned. Notwithstanding the above incident, my mind has been favored to feel a degree of peaceful quiet, for which, as well as all other favors, I desire to be thankful.

3d Month, *3d.* — While at the agent's last week, having been very anxious to talk more understandingly with the Kiowas, I spoke to the agent to send G. Conover to the camp with me for a few days as interpreter, which being assented to, he yesterday came with a wagon prepared to move my tent, as the Indians were about to move camp soon.

A party of Pawnees came in last evening, giving notice of their arrival by their head man and two or three others coming into camp immediately, while the main body remained two or three miles distant. This morning a public reception was given them.

The party was seen coming over a ridge in single file, bearing a white flag. Approaching to within twenty rods, they planted their flag, upon which was painted the single letter P, and sat down in a line on each side of it, facing the village.

After sitting in this manner for perhaps half an hour,

during which they maintained entire silence, and preliminary arrangements for their reception were made in the camp, the chiefs, followed by most of the head men, and these by the young men, women, and children, went forth to welcome them.

Upon drawing near to them, the Kiowa chiefs walking with a slow step and dignified mien, some of the old women set up a chant in a shrill voice, whereupon the head chief of the Pawnees, and two or three others perhaps the nearest in rank, arose, and with a quick, firm step approached the Kiowa chiefs, and, after embracing them, retired to their former position.

Others of the Pawnees came forward, a few at a time, until all had embraced and been embraced by the Kiowa chiefs and head men. The women, remaining some distance behind, renewed their shrill chant from time to time. Some of the Pawnees occasionally placed a shawl or embroidered blanket upon the shoulders of a Kiowa, while several of the old men passed along in front of the whole line of the visitors, shaking hands with them. After this the Pawnees set up a weird song, during the continuance of which Kiowa fathers, each carrying a small child in his arms bearing a piece of stick in its little hands, young girls, and occasionally a woman, would approach the Pawnees, and, selecting some one, would present themselves before him, holding out the stick. Thereupon he would arise, place his hands upon the donor's head in a solemn, reverential manner, as if blessing, pass them down the sides, following the arms, take the stick, and sit down. Each stick thus given was a pledge from the giver to the receiver for a pony, to be given when the visitors are ready to return to their country. Old men, from time to time addressing the Kiowas, urged them to liberality — to show the largeness of their hearts, the warmth of their friendship, by giving ponies to these poor Pawnees who had come so far to see them and renew their friendship, and not allow them to return on foot as they came. I know not how many ponies were thus pledged to them, but there must have been many.

At the conclusion of the ceremony the Pawnees arose in a body, ceased their singing, took up their flag, and a part following one Kiowa chief, and a part another, accompanied them to their lodges to partake of their hospitality. The head chief, with four or five others, including the flag-bearer, accompanied Kicking Bird to his lodge, thus becoming his guest.

Late in the afternoon our visitors gave an entertainment by which they received pledges for several more ponies. Having erected a kind of canvas amphitheatre, about six feet in height, by setting poles in a circle perhaps forty feet in diameter, and stretching the canvas around them so that it could be slipped down sufficiently to allow of looking over it, they proceeded to exhibit the Pawnee war dance to the music of a drum, a string of bells, and their own voices toned to the highest pitch of anger. They were fiercely painted in bright colors, and while dancing they appeared to be searching in every conceivable place for the enemy, their uplifted implements of war, consisting of revolvers, tomahawks, war-clubs, bows and arrows, knives, aud even swords, with their fierce and angry looks, showed but too plainly how they would be treated when found. Individuals occupied the intervals between the dances by narrating their own former valorous exploits, not even omitting to mention that their victims were in some instances Kiowas, concluding by throwing their war implements upon the ground with such force, in case of tomahawk or hatchet, as to cause the metal to ring again. Then, with gestures of covering it up, they would go away leaving it to lie there; thus intimating that, though they had been foolish, and fought, they now rejoiced in the beams of peace, and hoped that the red men everywhere might live in peace one with another; all of which was received by the Kiowas with the loud response of "*How, how!*" — "Yes, yes!"

In mentioning the dance and the music, words fail to convey any idea of it; and I shall not render myself ridiculous by attempting to describe that which is indescribable.

The reader should imagine himself placed in some of the most wild recesses of America, far from the abodes of civilized man, surrounded by hundreds of these untamed sons of the wilderness, ornamented in all the wildness of their unrefined tastes with tinsel and gaudy-colored paints, — the most diabolical gestures of nearly nude men as though searching an enemy, or actually engaged in deadly fray, — running, jumping, fleeing, dodging, brandishing their long knives, plunging their swords, striking with their tomahawks and war-clubs, drawing their arrows in their bows, being enacted before his eyes; — while his ears are filled with the most unearthly combination of noises — the twanging of bow-strings, beating of drums, jingling of bells, piercing, angry shrieks and yells, — in order to form even a faint idea of these heathenish practices.

15*th.* — On account of having so many Pawnees (forty-five) and for so long a time, our rations so far gave out as to necessitate some arrangements for our living, other than that issued by the agent. After seeing a young colt dressed and brought in for food, I was willing to accept of the proposition of Kicking Bird to go into the Agency for a while. Yesterday I took several Kiowa chiefs to visit the school, see how the children are fed, clothed, sleep, and are cared for generally; informing them that their children, would they but send them to school, would not only learn as those children are being taught, but they would be taken care of in all respects as these were.

What the effect may be on their minds I know not, and must leave for the present.

Last evening, Agent Richards and wife came here from the Wichita Agency, and to-day I accompanied them on a visit to Mount Scott.

We passed through some beautiful valleys, arable, and clear of stone, bounded by mountain ridges, so that, but a few rods from good, arable prairie, in all appearance clear of rock and suitable for agriculture, those immense piles of boulders arise with only enough soil to supply a foothold for the most scanty vegetation, among which are several varieties of cactus. Mount Scott is supposed to be the most elevated of the Wichita Mountains, and is an immense pile of rocks, which, notwithstanding its smooth, dome-like appearance, is in many places very precipitous and difficult to climb. The top is slightly convex, and covered with huge boulders of red or flesh-colored granite, and rises probably about twelve or fourteen hundred feet above the surrounding plains. The whole mountain appears to be composed of the same material, clothed with a shrubby dwarf-oak but a few feet in height, while the very top is sparsely covered with a low-spreading cedar. Numerous wild flowers were scattered about here and there on all parts of the mountain.

The view from the top is magnificent, embracing hundreds of square miles of mountain scenery, beautiful and wide-spreading valleys, and extensive plains. To the westward, point after point of the rocky Wichitas extend as far as the eye can reach. The boulders on the sides and tops of these mountains are rounded and smoothed as if by water, undoubtedly having lost their sharp corners in the immense ice-fields of the glacial period. Yet there is no doubt but that the modest, unassuming lichen — the rock-destroyer of every age and clime — has had a hand in rounding the rough and jagged corners of these adamantine rocks.

CHAPTER VIII.

AGENT TATUM. — HIS ADMINISTRATION AND LABORS. — RELEASE OF MEXICAN CAPTIVES. — COUNCIL WITH KIOWAS AND COMANCHES RELATIVE TO RELEASE OF PRISONERS. — DISMISSAL OF MILITARY GUARD. — DEATH OF DANGEROUS EAGLE'S WIFE. — SAND STORM. — TARANTULA. — CENTIPEDE. — SCORPION RATTLE-SNAKE. — BIG BOW. — RAIDING PARTY OF COMANCHES STOPPED. — VISIT TO WICHITA AGENCY.

4th Month, 4th. — After taking leave of Agent Tatum and wife, who will probably leave the Agency for their home before I shall come in again, I this day left for camp, where we arrived a little before sundown.

In thus parting with our much esteemed agent, whose term of office has expired, and from whose hands, with those of his excellent wife, I have received so many favors and attentions, my mind naturally reverts to the past, reviewing the various trying scenes of his administration. In so doing, I am persuaded, that, whatever errors there may be discovered in his management of the affairs of this Agency, they will be found to be of the head, and not of the heart.

The Indians, who are now beginning to understand and appreciate his labors for their good, very much regret his leaving them at this time; many of the better disposed among them often saying that he has had a hard time with them for many years, and now, when they themselves are just ready to leave their old ways and start on a new and better road, it is too bad to leave them.

Indeed, his steady, upright, straightforward dealing, his firmness and decision of character, coupled with great coolness and kindness of heart, have procured for him many friends, not only among the Indians, but also among the frontiersmen of Texas.

Many of these latter have abundant cause to remember him with gratitude for the assistance he has rendered them in the recovery of their captured children and stolen stock.

Even in the arrest of Satanta and Big Tree, for which he has been much censured, I cannot see how the dignity of government can be maintained if capital criminals may be permitted to come forward boldly to government officials and boast of their crimes, and he not cause their arrest, if means to effect the same be at hand.

I know that in his own estimation his administration has not been a successful one, and perhaps, in some respects, it has not. Yet, in looking at the wild, savage state of the Indians of this Agency at the commencement of his term of office, their hostility to the whites, their thievish, predatory propensities, their ferocious, warlike dispositions, — then considering the amount of stolen property he has recovered, the number of captives he has redeemed,* and the general quiet which now prevails, — it cannot be denied that a marked degree of success has attended his administration.

In the simple matter of the recovery of captives, easy as it may appear, to an observer at a distance, for the agent to sit quietly in his office and receive at the hand of a chief, captives as they are brought in at his demand, the practical working of the concern is a very different affair. From my knowledge of facts in connection with the recovery of those captives who have been redeemed since my coming within the limits of this Agency, it has been attended with unwearied exertion, and required, on the part of the agent, skilful management, together with an endowment of something more than mere human wisdom to accomplish.

Especially has this been the case in the recovery of the Mexican captives, eleven of whom have been brought in only upon condition that they should be at liberty to return with the Indians if they expressed a desire to do so.

In some instances the lives of the captives have been threatened; ten or fifteen young warriors have accompanied them to the office, apparently to carry their threat into execution if they expressed their preference to remain with the agent, or to go to their relatives. Various

* He has delivered eighteen captives and one hundred and sixty-four horses and mules within the last eight months.

schemes have been resorted to to deceive the agent into the belief that there were no more captives among them; but he has been favored with wisdom to detect them, so that it is now believed that all the captives who have not been adopted into the tribes, and have families around them, have been given into the hands of the agent. Perhaps I can illustrate the difficulties of this undertaking in no better way than by narrating the case of

LEVANDO GONZALES,

a Mexican boy, aged about sixteen years, which came particularly under my own observation.

The Indians had, as on previous occasions, denied having any more captives; but the agent, obtaining reliable information that there was at least one more, made the demand for him. He was brought in, in the evening, dressed as a young warrior, highly decorated with ornaments, accompanied by one or two chiefs and a party of fifteen or twenty young Comanche braves, the latter evidently for the purpose of intimidating him, and thereby secure his return with them, they being the very class whom he would have most reason to fear. He was placed in the middle of the office, while the others were seated around; and in reply to the question put to him by one of the chiefs, whether he would prefer to go back with them to staying with the agent (whom he had never before seen), answered he would return with them. Though the agent was sensible that the Indians would not hurt him, yet, as the boy could not know this, he saw the necessity of cautious management. Accordingly, he sent for a Mexican to interpret for him, and seeking for ability to treat the case with wisdom and discretion, gave him a good meal; then, after the arrival of the interpreter, instead of putting the question whether he would go back with the Indians or remain with him, opened conversation with him respecting his relatives — his father, mother, brothers, sisters, what their feelings must have been upon his capture, the happiness his return to them would occasion. Having thus aroused the young man's feelings of attachment to his near relatives, he proposed the question whether he would not prefer to live with them to living with the Indians; telling him that he need not be afraid to tell him the truth ; the Indians dare not hurt him, whatever they had threatened to do, — not knowing that they had threatened his life did he not answer in accordance with their wishes. Thus assured, he answered in favor of living with his friends. This answer being made in Comanche, he was immediately stripped of his ornaments, and then given up. From him the agent afterwards learned that there were other Mexicans in captivity who wished to escape. These were brought in at the demand of the agent, thus securing the liberation of all the captives.

I should have mentioned under date of the 28th ult., that a council was held with the Indians of this Agency by Cyrus Beede, who was duly authorized by the department to promise the speedy release of Satanta and Big Tree, and the Quahada women and children, provided the Indians, on their part, would but continue to be quiet and peaceable. They readily pledged themselves to abstain from acts of hostilities, and to maintain friendly relations towards the government and the white people, being given to understand that the prisoners would be delivered to them about the 1st of the sixth month next.

4th Month, 24th. — At the Agency. Agent Haworth having removed the military guard from about the Agency buildings soon after his arrival, the Indians look upon the move as an indication of confidence in them, and feel much pleased with it. Though there are several hundred of them around, including Kiowas, Comanches, and Apaches, — they having come in for rations, — they are more quiet than I have ever seen them on a day for issuing rations. Only the chiefs in the commissary ; no wandering and peeking through the house, climbing of the fences into the yard, trying this door and that to get in ; but all are quiet and orderly.

An old man is slowly riding round and round the buildings, all the time the crowd was so great, evidently to hold their wild young men in check, thus establishing a guard of their own to keep order, in lieu of the military guard heretofore employed — a convincing evidence that proper treatment will not only be appreciated, but reciprocated even by Indians.

Since my last entry, we have changed camping-grounds a number of times, remaining but a few days in a place ;

which, with the difficulties arising from their superstitions, has caused me to relinquish the school for a season, feeling that they are not yet so prepared for it as to admit of its being of much benefit to them. I also find a necessity of being more with and among the young men — the warriors of the tribe — than would be possible were I to attempt to continue the school longer.

29th. — Having been camped for a few days on Sulphur Creek, we yesterday removed to the Washita River, above the mouth of Rainy Mount Creek. The day before removing from our encampment on Sulphur Creek, I noticed a small mound of fresh earth, surmounted by a buffalo skull, near the lodge of Dangerous Eagle, which I took to be the grave of a young child; but not having heard any lamentations, I did not know what it meant; but now understand that Dangerous Eagle's wife had lost a young child, and, being herself very sick, could not make the usual lamentations. This mound, however, as I afterwards learned, contained buried medicine.* A couple of lodges were left at Sulphur Creek on account of her illness; but to-day they came into camp, bringing the sick woman in a kind of litter, formed upon long, springing poles, one end of which was fastened to the sides of a mule, while the other end dragged upon the ground. Cross-pieces were firmly lashed to these poles behind the mule, upon which coarse grass, buffalo robes, and blankets were spread, making a soft bed, surmounted — upon a framework of willows, through which the air could circulate freely — by an awning of muslin, making

* A sacrifice to their mother the Earth.

a cool shade from the rays of the sun. Inside of this rudely constructed vehicle the sick one is placed, and conveyed from camp to camp with comparative comfort, if not with the refined elegance of more highly civilized life. I have seen on some occasions several young children carried in one of these litters.

Upon leaving this place on the 30th, Dangerous Eagle was again compelled to remain behind on account of his wife's illness, which continued for several days before she expired. Before leaving, I saw the women engaged in digging her grave. This led me to fear that the patience of her husband was so nearly exhausted by his repeated detentions on her account, that violent means would be resorted to if she did not soon die. I have known instances among these people — though not among Kiowas — of men becoming discouraged, and killing their wives with their own hands, when they have been for some time sick, and their medicine (jugglery) failing to effect a cure. Indeed, I know a Comanche chief who cut the throat of his wife for that reason. She was sick a long time, and their medicine did not cure her; so, to avoid the inconvenience of caring for a sick wife, who was not able to care for herself, after making "medicine of preparation," to fit her for a happy reception in the unknown land of spirits, he took her life, though mourning her untimely death. Such deeds are rare among them, but are still sometimes practised, they setting but small value upon human life, and sick or very aged people are a great hinderance to their wild, roving, unsettled way of life.

5th Month, 8th. — Arrived at the Agency, after a journey of two days in coming from camp, which is now upon Pecon Creek. The removal occupied several days, so that we have been travelling most of the time since last date.

On first leaving the Washita, we passed over some rough, hilly country, underlaid in part with red sandstone, and in places with gypsum, with occasional petrifactions of wood of various qualities, and some crystallized gypsum. This land gradually gave place to high, elevated plains, from which very extensive views may be obtained. From one place, nearly the whole system of the Wichita Mountains was in full sight, — from those in the distant east, near Fort Sill, to those in the south-west, — embracing in the range Rainy Mountain, Mount Webster, or Rattlesnake Mountain, so called by the Indians from the immense number of rattlesnakes inhabiting its rocky sides; while in the east, north, and west, stretched out the ever-varying monotony of the plains. Slight elevations and depressions of but a few feet are distinctly marked, one beyond another, for miles and miles. In travelling over these, the scenery is ever changing, and yet unchanged. One is constantly meeting with depressions, ravines, cañons, &c., not discernible at a short distance, all varying one from another, and yet strikingly alike. In looking over the plains, one looks over these, seeing nothing of them;

and the sudden abruptness with which the traveller sometimes comes upon them gives endless variety and surprise, without changing the appearance of the general contour. On account of the almost constant optical illusion produced by the deflection in the perspective of the plains, together with the refraction of the atmosphere, the judgment is almost constantly in error, not only as to the distance of an object, but also as to its appearance and outline. One may travel for hours directly towards an object, without any apparent diminution of the distance; then, in a little time he may find himself close upon it.

A mountain will at one time appear high, with abrupt perpendicular sides, rising like a rocky island from the waters of a lake or sea, without visible connection with land, while but a short distance of travel will suffice to change it to a low hill, with long, sloping sides, rising but a few feet above the general level of the plains. This is particularly the case if one be travelling on ground that is slightly rising.

Occasionally we come to a more broken country, with high sand-hills; at the summit of these, deep gullies are cut out, apparently by the action of water, but in reality by the wind. This accounts for the clouds of sand one sometimes encounters in traversing these plains. One of these overtook us this afternoon, as we were coming in. Kicking Bird pointed out to me a red haze in the west, exclaiming, "Hoodlety! hoodlety!" (hurry! hurry!), at the same time putting his horse upon the gallop, which example was followed by the whole party.

Though this haze looked distant to me, it was but a few minutes before we were enveloped in blinding clouds of dust and sand, which, fortunately for us, were driven the same way we were travelling. The sand and small pebbles, furiously driven by the wind, stung our ears and the sides of our faces, and rendered our horses almost unmanageable by their continuous pelting; but being at our backs, we held rapidly on our way. Dense clouds of dust filled the air, obscuring all surrounding objects to within a few feet, filling our eyes, noses, ears, and mouths, and literally covering us with dust. These sand-storms are most frequent in the spring and early summer, but are of occasional occurrence at other times of the year.

To-day we passed over a level plain south-east of Rainy Mountain, sparsely covered with musquito (mus-keet) timber, which gave it, for many miles, the appearance of a broken down or badly kept peach orchard, with mountains on either side. This plain gradually gave place to gravelly ridges and rocky ravines, north-west of Mount Sheridan, and this again to fertile prairies and rich valleys, well watered by fine streams of pure water, and bounded on all sides by rocky mountains, among which we travelled in a south-westerly direction, towards the Agency, where we arrived about four o'clock P. M.

5th Month, 12*th*. — As the Indians' beds in their

lodges are either upon the ground, or at best elevated but a few inches by means of poles, — the space between them often filled in with weeds and dry grass, which one would naturally suppose would form a harbor for the poisonous insects, reptiles, and snakes, with which this country is infested, — scorpions, centipedes, tarantulas, rattlesnakes, &c., — I have wondered that they have not got poisoned by them. But they nearly or quite always turn the skins and blankets with which their beds are made, and shake them well, before retiring for the night. Early this morning, however, I was awakened by the groans of Couquet, whose lodge is but a few steps from my tent, who had been bitten, as was supposed, by a tarantula. He suffered intensely, cramping and vomiting; still the part did not look inflamed. I was not permitted to witness the performance of the medicine-man, as he manipulated the case, but as the lodge is but a few steps from my tent, I heard some strange noises from him, and eventually the suffering man went through the process of the steam bath, and this evening he appears to be much better.

The tarantula is a large hairy spider, the body of which is over an inch and a half, and sometimes two inches, in length, and the legs spread over a surface of from three to four inches square.

The scorpion is a less ferocious looking, as well as less venomous reptile, and is of an elongated egg shape, armed with formidable pincer-like claws, and a long, jointed tail, terminating in a curved, horny sting-sheath; the whole animal is about four inches in length, and of a green color.

The centipede is a flat jointed worm, frequently six inches in length, and is very poisonous. It not only communicates its venom by biting, but its feet are armed with sharp poison points, which inflict dangerous ulcerating wounds, as it crawls over the flesh.

These reptiles could easily secrete themselves in the rubbish which forms part of the beds upon which these people sleep. The rattlesnake is much larger than his northern namesake, and is thought to be more venomous. I have seen them on the plains, occupying prairie dogs' holes, which measured from five to seven feet in length, and from nine to eleven inches around. A most formidable looking reptile.

I have known of several Indians being bitten by them, but of no case proving fatal; though I have no doubt but that it would, were it not for the application of a remedy for animal poisons, with which their medicine-men are familiar, and which grows in great abundance in this country.

The steam bath is resorted to on all occasions of sickness. A round hole is dug near the stream on which the camp is located, similar to the fire-holes in their lodges, but smaller; willows are stuck in two rows, about six feet apart, the tops brought down and twisted together, so as to form an archway about eight feet in length and four and a half in height, with this hole in the middle; long, dry grass is spread on the ground within, a fire is made near by, in which a number of stones are heated to a red heat; these are then placed in the hole, and arranged in a pile over it. An old tent-skin is spread over the archway, and fastened at the bottom, except at one end. The patient now enters it entirely naked, and a bucket of water being introduced by an attendant, the end is closed. He then, with a wisp of the grass, sprinkles water upon the hot stones, and the apartment is soon filled with hot vapor. When the patient is sufficiently steamed, he rushes out, jumps into the stream of water, resumes his blanket, and returns to his lodge, from whence the evil spirits that caused his sickness have been driven by the medicine-man during his absence.

5th Month, 14th. — Removed to the North Fork of Red River, called by the Kiowas Pēē-pōh, about eighty miles from the Agency. Just at starting, this morning, an Indian rode up to me, asking me if I knew him. I at once recognized in him the notorious Kiowa raider Big Bow, who has, probably, killed and scalped more white people than any other living Kiowa; and who, with his brother raider, White Horse, has been for years the terror of the frontiers, not only of Texas, but of Kansas, Colorado, and New Mexico. These two men, with small companies of their braves, have been continually going up and down, not as roaring lions, but prowling about in secret, seeking whom they might destroy; and woe to the white man, woman, or child, who fell in their way.

The last of their terrible deeds, of which we have any reliable information, took place nearly ten months since. One beautiful summer morning, a frontier settler, about sixty years of age, by the name of Lee, was sitting near the door of his home, in Texas, reading; his wife and family were about their morning duties, little thinking of the terrible things in store for them, even now at the door. The crack of a rifle is heard, and the old man lies dead upon the floor; no one is seen; the good wife flies to the open door, and is met by a similar missile of death; one or two other members of the family share a similar fate; the others, three in number, betake themselves to a field of corn for concealment, but are discovered and carried into a cruel captivity. The two eldest of these were daughters, aged sixteen and twelve; the other was a son, some years younger. They were continued in captivity for three months, when Kicking Bird effected a purchase of them, and delivered them at the Wichita Agency. The perpetrators of this horrid deed were Big Bow and White Horse.

Big Bow has a more treacherous and ferocious countenance than when I last saw him,—quite the reverse of his brother raider, White Horse, who wears an open, smiling face, and is a much more powerful man physically, as well as many years his junior. Neither of them are likely to atone for the evil they have done. At present they appear disposed to be friendly to the white people, and have for some months abstained from acts of hostility. Big Bow, however, still refuses to go to the Agency, while White Horse has gone repeatedly. The latter, though terrible as an enemy, I think is capable of warm friendship.

5th Month, 18*th*. — Removed to a point about fifteen miles up the river, and camped for the night on the south side of it. Our course to-day lay over an uneven, sandy country, covered with a small kind of oak, not over one or two feet high, yet having abundance of last year's acorns upon them. Over miles of this miniature forest we travelled, with little regard to the proverbial sturdiness of the timber, of which it was composed.

Late in the evening of the 15th instant, a party of Comanches, belonging to Tabananika's and White Wolf's bands, came into camp, on their way into Texas on a raiding expedition, and stopped to give the Kiowas the privilege of participation. A council of the war-chiefs and chief warriors was immediately called, in which they determined to punish any Kiowa who should attempt to go raiding in Texas, by killing his war-horses, destroying his saddle, bridle, blankets, and lodge. The principal chiefs approved of this resolution when informed thereof the next morning.

To-day, while on our journey to this place, a party of Comanches were discovered and surrounded; these had also started on a raid to Texas, and belonged to Tabananika's and White Wolf's bands. After surrounding them, the Kiowas told them they would give them four talks; then, if they were determined to go on their contemplated raid, they should kill their horses, tear their blankets, and let them go raiding naked and on foot — a condition in which they will not be very likely to go.

Not the least remarkable of events is this determination of these wild people, who have always hitherto been ready to join in, if not to lead, any hostile enterprise, now to stand firmly against all the influences of their old friends and allies, the Cheyennes and Comanches. The former of these have not been wanting in endeavors the past winter, as well as this present spring, to induce the Kiowas to join them on their war-path against the Agencies, while the latter are now endeavoring to seduce their young men to join them in their raiding expeditions, in order to renovate their stock of mules and ponies. But there is One who rules in the hearts of the children of men, and whose power is sufficient to bring under control the heathen who know Him not.

28*th.* — Arrangements were made, on the morning of the 19th instant, for me to come in to the Agency in company with a brother of Stumbling Bear, who, with several others, was going in after rations, while the main body of the tribe should journey on towards the north-west, to some place understood among themselves. It was also arranged for me to go to the Wichita Agency, there meet with Tofe-ko-neg Kiowa, and return to camp with him, — our camp being now about one hundred miles from the Agency. Accordingly I came in, and in due time proceeded to the Wichita Agency, where I visited both schools. These are in a flourishing condition, particularly the one for the Caddoes, which is really an interesting institution.

The one for the Wichitas being a day school, and the scholars going home every night, they are irregular in their attendance, which adds to the labor of the teacher, while it retards the progress of the children. Home influences being naturally strong, the children under our care should be removed as much as possible from them, in order to make much improvement in the ways and arts of civilized life. It cannot be expected that a stranger, in whom they have very little confidence, can successfully counteract the superstitious customs and heathenish practices in which their parents instruct them.

The Caddoes have opened several new farms this summer; their corn looks well, and many of them are turning considerable attention to raising cattle and hogs.

The wife of Tofe-ko-neg Kiowa being sick, he could not come in according to his expectation, and failing to meet him, I returned to the Kiowa Agency, to meet with Lone Wolf, who, I understood, was there, in order to return to camp with him. But he having gone before my arrival, I was, consequently, left at the Agency.

CHAPTER IX.

COUNCIL. — THOMAS WISTAR'S LABORS. — MEXICAN AND WIFE. — CHANGE OF INTENTIONS RESPECTING RELEASE OF SATANTA. — LETTER TO THE AGENT. — LETTER FROM WASHINGTON. — ARRIVAL OF COMANCHE WOMEN AND CHILDREN. — CAPTAIN McCLERMONT.

A PORTION of the executive committee having come to the Agency, a council was called on the 30th, in which Thomas Wistar was principal speaker. Alluding, in his speech, to his old age, and his long-continued labors for the Indians, he stated that over fifty years ago he visited the Indians in the south. Then there were thousands of Indians there — Creeks, Choctaws, Cherokees, Seminoles, &c.; now there are no Indians there, but thousands and millions of white people. He afterwards visited the Six Nations, in the north; there were the Mohawks, the Senecas, the Oneidas, the Onondagas, the Cayugas, and other tribes by thousands; now there is but a little handful of Indians there, but in their place are thousands and millions of white people. He afterwards visited the west, where St. Louis now is, saw the Indians there; but they are now gone from thence, and the towns and cities of the white people are there instead. Now, he had come here to tell these Indians why this has been so, in order that they might continue in their country forever. It is because the Indians of those countries would not work; they lived by the chase, and when the buffalo, the deer, and the antelope were gone, their old way of life would not afford them a subsistence. The white man finds his subsistence in the soil, but he has to work to get it out; and the Indian, would he but do the same, might continue in his country forever.

Late last evening, a Mexican man and his wife, who were captured when they were but children, and always held as slaves by the Comanches, came to the Agency for protection.

Perhaps a year since, the Comanches were about to kill the woman, and they ran away from them, and went for protection to J. Chandler, who took care of them while he lived. But, about two months ago, their retreat was made known to the Comanches by a white man, and a party proceeded to the widow Chandler's, for the purpose of killing them, or taking them back into captivity. They belonged to a brother of Tabananika, a Comanche chief. The widow Chandler, who was herself a Mexican captive,—having been stolen and brought up among the Comanches,—secreted them under the floor of her house, where they were discovered; but, as the Indians knew not how to get at them, they were willing to make a compromise with her, to the effect that their lives should be spared if she would give them up, to which she agreed. Subsequently the man was brought in at the demand of Agent Tatum ; the woman, being sick, was not brought in. He expressed a preference for returning with the Comanches, and was allowed to do so on the express condition that at any time when they wished to come in, or leave the Indians, they should be permitted to. He now says that he did not dare to express his actual feelings at that time as his wife was sick in camp, and he feared to leave her, or say anything to endanger her. The Indians had threatened to shoot him on the spot, if he expressed a choice for remaining at the Agency; two of them entered the office with him, having revolvers concealed under their blankets for that purpose. The same men accompanied him to the doctor's, and wherever he went, giving him no opportunity of stating his real inclination, or the true reason for his wishing to return to the camp, which was on his wife's account. They have now travelled six nights, keeping themselves concealed by day, during which time they have had but little to eat.

These Mexicans were taken care of by the agent for some time, until an opportunity occurred of sending them to a place of safety.

31*st.* — The agent received official information from the head of the department, that government, in consequence of the Modoc tragedy, contrary to its promises made to the Kiowas to release their chiefs, Satanta and

Big Tree, had countermanded its order for their release. This appears to me as unjustifiable an act as it would be to violate the treaty stipulations with Mexico on account of misdemeanors of the people of England or France. The Kiowas had never even heard of the Modocs.

Having had an opportunity of knowing their determination to follow out, to the best of their understanding, the instructions received from Washington, and fearing that a breach of faith, in a matter regarded by them as of so great importance as the release of their chiefs, will have a tendency to weaken, if not entirely destroy, the confidence they are beginning to repose in the government, — to their own hurt, and, perhaps, to the shedding of much blood, — I believed that it would be right for me to write a condensed statement of facts, that have come under my own observation, to be forwarded by the agent to the head of the department. Accordingly I wrote the following letter for the purpose: —

KIOWA AGENCY, FORT SILL, 5TH MONTH, 31st, 1873.

JAMES M. HAWORTH, *United States Indian Agent.*

RESPECTED FRIEND: Having an opportunity, possessed perhaps by no other individual, to know the state of feeling of the Kiowa Indians towards the Agency and general government, also their great anxiety for the restoration to them of their chiefs, Satanta and Big Tree, and believing, from my acquaintance with the tribe, that the latter act, on the part of the government, would go far towards their settling down and ultimate civilization, I thought it might not be improper for me to lay a few facts before thee in writing, respecting their *willingness* at least to comply with the requisitions of government.

About the time of my first going among them, in the 12th month last, that portion of the tribe with whom I was located was making great exertions to collect and return the mules stolen from the government, and many were returned, probably to the extent of their ability.

The subject of their frequent raids in Texas was freely talked over in their camps, and discouraged by their chiefs and principal men. Later in the winter, when a proposition was made to them by a party of Cheyennes — who came to them in the name of the tribe, professing to have been sent by their chiefs — to join them in the spring in a descent upon the Agencies, notwithstanding our rations were insufficient to prevent the gnawings of hunger, — they frequently having to kill their horses and mules for subsistence, — and the representations of the Cheyennes of plenty in their camps, with their solicitations immediately to join them in the buffalo country, they utterly refused to listen to them, and gave immediate information to the agent of the designs of the Cheyennes.

Subsequently to the murder of the four men belonging to the surveying party, the Cheyennes removed to the south side of the Washita River, and encamped near some of the Kiowas who were away from the main body, remaining there some weeks, until the main body of the Kiowas removed to a place near by, when three of the Cheyenne chiefs visited our camp, and had a council with the Kiowas; in which the Kiowa chiefs informed them that they understood the road Washington had made for them; that they believed it to be a good road, and should travel in it. They knew that their agent was a good man; the Wichita agent was a good man, and the Cheyenne agent was a good man (referring to the proposition of making a descent upon these Agencies); that they were doing all they could for the Indians; that only the Cheyenne Indians were bad; finally advised them to go home to their agent, sit down, and not come around trying to get their young men into trouble by inducing them to go on the war-path.

On the night of the 15th instant the war chiefs held a council in consequence of an invitation to join a raiding party into Texas, and the next morning, in my presence, informed some of the chiefs that they had determined to punish any Kiowa soldier who should go, or attempt to go, raiding into Texas, by killing his ponies and burning his lodge.

On the 18th inst. the Kiowas intercepted a band (not Kiowas) who had started on a raid, surrounded them, told them they would give them four talks, and then, if they still persisted in going on the raid, they should kill their horses, tear their blankets, and they should go naked and on foot.

They often tell me, that, if government does not return Satanta and Big Tree at or about the time specified by Beede in his council two months since, they can put no further confidence in the white man's word, and that they are waiting to see the fulfilment of that agreement before settling down; that, if they are delivered up, they will settle down, raise corn, send their children to school, and do just as their Great Father at Washington wants them to; provided they can have a school-house away from the military post.

Thy friend, respectfully,

THOMAS C. BATTEY,
Teacher in Kiowa Camp.

After about five or six weeks, the agent received the following communication from the Commissioner of Indian Affairs, which, as it refers directly to the foregoing letter, and, by being translated to the Indians, gave them the idea that the renewed action of government in relation to the release of their imprisoned chiefs was mainly owing to the information contained in it, thereby giving me an influence not before possessed, though somewhat out of place, I may be excusable for transcribing it in these pages.

Department of the Interior.—Office of Indian Affairs.

WASHINGTON, DISTRICT OF COLUMBIA,
June 26, 1873.

SIR: Referring to the letter addressed to you by Thomas C. Battey, teacher in Kiowa Camp, relative to the compliance of the Kiowas with their promises, their friendly attitude towards the government, their efforts to restrain hostile Indians from raiding, &c., and their anxiety for the return of Satanta and Big Tree, I have to inform you, by direction of the Honorable Secretary of the Interior, that the government is now engaged in the necessary steps to consummate the release of those prisoners, and their return to their tribe at an early day; and also that you will inform the Kiowas that all necessary measures are being taken to that end which are in the power of the department; but that the final decision rests with the governor of Texas, who is expected to visit Washington in a few days, when the subject of [their] release will be urged upon him, and it is confidently expected that the chiefs will be set at liberty.

Very respectfully, &c.,

ED. P. SMITH,
Commissioner of Indian Affairs.

JAS. M. HAWORTH, *U. S. Ind. Agt.*

6th Month, 10*th*. — This day arrived the Comanche women and children captured by Colonel McKenzie last fall, and held as prisoners in Texas since that time. Some two months ago, orders were issued for their release, of which the Indians were notified. Since then, no tidings had been heard from them, and the Indians were getting restless and uneasy, which was in no wise diminished by the inability of the agent to give them any information respecting the captives. Day after day, and week after week, passing by, and still no tidings, their faith as well as patience was well nigh exhausted, and they were ap-

11

pearing dejected and sad, many of them not believing that they were to be released. But while a large company were lying around the commissary, about noon to-day, giving impatient utterances to their feelings, the train bringing their women and children came in sight upon a distant hill. They were at once recognized by them, and the ominous gloom which had hung as a dark cloud upon their countenances was at once dispelled, and a joyful expression took its place as the whole party, accompanied by an interpreter, set off at full speed to meet them. The change in feeling was complete, affecting not the Indians alone, but the employees at the Agency, and all the white people around.

The news of their arrival was carried to the Comanche camps about as soon as horse-flesh was capable of doing it.

They have been seventeen days on the road, having had a rough, tedious journey, wading through mud, swimming rivers, &c. They look well, and say that they have been very kindly treated the whole time of their captivity, and have lived well. Five women ran away two or three nights before they started from Fort Concho, and have not yet been discovered, nine died in captivity, four were returned last winter, and there are just one hundred who arrived to-day, making one hundred and eighteen as the whole number captured. In order to give the whole tribe an opportunity to be present, they are not turned over to their friends, which, with the reception talk, is deferred until to-morrow.

11*th.* — A great many Comanches came in this morning to receive their women and children; and it was affecting to witness the meeting of parents with children, husbands with wives, brothers with sisters, &c.

The prisoners had informed their people of the kindness of their treatment, and of the difficulties encountered on their return from the high waters along the whole journey. The Indians expressed their joy and thankfulness for the return of their friends, stating over and over again that now they are strengthened to walk in that good, white road Washington is making for them.

Now they know and believe that Washington and Texas are their friends, and they want to take all white people everywhere by the hand.

Captain McClermont, who brought them through, deserves high credit for the kindness of his treatment, and the promptitude with which he met and overcame every obstacle in the way. He was supplied with but twenty-one men, two of whom were brought in in irons for having offered abuse to the prisoners. With this small force he had to head rivers, make roads at fording-places, and, most of all, to make his way for nearly three hundred miles through a country of enemies to the Indians, where the rule is to shoot an Indian at sight. On arriving near Jacksboro', he found that a force of three thousand armed citizens had assembled to oppose further progress, and prevent the return of the prisoners. He, being well acquainted with the country, secretly sent his train a by-road, while he drove his ambulance into town, and waited, as if in constant expectation of his train, until he knew that they were far enough advanced to avoid pursuit by the drunken mob, when he left them to look after his train. He stated, at the opening of the council, that he had been seven years in Texas fighting the Indians, and had never before met an Indian in peace.

The Indian chiefs, one by one, came forward, and took him by the hand. Some of them, embracing him, expressed their gratitude and thankfulness for his care, attention, and uniform kindness to their women and children, as well as for bringing them back in safety. One of them told him that he should always respect a white soldier for his sake.

At the conclusion he told the Indians that to-day, for the first time in his life, he had taken the hand of an Indian in friendship; but that, having so taken their hand, he should never expect to meet a Comanche on any other ground; that he should report to the "big war chief" what he had seen and heard to-day, and tell him that the Comanches were enemies no more.

The chiefs said they would hide nothing: there were a few young men — only a few — whose leader killed his father, and all of them outlaws, without father or mother (an expression they use, signifying that they are not connected with any band of the tribe), who were away from the tribe, they knew not where, and did not wish to be held accountable for their deeds. They considered these men enemies to the tribe as well as to everybody else, the same as some white people are, who are continually prowling about, stealing ponies, &c. If any

Comanches brought in horses or mules from Texas, they should be immediately turned over to the agent, in order to be restored to their owners; and they wanted the Texan chiefs to do the same for them when white people steal their ponies and take them into Texas. Then there would be no more occasion for war between them.

After the council, Captain McClermont informed the agent that he had never before witnessed the practical working of the peace policy, and was a thorough convert to it, as being the only correct way of treating the Indians.

I might here state that the five women who ran away from Fort Concho made their way back to their people in safety, travelling on foot, and swimming rivers, at last arriving at their camps only two days after those brought by Captain McClermont.

It may be a matter of wonder how they could sustain life for such a length of time; but to one acquainted with their mode of life, and the productions of the plains, there is nothing surprising in this, as an Indian would find a bountiful living among the various roots which abound, where a white man, for the want of knowing them, might starve to death. Moreover, the plains abound with tortoises, which by the Indian are esteemed a delicacy.

CHAPTER X.

JOURNEY TO THE KIOWA CAMP. — BUILDING OF MEDICINE HOUSE. — SITUATION OF CAMP. — MEDICINE DANCE, ETC.

6th Month, 16*th*. — Arrived at the Kiowa camps, after three days of hard travel, with a small party of Indians, who were sent in to the Agency for me, and to get rations. The distance from the Agency is about one hundred and fifty miles in a north-westerly direction. They are here making preparations for the great Medicine Dance.

The whole Kiowa tribe, as well as nearly all the Apaches, about five hundred Comanches, several Cheyennes and Arapahoes, and other Indians, being together, makes a very large encampment.

This is situated in a beautiful broad valley, through which flows a fine stream of clear water nearly devoid of alkali. It is called by the Kiowas Yoū′-guoo-ō-poh′ (Rice Creek).

Had a talk with several of the head men of the tribe respecting the change in the intentions of government as regards the release of Satanta and Big Tree. They cannot comprehend why government should violate its pledge to them in consequence of the misdemeanors of the Modocs, a tribe living so remote from them that they did not even know of their existence. It looks to them as though Washington was very willing to class them as enemies, while they are doing all they can to prove their friendly intentions. I informed them of my writing to Washington (p. 157), desiring them to refrain from any hostile manifestations until they should learn what Washington will do when he reads my letter.

The warriors are busily engaged hauling cottonwood trees for the medicine house, accompanied by music and dancing.

17*th.* — The music of the soldiers, who, if I rightly understand, are not allowed to sleep during the erection of the medicine house, continued through the night. On going out early this morning, crowds of Indians, old and young, were marching in companies towards a grove of small cottonwood trees, and, being invited to join them, I accompanied them.

Soon several small cottonwoods were cut down by the women, ropes attached to them, several hands to a rope making light work of the hauling, particularly as it was made a frolic, with music and dancing.

After breakfast, the hauling of larger trees was proceeded with. They were drawn by horses by means of ropes attached to the saddles; a warrior, or brave, and a young woman upon the horse, several of which were hitched to one tree, drawing abreast, some of the riders beating drums, and all singing.

The duties of the young woman were to hitch and unhitch the horse she was permitted to ride, so that the brave with whom she rode could maintain his dignity without dismounting. This business continued through the day, except for an hour or two in the middle of the afternoon, when the old women — the grandmothers of the tribe — had a dance.

The music consisted of singing and drumming, done by several old women, who were squatted on the ground in a circle. The dancers — old, gray-headed women, from sixty to eighty years of age — performed in a circle around them for some time, finally striking off upon a waddling run, one behind another; they formed a circle, came back, and, doubling so as to bring two together, threw their arms around each other's necks, and trudged around for some time longer; then sat down, while a youngish man circulated the pipe, from which each in turn took two or three whiffs, and this ceremony ended.

18*th.* — Work at the medicine house drew to a close.

The large trees and brush were all hauled by the middle of the forenoon. The putting up of the long cottonwood poles, to support the covering, was work requiring strength to perform. They were thirty-five or forty feet in length, green and heavy, and required a great amount of noisy talking, loud hallooing, and hard lifting to get them to their places. This being done, and the brush thrown over them for a shade, the medicine house was completed about noon — the side shade having been previously put up.

The soldiers of the tribe then had a frolic in and about it, running and jumping, striking and kicking, throwing one another down, stripping and tearing the clothes off each other. One tall Indian clasped me around for a back-hold wrestle; but, though I did not attempt to throw him, by exerting my little strength in the right direction, he found it too much resembling work to lay me on the ground, to suit his ideas of dignity, and so gave it up.

Before this frolic was over, a party of ten or twelve warriors appeared, moving a kind of shield to and fro before their bodies, making, in some manner (as I was not near enough to see how it was done), a grating sound, not unlike the filing of a mill-saw.

The medicine house is situated nearly in the centre of the encampment, is circular in form, and about sixty feet in diameter, having its entrance towards the east. It is built by erecting a forked post, twenty feet high perhaps, for a central support. Around this, and at nearly equal distances, are seventeen other forked posts, forming the circumference of the building.

These are from twelve to fifteen feet in height, and all of cottonwood. Small cottonwood trees are tied on the outside of these, in a horizontal position, with ropes of raw hide, limbs and leaves all on them. Outside of these, small cottonwood trees are placed in an upright position, thus forming a wall of green trees and leaves several feet in thickness, in the midst of which many hundred spectators afterwards found a cool retreat, where they could observe what was going on without making themselves conspicuous.

Long cottonwood poles extend from each of the posts in the circumference to the central post, and then limbs of the same are laid across these, forming a shady roof one third of the way to the centre.

The central post is ornamented near the ground with the robes of buffalo calves, their heads up, as if in the act of climbing it; each of the branches above the fork is ornamented in a similar manner, with the addition of shawls, calico, scarfs, &c., and covered at the top with black muslin. Attached to the fork is a bundle of cottonwood and willow limbs, firmly bound together, and covered with a buffalo robe, with head and horns, so as to form a rude image of a buffalo, to which were hung strips of new calico, muslin, strouding, both blue and scarlet, feathers, shawls, &c., of various lengths and qualities. The longer and more showy articles were placed near the ends. This image was so placed as to face the east.

The lodges of the encampment are arranged in circles around the medicine house, having their entrances towards it, the nearest circle being some ten rods distant.

In the afternoon, a party of a dozen or more warriors and braves proceeded to the medicine house, followed by a large proportion of the people of the encampment. They were highly painted, and wore shirts only, with head-dresses of feathers which extended down the backs to the ground, and were kept in their proper places by means of an ornamented strap clasping the waist. Some of them had long horns attached to their head-dresses. They were armed with lances and revolvers, and carrying a couple of long poles mounted from end to end with feathers, the one white and the other black. They also bore shields highly ornamented with paint, feathers, and hair.

They took their station upon the side opposite the entrance, the musicians standing behind them.

Many old women occupied a position to the right and near the entrance, who set up a tremulous shrieking; the drums began to beat, and the dance began, the party above described only participating in it.

They at first slowly advanced towards the central post, followed by the musicians, several of whom carried a side of raw hide (dried), which was beaten upon with sticks, making about as much music as to beat upon the sole of an old shoe, while the drums, the voices of the women, and the rattling of pebbles in instruments of raw hide filled out the choir.

After slowly advancing nearly to the central post, they retired backward, again advanced, a little farther than before; this was repeated several times, each time advancing a little farther, until they crowded upon the spectators, drew their revolvers, and discharged them into the air.

Soon after, the women rushed forward with a shrieking yell, threw their blankets violently upon the ground, at the feet of the retiring dancers, snatched them up with the same tremulous shriek that had been before produced, and retired; which closed this part of the entertainment. The ornamented shields used on this occasion were afterwards hung up with the medicine.

Soon after followed the great buffalo medicine. Ninety Indians, — men, women, and children, — disguised in buffalo robes, having the pates and horns on them, in imitation of living buffalo, collected upon the side of a hill just outside the camp. At the proper signal, — the great medicine chief, standing some distance to the left of the entrance to the medicine house, holding something in his hand that made a smoke, — they came in a long procession, followed in the rear by one very old and weak one, which continued to fall back from the others, and, to keep his position, would endeavor to run; but would fall down, get up after several efforts, and jog along again.

After the others had reached the medicine house, they took several turns around it before apparently, finding the entrance, when they cautiously entered, before the old, feeble buffalo in the rear came up, which, after considerable exertion, and several times falling down, accomplished three entire circuits of the building before entering it. As soon as all the buffalo had entered, nearly the whole population of the encampment, who had been standing about midway between the first circle of lodges and the medicine house, started upon the double quick for the medicine house.

Upon entering it, the buffalo were found lying down,

huddled together around the central post, with their heads either towards it or directly from it, except the old veteran of the rear; he lay near, and with his head towards the entrance, forming a most ludicrous spectacle, as we entered. The hair of his sides and back had been partially rubbed off, and hung in shabby tags, while his head was shaggy and his horns enormous.

The great medicine chief, painted white, wearing a buffalo robe and fur head-dress, stood opposite, and facing the entrance, holding in his hands something similar to the squirt-gun of my boyhood days.

He was accompanied by two old men, also wrapped in buffalo robes. After some fifteen or twenty minutes of profound silence, the two old men advanced, and commenced a minute examination of the buffalo — feeling them, punching them, and talking to them; occasionally holding up a small stick, apparently pulled out of the side of a buffalo, and addressing a few words to the medicine chief, *he* would step forward, and squirt a small quantity of the contents of his gun into the hair of the animal; one of the old men would then make a short speech, holding up the stick to view, and conclude by placing it upon the buffalo from which it was first taken. Hereupon the wild, tremulous shrieking of the women rent the air. This was repeated several times, and finally, at a signal from the medicine chief, the ceremony ended, and I saw no more medicine to-day.

19*th.* — Music and dancing continued in the medicine house through the night. At an early hour this morning I went thither with Couguet, and witnessed one dance throughout. The ground inside the enclosure had been carefully cleared of grass, sticks, and roots, and covered, several inches deep, with a clean, white sand. A screen had been constructed on the side opposite the entrance, by sticking small cottonwoods and cedars deep into the ground, so as to preserve them fresh as long as possible. A space was left, two or three feet wide, between it and the enclosing wall, in which the dancers prepared themselves for the dance, and in front of which was the medicine. This consisted of an image, lying on the ground, but so concealed from view, in the screen, as to render its form indistinguishable; above it was a large fan, made of eagle quills, with the quill part lengthened out nearly a foot, by inserting a stick into it, and securing it there. These were held in a spread form by means of a willow rod, or wire, bent in a circular form; above this was a mass of feathers, concealing an image, on each side of which were several shields, highly decorated with feathers and paint. Various other paraphernalia of heathen worship were suspended in the screen, among these shields or over them, impossible for me to describe so as to be comprehended. A mound had also been thrown up around the central post of the building, two feet high, and perhaps five feet in diameter.

The musicians, who, if I mistake not, are the war chiefs, were squatted on the ground, in true heathen style, to the left, and near the entrance, having Indian drums and rattles. The music was sounding when we entered.

Presently the dancers came from behind the screen; their faces, arms, and the upper part of their bodies were painted white; a soft, white buckskin skirt, secured about the loins, descended nearly to the ankles, while the breech-cloth, — blue on this occasion, — hanging to the ground, outside the skirt, both in front and behind, completed the dress. They faced the medicine — shall I say idols? for it was conducted with all the solemnity of worship, — jumping up and down in true time with the beating of the drums, while a bone whistle in their mouths, through which the breath escaped as they jumped about, and the singing of the women, completed the music. The dancers continued to face the medicine, with arms stretched upwards and towards it, — their eyes as it were riveted to it. They were apparently oblivious to all surroundings, except the music and what was before them.

After some time, a middle-aged man, painted as the others, but wearing a buffalo robe, issued from behind the screen, facing the entrance, but having his eyes fixed upon the sun, upon which he stood gazing, without winking or moving a muscle, for some time, then began slowly to incline his head from side to side, as if to avoid some obstruction in his view of it, swaying his body slightly, then, stepping slowly from side to side — forward — backward — increasing his motions, both in rapidity and extent, until, in appearance nearly frantic, his robe fell off, leaving him — except his blue breech-cloth — entirely naked. In this condition he jumped and ran about the enclosure, — head, arms, and legs all equally participating in the violence of his gestures, — every joint of his body apparently loosened, his eyes only fixed. I wondered how, with every joint apparently dislocated, and every muscular fibre relaxed, he could maintain the upright position.

Thus he continued to exercise without ceasing, or once removing his eyes from the sun, until the sweat ran down in great rolling drops, washing the white paint into streaks no more ornamental than the original painting, and he was at length compelled to retire, from mere exhaustion, the other dancers still continuing their exercises.

Presently another man entered from behind the screen, wearing an Indian fur cap and a blue breech-cloth reaching to the ground. He was unpainted, and had a human scalp fastened to his scalp-lock, the soft, flowing hair of which, spreading out upon his naked back, bore mute testimony to the tragical death of some unfortunate white woman. This man, with a kind of half running jump, still in step with the music, went around all the dancers, who did not notice him, with one arm stretched out over their heads, first in one direction, then the other, turning his course at every time, after stopping in front of the medicine, and making some indescribable motions before it. He sometimes parted the feathers concealing the small image, appearing to examine it minutely, as if searching for something, and sometimes putting his lips to it, as if in the act of kissing it. At length, after repeated examinations, he, apparently for the first time, discovered the fan, and took hold of it hesitatingly, and as if afraid.

This was loosed from its fastenings by a hand behind the screen, and he slowly raised it up, looking intently at it, while the expression of his countenance indicated a fearfulness of the result of handling an object whose hidden and mysterious powers were so far beyond his comprehension. He held it up before the medicine, waved it up and down, and from side to side, then, turning round so as to face the dancers and spectators, waved it from side to side near the ground, once around the dancers; then, raising it above his head, he waved it in the same manner, performing another circle around the dancers.

Then, with gestures of striking, and a countenance scowling as with fierce rage, he began to chase them around and around the ring, from left to right. Finally, getting one of them separated from the rest, he pursued him with the most fiend-like attitude, fiercely striking at him with his fan. The pursued one fled from him with a countenance expressive of almost death-like terror, until, after several rounds, he stumbled and fell heavily to the ground. Another and another were thus separated from the dancers, pursued, and fell before the mystical power of the fan, and the act closed.

Being called to a council of the war chiefs, I went no

more to the medicine house to-day, though the music and dancing continued the whole time, by day and by night, with short intervals between the different acts, to give opportunity for rest, arranging dress, painting, and such other changes as the programme of the ceremony demanded.

20th. — Saw but one dance to-day. Quite a quantity of goods, such as blankets, strouding (blue and scarlet list-cloth), calico, shawls, scarfs, and other Indian wares, had been carried into the medicine house previous to my entrance. The dancers had been painted white, three of them ornamented with a green stripe across the forehead, and around down the sides of the cheeks, to the corners of the mouth, and meeting on the chin. A round green spot was painted on the back and breast, about three inches in diameter, while on either side of it, and somewhat elevated above it, was a crescent of the same size and color. Two small, hollow mounds of sand and clay had been made before the medicine, in which fire was placed, and kept just sufficiently burning, with the partially dried cottonwood leaves, cedar twigs, and probably tobacco, to produce a smoke. A small fire was burning near the musicians, for lighting pipes, tightening drums, &c.

When all was ready, the three young men, who were painted as described, were led, each by a man clad in a buffalo robe, near to the smoking mounds in front of the medicine. An ornamented fur cap was, with some ceremony, placed upon the head of one of them; wisps of green wild wormwood were fastened to the wrists and ankles, which being done, he reverently raised his hands above his head, leaning forward over one of the mounds, brought them down nearly to it; then, straightening up, passed his hands over his face and stroked his breast. This was repeated several times; then, after holding one foot, and then the other, over the mound, as if to warm them, two or three times, he went around the central post, and back to the other mound, where the same ceremony was repeated. During this whole ceremony I could perceive that his lips moved, though he uttered nothing. I afterwards learned that it was in prayer to this effect: "May this medicine render me brave in war, proof against the weapons of my enemies, strong in the chase, wise in council; and, finally, may it preserve me to a good age, and may I at last die in peace among my own people." The others, one at a time, were similarly brought forward, and went through with the same ceremony. Three bunches of wild wormwood were then placed on the ground in a row, crossing the line of entrance, and between it and the central post, upon which the three young men were placed by their attendants, who stood behind them, with their hands upon their shoulders, the music playing all the time. Two or three men then approached the pile of goods, selected therefrom some plaid shawls, strouding, blankets, scarfs, and an umbrella, and hung them over the medicine; this being done, the six men began to dance, — the three foremost ones upon the wormwood, with their arms stretched towards the medicine, the three others with their hands still resting upon the shoulders of the former. After some time the latter retired; the other dancers came from behind the screen, and joined in the dance, which continued until they were driven off by the medicine chief, as described in yesterday's dance. All these ceremonies had a sacred significance, which I did not understand, but have been informed that they believe any article of wearing apparel, or of harness for their horses, hung up by the medicine during these ceremonies, receives a charmed power to protect their wearers from disease, or the assaults of their enemies, during the year.

21*st.* — At one of the dances to-day, all but one retired behind the screen, who continued to dance by himself for a long time. Various articles were brought forward, and laid upon the ground, which he took up and hung in proximity to the medicine. After a long time, the other dancers reappeared, and he retired; these continued their exercises, until driven off as before. The last dance differed from the preceding in this: the last man selected and separated from the others by the medicine chief to be driven off, though he ran from him, did not appear terrified, and would not fall down, but retired, with the medicine chief, behind the screen.

At one of the dances to-day, five human scalps were exhibited, — one attached to each of the right wrists of two men, and one to each wrist of another, besides the one worn attached to the scalp lock of the medicine chief. Two of these scalps were from the heads of Indians. They had all been tanned, and evidently belonged with the medicine fixtures.

The whole ceremony closed about four o'clock in the afternoon. The medicine was packed away by the medicine chief, and the several articles which had been hung about it — medicated, I suppose, or, in other words, sanctified by proximity to the sacred things during the ceremonies, and consequently having power to protect their possessors from evil — were restored to the proper owners. They then packed them, took them upon their backs, formed into a procession, and marched, to the music of the drums, around and out of the medicine house, whence every one took the direction of his or her own lodge, and the ceremonies of the great medicine dance were ended.

There was no time during the dance but women were present at the medicine house, participating in the music, but not in the dance. The same individuals appeared in every dance, from the beginning to the end. Though they were not permitted to taste food or drink, from the commencement of the dance until its conclusion, they were allowed to smoke from time to time, which was done with great solemnity and ceremony. The pipe was filled, brought forward, and laid upon the ground; the person, carefully turning the stem towards the fire, and bedding it in the sand, so that the bowl should remain in an upright position, arose and stood with his back towards it, or facing the medicine. It was then approached by one of the musicians, who, in a squatting position, raised his hand reverently towards the sun, the medicine, the top of the central post, or buffalo; then, passing his hands slowly over the pipe, took it up with his left hand, and taking a pinch from the bowl with the thumb and fore finger of the right, held it to the sun, the medicine, the top of the central post, then the bottom, and finally covered it up in the ground. He then proceeded to light the pipe, blowing a whiff of smoke towards the several objects of adoration, and placed it carefully where he found it, in reversed order, that is, with the stem from the fire. The person who brought it had stood waiting all this time for it. He now took it up and retired to the dancers, who, wrapped in buffalo robes, were waiting, in a squatting position, to receive it. The sand where the pipe had lain was carefully smoothed by the hand, and all marks of it wholly obliterated. I might also add that no one crossed the medicine house without first removing his moccasons from his feet.

I have but faintly described what I saw and heard of this pagan rite; neither did I see all, being at the medicine house but a small part of the time; but I saw enough to cause my heart to swell with deep and conflicting emotions in beholding the depth of heathen superstition into which this people have fallen.

Forgetting the true and living God, they have substituted in His stead a mass of fantastic objects, before which their wild orgies are solemnly and devoutly performed. At the same time a feeling of thankfulness pervaded my mind, to the Great Disposer of all things and events, that in His mercy He saw fit to cast my lot on earth in a land where the blessed light of the gospel of truth shines, mingled with a hope that the day may not be far distant when the darkness enshrouding this portion of our country may be dispelled by the beams of the everlasting Sun of Righteousness, the great Fountain of light and life, and the Dispenser of every blessing. May the day hasten, saith my soul.

Although there have probably been no less than three thousand Indians of all ages, and of different tribes, congregated here since being encamped at this place, and I was round among them most of the time by day, I saw not a single instance of disagreement; on the contrary, everything moved on harmoniously and quietly, and the tribes dispersed with apparently friendly feelings.

One circumstance I must not fail to mention, as corroborating their superstitious ideas. The leaves forming the shady roof of the medicine house wilted. The heat of the sun preyed upon the naked dancers. To-haint (no-shoes), the great medicine chief, made medicine for clouds and rain. The rain came, with a tempest of wind and the most vivid lightning. Peal after peal of thunder shook the air. The ground was literally flooded. Two Cheyenne women were killed by the lightning. The next morning To-haint apologized for the storm.

He was a young man, and had no idea of making such strong medicine. He hoped the tribe would pass by his indiscreetness. He trusted that, as he grew older, he would grow wiser. The Cheyenne women were dead, not because of his medicine, but because of their wearing red blankets. All Indians know they should not wear red during the great medicine dance of the Kiowas.

The apology was accepted, and it is to be hoped that all Indians who may in future incline to attend this, the great annual assembly of the Kiowas, will remember not to wear red blankets.

CHAPTER XI.

MILITARY SYSTEM OF THE KIOWAS. — BUFFALO HUNT. — DRESSING THE HIDES FOR LODGES AND FOR ROBES. — DANGERS OF THE BUFFALO HUNT. — SICKNESS. — PETROLEUM SPRING. — REPORT. — CONTINUE SICK. — JOURNEY HOME.

AFTER the close of the medicine dance, I continued in the Kiowa camp some three weeks, during which time the men were busy in killing buffalo, and the women in curing the meat and preparing their skins for making lodges.

Being determined that none of their thoughtless young men should go raiding in Texas, and thereby bring trouble upon the tribe, the Kiowas, immediately after the whole tribe got together on Pecon Creek, organized a military system, under the control of the war chiefs, which was put immediately into operation. By this a strong guard of their soldiers were continually watching, day and night, while in camp, to prevent any such enterprise from being undertaken. In moving from place to place, these soldiers marched on each side of the main body, while a front guard went before, and a rear guard behind, thus preventing any from straggling away.

Their buffalo hunts were conducted in the same military order. The soldiers, going out first, surrounded a tract of country in which were a large herd of buffalo; and no one might chase a buffalo past this ring guard on pain of having his horse shot by the soldiers.

Within the ring, hundreds of men on horseback were chasing and shooting those huge creatures, with revolvers, or bows and arrows, until each had killed as many as his female attendants could skin and take care of; when the day's sport is ended.

Not so the work of the woman. When her lord has killed a buffalo the woman's work begins. She has to skin it, the meat to secure, and all to pack upon ponies or mules, and carry to camp, where the meat must be cured. This is done by cutting it into thin sheets, and hanging it over poles in the hot sunshine, where it is soon dried thoroughly; then it is packed fresh, in packages of about one hundred pounds each, and enclosed in a nice folding sack of thick buffalo skin, prepared especially for the purpose. This is not dressed down thin after being fleshed, but well tanned, and of the full thickness of the skin; the hair side nicely ornamented with paint, for the outside of the sack. This is cut out like a huge envelope, so that the ends and sides will fold over whatever is put in them, and secured by strong buckskin strings. By being thick it retains its form, and is very useful for carrying other things besides meat and tallow.

After the meat is taken care of, the skin must be looked after. Those taken at this season of the year are mostly dressed for lodges. They are first staked on a smooth spot of ground, and water put upon them, when they are ready for fleshing. This consists in removing the flesh with an instrument made of a straight bar of iron, about a foot in length, flattened at one end and filed to an edge. This being grasped in the hand, and a succession of quick blows given, the work slowly proceeds. The skin is then dried, after which the hair is removed in a dry state, and the skin reduced to the proper thickness by dressing down on the hair side. This is done with an instrument made by firmly tying a flat piece of steel, filed to a bevelled edge at one end, and with the corners rounded, to a large prong of a deer's horn. This is so trimmed, in connection with the body of the horn, as to form an elbow, and is used a little as a carpenter uses his adze. This work is usually done in the cool of the morning.

The brains of the animal, having been properly taken care of for the purpose, are now soaked and squeezed by the hand until reduced to a paste, and applied to both sides of the skin, which is afterwards worked and rubbed until flexible.

The preparation of robes is from winter skins, and differs from the foregoing only in being dressed down on the flesh side, so as to leave the wool and hair upon the robe, and is more thoroughly worked and scoured by means of a sharp-gritted stone.

The hunting of the buffalo, as practised by these Indians, is a wild and exciting sport, not unattended with danger. This arises from different sources, as the character of the ground on which they run, the training of their horses, and the temper of the animal pursued.

Sometimes the horse, having his eyes fixed on the animal he is running, sets his feet into a hole, and falls; being under full headway, the rider is thrown with great violence upon the ground, often breaking an arm or a leg, in which case, as they know nothing of the art of setting bones, the limb is deformed for life, or never gets well, and the patient, after lingering for months, and suffering excruciating pains, is released by the hand of death. I have seen the bones of the fore-arm shoved down into the hand to the knuckle joint, an ankle turned over so that the foot was bottom upwards, and placed upon one side of the lower ends of the leg bones.

But perhaps the greatest danger to the hunter arises from the temper of the buffalo when wounded. The hunter rides up nearly alongside of the animal, in order that his arrow may pierce his heart, and shoots; the arrow wounds the animal, but not fatally, and he turns upon the horseman before the horse can change his course, and, with a desperate plunge, sometimes overturns both the horse and his rider. The greatest coolness is essential to effect an escape in such cases. The rider has been known, after seeing that the buffalo is

KIOWA BRAVE AND WIFE (LONE WOLF'S DAUGHTER.)

about to toss his horse, to leap from the opposite side and escape, while the huge beast was reducing the horse to a jelly. The horse, if well trained, will always, upon hearing the twang of the bow-string, spring from the buffalo, in which case, if the rider retains his seat, he is safe; but if he is left on the ground, he is at the tender mercy of the infuriated beast. The Kiowas declare that the buffalo does not attempt to injure a man who has been thus thrown, if he lies perfectly still and will hold his breath, but, after watching him for a moment, will go away and leave him; but if he stirs while the buffalo is watching him, he plunges upon him, pawing him with his feet, and mangling him with his horns, until the remains will have no appearance of a man.

Having been taken sick, about three weeks after the medicine dance, the Indians carried me into the Agency, where I remained for some time in a feeble state, occasionally visiting the Comanche and Apache camps as my strength permitted.

On one occasion I went with the agent to visit the cornfield of Asa Toyett, a Comanche chief; also to select a location for his house and village; after which the chief took us to see a place on Medicine Creek, where there was a "heap of medicine—good, black medicine." This "good, black medicine" proved to be a spring of petroleum, unmixed with any foreign substance. Patches of oil were floating upon the water, while petroleum was oozing from a small hole in the ground.

Were this spring in Ohio or Pennsylvania, it would be

a fortune to the owner. There are other places in the vicinity where petroleum is found. I know of two within ten miles of Fort Sill; but there being no means of cheap transportation, it is here valueless, except as an application to the sore backs of mules and ponies.

There are undoubtedly many minerals existing among the mountains, as well as upon the plains, which will in time prove valuable. Iron exists in the form of a black sand, and salt is found in immense quantities, on what are called the salt plains, in the western and north-western parts of the territory, in the form of common barrel salt, being formed by the evaporation of salt water arising from beneath. It is as pure, if not purer than the salt of commerce. Farther south, on the Salt Fork of Red River, it exists in solid rocks in immense quantities and easy of access.

My health not improving sufficiently to admit of my going to the Kiowa camps, I drew up the following report of my services there, and submitted it to the agent.

REPORT.

KIOWA AGENCY, FORT SILL, 7th Month 31st, 1873.

J. M. HAWORTH, *U. S. Ind. Agt.*

RESPECTED FRIEND: Notwithstanding I have not succeeded according to my anticipations in the work which I undertook among the Kiowas, and possibly have not answered the designs of the department in my employ, that my position, the difficulties attending it, and the attitude of the Kiowas in relation to the government, may be fully understood, I make the following report: —

After the necessary preliminary arrangements had been made, I first went to the Kiowa camps on the first day of the 12th month, 1872, but did not attempt to open a school among them until the 23d of the 1st month of the present year.

Having erected a tent, and fitted it up, I commenced a school, with twenty-two children in attendance, which continued for something over a week, during which time the children manifested their aptitude to learn by the progress they made. The elder people also manifested much interest in it by their frequent visits, their attention to the exercises, and their encouraging words to the children. About this time, much sickness prevailing among the children in the camp, some superstitious Caddoes, who happened there, attributed the sickness among them to me, telling them I was a bad medicine man, and had made some of their children sick when I was with them, two of whom died. This had the effect to entirely break up the school, though I continued my efforts to renew it for nearly two months. Sometimes, when I would get a few children collected, they would be driven out by their old men. Sometimes young men would come in, laugh at them, and abuse them until they would leave. After about two months they became more unsettled, moving from place to place almost continually, searching for better grass for their stock, better water, more wood, to get buffalo, &c., &c. As we were seldom but a day or two in a place, I gave up all effort to sustain a school; but being encouraged to remain with the tribe, I have done so, moving with them as they moved from place to place, endeavoring to aid them in acquiring the English language, while I myself was becoming to a very small extent acquainted with theirs. Gradually, as I could make myself better understood, I would explain the advantages of living and dressing like the white people, giving up raiding, raising cattle and hogs instead of so many ponies, cultivating corn, and living in houses.

They usually listened attentively to my talk, but mostly consider their own mode of life far preferable for them. They have, since the 1st of the 6th month, objected to sending to school on account of government not complying with the terms of agreement with them in relation to Satanta and Big Tree, saying, "Washington talk good, but does not do as he talk." If they could rely upon his doing as he talks, they would settle down, work farms, send their children to school, and do as he wants them to in all respects. However, they promise to keep quiet until after the time appointed for the council in the 10th month next. I can but believe that the early release of their imprisoned chiefs would have a very great effect upon their immediate settlement and ultimate civilization, though much patient and long continued labor must be exerted before they can be fully brought off from their heathen traditions, superstitions, and practices; and the first effectual step in this direction is to secure their confidence by the truthfulness and sincerity of all concerned in their management.

Though I was with the tribe about six weeks while all the different bands were together, owing to their superstitious fears in regard to being numbered, I could not obtain a correct account of their numbers band by band; but, admitting six to the lodge, the Kiowas must number from one thousand six hundred to one thousand six hundred and fifty (1600 to 1650).

There are many Mexicans among them, who, having been taken by them while young, and grown up among them, have now no inclination to leave them, and may be considered as incorporated into the tribe.

Submitted respectfully by thy friend,

THOMAS C. BATTEY,
Teacher in Kiowa Camps.

8th Month, 5th. — My health continuing very poor, the doctor and my friends generally advise my return home for a while, in order to recruit my health and strength.

The agent also being anxious to send a messenger to the superintendent's office, though I have not been able to sit up the whole day for some weeks until within two or three days, I finally made up my mind to undertake the journey. Accordingly I took passage on the stage-coach for Caddo, on the M. K. and T. R. R., where I expect to take the cars for Lawrence, and thence home.

7th. — Arrived at Caddo about noon. The journey so far has been very rough, and, feeling very weak and tired, my observation of the country through which I was passing was limited ; but noticed in both the Chickasaw and Choctaw nations much excellent country, as well as much that was poor and rocky. Smith Paul's valley, — so called from a half-breed Chickasaw, — on the Washita River, is a broad bottom, with a soil of unexampled quickness and fertility. It produces bountiful crops of corn and other grain, but is badly cultivated by a poor class of whites and mixed bloods abounding in this part of the Territory.

The Indians of these nations, as well as the Cherokees, were slaveholders before the war ; their slaves were emancipated, and remain in the country, together with many whites, who have married Indian women in order to secure a home in this land. This gives as heterogeneous a population as can be found probably in any country. Governor Harris, who is a Chickasaw, has a good farm, lives in a comfortable frame house, has quite a stock of cattle and hogs, and good orchards. In the Choctaw nation there is much land of a superior quality, and the best timber I have seen for many years.

In the afternoon I took passage on the cars for Lawrence, passing through some of the most beautiful country I ever beheld, abounding in excellent timber, good water, and rich prairies sparsely settled by the more civilized Cherokees and Creeks, who are engaged in stock-raising and agricultural pursuits.

Saw several fields of cotton, the first I had ever seen growing. It has a very pretty and novel appearance, especially to a Northerner. The country in the Verdigris and Neosho valleys appeared to want nothing but improving by an intelligent and energetic people to render it one of the most desirable localities to live in I have ever seen, so far as relates to climate, soil, water, and stone, while timber is not scarce, and may be easily raised.

8th. — Arrived at Lawrence in the afternoon, and proceeded to the superintendent's office and reported my business; but feeling very weak and worn out, every way unequal to proceed on my journey for the present, I was compelled to lie over a few days.

Arrived at home on the 12th, having left Lawrence in the afternoon of the 11th. Found my family anxiously awaiting my arrival, and I may say that I was indeed thankful to the Great Giver of every blessing that we had been spared to meet again.

Remained at home, much of the time sick, until the 28th of the following month, when, being very anxious to be at the great council at Fort Sill, between the Indians, Commissioner Smith, and Governor Davis of Texas, — relative to the release of Satanta and Big Tree, who have been removed to Fort Sill, — I again left home for the country of the Kiowas and Comanches. Arrived at the Kiowa Agency in the night of the 4th of 10th month, 1872.

CHAPTER XII.

SATANTA AND BIG TREE. — COUNCIL. — DEMAND FOR FIVE RAIDING COMANCHES. — COMANCHES REFUSE COMPLIANCE. — AGREE TO JOIN A PARTY OF SOLDIERS AND GO INTO TEXAS. — COMANCHE HORSES STOLEN BY WHITES FROM TEXAS. — JOURNEY TO KIOWA CAMP. — MEDICINE. — CONSTERNATION IN CAMP. — TELEGRAM RENEWING DEMAND FOR FIVE COMANCHE MEN.

SATANTA, concerning whom much has been said, and whose name has often occurred in these pages, was perhaps the most influential of the Kiowa chiefs, a notorious raider and a great lover of whiskey, but not without good qualities and marked ability.

His name is a corrupt pronunciation by the whites of See-tĭ-toh (White Bear), but eventually became adopted by the Kiowas themselves.

He was taken prisoner in 1869, but released by General Sheridan at the place where Fort Sill now stands. Afterwards, in 1871, at the head of a hundred warriors, he made an attack upon a corn train in Texas, killed seven teamsters, one of whom was tied to the wheels of a wagon and burned over a slow fire. Boasting of this act to General W. T. Sherman and Agent Tatum, they simultaneously ordered his arrest. This was effected, together with that of Satank and Big Tree, his boasted accomplices, and they were turned over to the authorities of the state of Texas. Immediately after leaving Fort Sill for that state, under guard, and while in sight of the Agency buildings, Satank, who had been singing the death-song, or making medicine of preparation for death, slipped his hands from the handcuffs, seized a knife, and struck at one of the guards, wounding him in the leg, and was killed by the soldiers on the spot.

The other prisoners — Satanta and Big Tree — were taken to Texas, tried for murder, found guilty by the jury, and sentenced to be hanged. This sentence was afterwards commuted to imprisonment for life.

Thus matters stood until the autumn of 1872. At that time, when the Kiowa and Comanche delegation were at Washington, they were assured that, if they remained at peace till the following 3d month, gave up the stock they had stolen from government, and the captives held by them, their prisoners, which now included the Comanche women and children captured by Colonel McKenzie, would be released. This promise was renewed in the 3d month, and the time of release fixed about the 1st of the 6th month. The Indians, as may be seen in the foregoing pages, faithfully complied with these requirements, giving up all the captives in their possession, and restoring the stolen stock to the extent of their ability; both tribes, except a small band of Comanche outlaws, refraining from hostile acts, with the full understanding that their prisoners should be restored to them.

This, so far as the restoration of the Comanche women and children was concerned, was done without difficulty, they being prisoners of war, and detained on the authority of the government itself; but with the imprisoned chiefs of the Kiowas — Satanta and Big Tree — the case was different. They had been surrendered to the state of Texas, and were in prison in accordance with the laws of that state, and could only be pardoned by its governor. The general government had no more right to promise the release of these two prisoners than to interfere with the operation of the laws of any state in any other respect. It had a right, however, to negotiate with the governor of Texas for their release, and promise to the Indians the result of such negotiation; and there would probably have been no difficulty in obtaining their release but for the excited state of the public mind growing out of the Modoc tragedy. This induced the governor to interpose new conditions for the release of these prisoners.

In the mean time, the Kiowas not being able to comprehend why the Comanche prisoners were restored, while their own friends were retained in prison, were very uneasy, and it was with difficulty that they were kept quiet.

While affairs were in this situation, much correspondence was going on between the officers of state and the governor of Texas, setting forth, on the one part, the faithful compliance of the Kiowas with all the imposed conditions for securing the release of their chiefs.

The governor, however, in order to render himself politically more popular with the people of his state, so as to secure, if possible, his re-election to the gubernatorial chair, constantly demanded additional conditions, which were wholly impracticable. This correspondence finally resulted in sending the two chiefs to Fort Sill, to be held there until a council should be had with the Kiowa and Comanche chiefs, early in the following 10th month, by the parties before mentioned, at which the question of release should be finally settled.

The Kiowas consented to keep the peace until that time, which it was made to appear at the council they had faithfully done.

The conditions which the governor of Texas proposed to the government, on which he would release the two prisoners, were, that not only the Kiowas, to whom the prisoners belonged, but "all of the horse [mounted] Indians bordering on Texas be gathered into reservations, their arms and horses taken from them, and supplies of food be issued to them for not longer than one day at a time." (See letter of Governor E. J. Davis to Hon. C. Delano, Secretary of the Interior.)

On the arrival of Governor Davis, he took up his quarters at the fort, and refused to meet the Indians except inside the garrison. This the Indians were opposed to doing, and strongly protested against, saying "some of their friends had been killed there; there the prisoners were arrested; it was a bad place; their thoughts would be bad if they went there; and it would be impossible for any good to come out of so bad a place." But as the governor would not yield, at the earnest solicitation of the commissioner and agent, who himself shared the feelings of the Indians, they yielded, and the council convened.

It should have been stated earlier in this account, as a further complication of these difficulties, that, early in the year, three young men of the Penhatethka band of Comanches, the leader of whom had killed his father, ran away from their tribe, becoming outlaws.

These were joined by two other boys and two women, making seven persons in all, who went into Texas, and commenced a system of raiding. Government was apprised of these circumstances in the spring, but, in view of their being held as outlaws by the tribe, did not consider it responsible for their deeds; hence did not allow them to interfere with the release of the Comanche women and children.

Afterwards some young men belonging to the two bands of which Tabananika and White Wolf are chiefs, not being sufficiently discouraged by their chiefs, joined this little band of outlaws in raiding in Texas, stealing horses and mules. These the other chiefs began to turn over to the agent, according to their promises, not countenancing the doings of the young men. In the course of the summer five persons were killed in Texas, supposed to have been done by Comanches, but not sufficiently proved to be positively known: two Comanche Indians were also killed in Texas. This was the situation of the affairs with these two tribes, at the opening of the council, on the 6th day of the 10th month, 1873.

On the first day of the council the governor made his propositions directly to the Indians, without having treated the representative of the United States government — the Honorable Commissioner of Indian Affairs — with sufficient consideration even to let him know what he was about to propose, — perhaps forgetting that the Indians were wards, and it was the government with which he must deal. Prominent among these propositions were the following, viz.: they must settle down upon farms near the Agency; government must put a white man in every camp, to watch them and report their behavior to the agent; they must draw their rations in person, instead of the chiefs as heretofore, once in three days; answer to the roll-call at the same time; place themselves under direction of the United States army, to assist in arresting all depredating Indians; dispense with the use of their arms, horses, and mules; raise cattle, hogs, and corn, like the other civilized Indians, — the Choctaws, Cherokees, &c.

In return, Satanta and Big Tree, who were present, were to be remanded to the guard-house at Fort Sill, and kept there under the charge of the post commander, to be released on the future good behavior of the tribe, whenever he should be satisfied that these terms were complied with. They were not to be pardoned, but subject to re-arrest at any time, upon the misdemeanor of the Kiowas, and returned to the authorities of Texas, saying, in the winding up of his speech, "I will not change these conditions."

The Indians agreed to all these conditions, provided the governor would release the prisoners immediately, without returning them to the guard-house, which he refused to do, and the council closed.

The following, though a bright, pleasant day outwardly, yet was a gloomy day at the Agency. The Indians were much excited, though this excitement was not manifested in words or noise; it was of the more deadly kind, which shaded the countenance and gleamed in the eye. The Kiowas were all about, with their bows strung, ready for use at a moment's warning. Kicking Bird said his "heart was a stone; there was no soft spot in it. He had taken the white man by the hand, thinking him to be a friend, but he is not a friend; government has deceived us; Washington is rotten." Lone Wolf said, "I want peace — have worked hard for it — kept my young men from raiding — followed the instructions Washington gave me to the best of my knowledge and ability. Washington has deceived me, — has failed to keep faith with me and my people, — has broken his promises; and now there is nothing left us but war. I know that war with Washington means the extinction of my people, but we are driven to it; we had rather die than live."

Much hard work devolved upon the agent, who saw the approaching storm, and succeeded in awakening the commissioner to a sense of the danger, who set earnestly to work, with the superintendent and others, talking with the frontier citizens of Texas, reasoning with the governor, and pouring oil, as it were, upon the turbulent spirits of the Indians. After much talk and some correspondence, on the part of the commissioner, with the governor, the latter, late in the evening, sent a note to the former, requesting the Indians to meet him again in the garrison, stating that the "final answer will be favorable."

Early the next morning, the Indians, who had been apprised of the governor's request to meet them, but kept in ignorance of his answer, assembled, and proceeded to the post, being determined to rescue the prisoners, even at the price of blood. They loaded their carbines and revolvers, strung their bows, between the Agency and the fort, ready for the emergency, fixing the time for the conflict when the guard should come to take the prisoners back to the guard-house. With full knowledge of the situation, I accompanied them to the post, saw them prepare themselves for action, placing their soldiers, as if by accident, in the most favorable position for shooting the governor and the guard; placing fleet horses convenient for the prisoners; and, to avoid suspicion, some of their women were on hand, mounted, it is true, so as to be out of the way at the right moment. But the arrangements had been completed between the commissioner and the governor, by which the immediate release of the chiefs was secured.

The commissioner pledged the government to return them, or other chiefs of equal rank, into the hands of the governor of Texas, at any time when it shall appear that the Kiowas have been raiding there; procure a roll-call of every male member of the tribe over sixteen years of age, with such frequency as to render it impossible for any warrior to be absent from the reservation without its being known, and to make information reliable as to the daily whereabouts of the Kiowas. The Comanches shall be reduced to the same daily inspection as soon as possible, and the government is pledged to use its force to compel the Comanches to surrender not less than five of the recent raiders of their tribe, to take the place of Satanta and Big Tree.

The governor, in his speech, alluded to the promises of the government to the Indians, the faithful adherence of the Kiowas to their agreement, and turned the chiefs over to the tribe, without a pardon. Satanta and Big Tree, after embracing the governor, proceeded to embrace the chiefs present, and immediately returned with them to the agent's office, from whence they went to their rude home in their camps.

The reunion of these chiefs with their tribe and families was impressive and affecting in the extreme. Joy beamed upon every countenance, and their happiness was exhibited, as might be expected, in the most wild and natural manner.

In the afternoon of the day on which these two chiefs were released, being the 8th of the month, the commissioner held a council in the agent's office, in which he spoke of the solemn engagements the Comanches entered into in the spring, also in the early summer, when their women and children were returned to them, that henceforth they would keep the peace with the whites, and not raid any more in Texas. They had violated their pledge, raided, stolen horses, and committed murders there, and now they must give him five of the guilty persons; giving them until the next morning to make their answer.

The next morning, the Comanches said they could agree to all the terms demanded of them except the giving up of the five guilty young men, which they could not do unless the commissioner would give the names of the men he wanted, which he did not do. They then offered to restore all the horses and mules they had stolen, but this was a new road which they could not accept.

Neither did the commissioner accept their proposition, and was so indiscreet in his remarks as to affront them, by calling them cowards. They denied the imputation of cowardice, telling the commissioner they could not give him the five men, and if he wanted them, there were soldiers at the fort, and their young men were there, — take them himself, and he would have them, if that was what he wanted. However, they wished it understood that they were anxious to maintain friendly relations with Washington, and would make one more proposition.

They were willing that a party of their young men, under their leading chief, should join a squad of military scouts in going into the raiding district of Texas, in search of raiding Indians, assist in capturing any that might be found, and turn them over as demanded.

To this the commissioner assented, and gave them thirty days in which to report. They were also told that if they did nothing, their rations would be stopped, and their annuities withheld.

Accordingly, a company was soon formed, who joined a party of soldiers under one of the officers of the fort, went into Texas, in search of Indian raiders, but finding none, they reported their want of success through the officer who commanded the expedition.

During their absence, a party of whites from Texas made a raid into the Indian country, and stole about two hundred head of ponies and mules from the Indian herds. A small number (thirty-seven) of these were recovered and one of the party arrested, through the prompt action of William H. H. Howard, acting agent for the time.

Affairs being in this unsettled condition, Kicking Bird was unwilling to assume the whole responsibility of taking me to his camp, but finally, after consulting with

Stumbling Bear and Sun Boy, — two prominent Kiowa chiefs, — they jointly agreed to my accompanying them, though with apparent reluctance, which I did not understand at the time.

11*th Month*, 15*th.* — Arrived at our camping-place, on Rainy Mountain Creek, after a journey of a part of three days. Yesterday, crossing a fresh trail, we noticed, by the tracks, that some of the horses had shoes on — an evidence that they must have been just coming from Texas; and last evening, a small party, consisting of four Comanches belonging to Asa Habbit's band, came to our camp on Sulphur Creek, very hungry of course, and their horses all tired out. They stated that they had been in the vicinity of San Antonio, and had a hard time in keeping clear of the soldiers. Kicking Bird said but little to them, further than to let them know that he did not approve of their going into Texas on any account. Not relishing his disapproval of their conduct, they left soon after supper.

Our route to this place has been varied by passing through rich and fertile valleys, between rocky and precipitous mountains, over beautiful rolling prairies and level sterile plains.

Our camp is situated on one side of a wide and beautiful bottom, of not very rich soil, upon the bank of the creek, which is skirted with timber, in which are hundreds of wild turkeys and many deer, while the plains on either side abound with the never quiet or silent prairie dogs, with their near relative, the tsi-at-kea, or burrowing owl, with an occasional straggling buffalo or two, and many antelopes. We are about forty miles north-west from the Agency.

Shortly after going into camp, the three chiefs, who had taken the responsibility of my being in their camp, spoke to me respecting their reluctance in taking me with them, telling me that the Comanches were not friendly to my being in the Kiowa camps, looking upon me as a spy, and that they might be disposed, if they were to meet me out anywhere, to put me out of the way; further saying that I might see some of them to-morrow, as they were encamped near by. Sun Boy rose up, and bade me follow him. I did so. He led the way, without the utterance of a word, some distance into the thick, brushy wood, to a large oak tree, where he had caused his medicine shield to be placed. This, as usual, was wrapped carefully in a blanket, and mounted upon poles, a little after the fashion of a painter's easel. Stopping at some distance from the shield, the chief bade me by signs to go forward and remove its covering. I did so, and found that it had still another covering of buckskin, with a painted representation of the sun in the centre, shedding rays of all colors, in straight lines, to the circumference. This he also bade me remove, himself still standing where he first stopped. But not understanding how it was fastened, and not being inclined to meddle with those things which they regard as sacred, and withal not fully comprehending the design of the adventure, after laying my hand upon it I hesitated. Upon this, the chief stepped forward, removed the covering, and desired me not only to pass before it and look at it, but to handle it.

With all this I complied, feeling the thickness of the shield, and handling the raven feathers and bone whistle which hung upon its face. This latter article is made of the principal bone of an eagle's wing.

He appeared satisfied, and proceeded very carefully to replace the coverings, doing it with all the gentle tenderness with which a mother would cover the face of a sleeping infant.

He then led the way back to the place from whence we started, where Kicking Bird and Stumbling Bear were awaiting our return, entire silence having been maintained throughout the proceeding. On our return, seating ourselves by the other chiefs, Kicking Bird explained the object of the adventure, which was to render me safe from the bullets or arrows of the Comanches and Cheyennes. I had looked the shield in the face, had handled the sacred ornaments, and the spirit residing in it had not been angry, and would now watch over and protect me.

From this explanation I was persuaded that they had a double design in what was done. First, that they might know whether the Great Spirit was pleased with my being in their camp, and secondly, for my safety. The Great Spirit resides in the sun. Sun Boy, or the sun's son, having his shield cover painted with a representation of the sun, is especially under his protection, and a portion of his spirit resides in this shield; hence, no doubt, they expected, in their superstition, that if he was not pleased with my being in their camp, he would have manifested his displeasure by striking me dead, when my polluted fingers took hold of the sacred ornaments of the shield, which, when uncovered, I recognized as one of those hung up by the image in the medicine house. As no harm befell me, this was to them an omen of his pleasure and my protection.

Soon after dinner, the camp was thrown into consternation by the announcement that white soldiers were approaching. Young men were at once sent out for the horses; women and children were running from lodge to lodge as if distracted; their valuables were arranged for a sudden departure, should such an event become necessary. The whole herd of horses and mules was soon run at full speed into camp, and many caught with the lariat; every one apparently secured a horse, pony, or mule, either to ride or pack with valuables. I had previously arranged with Kicking Bird to go with him and see the soldiers, before anything should be done, as I was of the opinion that there was no occasion for alarm.

Accordingly, a horse was led in for me to ride, my blankets were brought out of the lodge, and I was asked what should be done with them; I directed that they should remain where they were.

Soon a scouting party was ready to start out, with Kicking Bird and myself at its head. We went in the direction the soldiers were reported to have been seen, and scoured the plains for some hours, or until dark, without seeing any signs of human beings, except an Apache camp in the distance, and a small camp of Comanches near by. On our return in the evening, we found that tranquillity had been restored, and the horses and mules again turned loose to graze.

18*th.* — Remained in and about camp. I was more favored with a sense of Divine Goodness overshadowing my mind than for some weeks past, for which I desire to be thankful.

Though mine is very far from being a state of abounding fullness, yet I have learned that a crumb of the "true bread which cometh down from God out of heaven," administered at the right time, may be blest to the sustaining of the divine life in the soul, and is sufficient to preserve a relish for that which is good.

30*th.* — My health continuing very poor, I came into the Agency a few days since, and should resign my position but for the unwillingness of the agent to have me leave the Kiowa camps entirely.

Notwithstanding a party of Comanches went with a company of soldiers into Texas, searching for Indian raiders, in accordance with their agreement with the commissioner, and notwithstanding the raid made upon their stock, in their absence, by people living in Texas, as heretofore related, the agent this day received a telegram from Washington, to give the Comanches ten days in which to bring in five guilty raiders, as had been before demanded. In case of failure to comply, he is directed to cease issuing rations to them, and to withhold their annuities, as they will then be turned over to the military department. A messenger was sent out to the Comanche camps, requesting the attendance of their chiefs at an important council to-morrow. Thus are the clouds gathering, which may ere long rain blood upon this land. May they be dispelled, is the prayer of my soul.

12th Month, 1*st*. — Many of the Comanches came to the Agency, and the subject of the Washington despatch was explained to them; but how it will result it is impossible to foresee. It is not probable that they will make any effort to arrest the men, as that would be likely to produce war among themselves, and this despatch is looked upon by many of them as equivalent to a declaration of war against them.

It being well known that there are but two of the Comanche chiefs belonging to this Agency who have not discouraged their young men from raiding, it looks to me that this act of government might have been with propriety so modified as to issue rations and annuities to those chiefs and their bands who have not raided, and who, it is known, have not been committing depredations. They could then see that government means to reward well-doing and punish those who do wrong. Some of these chiefs have been friendly for many years, but are powerless to cause the arrest; and now to withdraw our care and protection from them, because of their inability to enforce the demand, and turn them over to the military, looks to me to be unjust, if not unwise.

Besides this, it is a well-known fact that Asa Habbit's band, belonging to the Wichita Agency, whose annuities have been issued to them, have been as deeply engaged in this raiding business, if not more so than any other bands, yet, because they belong to another Agency, they are not included in this arrangement.

It is very evident, as has been expressed by prominent citizens of Texas, that if the Indian policy that has been at work for the past few years — though but imperfectly the past season, on account of the pressure brought to bear against it by adverse circumstances — could be continued, there would be an end to these Indian difficulties. But if they are again thrown upon the war-path, the end of these depredations in Texas will be removed to an unknown and remote period, and much suffering must ensue.

It is admitted that fewer depredations have been committed by them the last year than has been the case for the past thirteen years, while the loss of their own stock by whites is far greater than ever before. In view of all these facts, it is seriously to be regretted that government could not have so modified its action as to have made a distinction between the innocent and guilty.

Since they have no confederate government, and one chief and band is as much independent of the others as one state is from another, the course adopted is calculated to have the effect to drive off those who have long been friendly to the whites, and instead of gathering to a civilizing influence, will tend to make enemies even of those who are, and have long been, our friends.

CHAPTER XIII.

AGENT'S MESSAGE TO THE KIOWAS. — NIGHT ON THE PLAIN. — LONE WOLF'S CAMP. — LONE WOLF'S SPEECH. — THE RETURN OF THE WARRIORS. — INTERVIEW IN KICKING BIRD'S CAMP. — KICKING BIRD'S SPEECH.

12*th Month*, 2*d*. — The agent having determined to send a message to the Kiowa camps, arrangements were made for the interpreter, George Chisholm, and myself to be the bearers of it. The following is the message: —

To the Kiowas and Apaches.

My Friends: I to-day send to you Thomas and Caboon, to ask you to come in near the Agency, so, if any trouble should come up between the soldiers and Comanches, you will not get into any of it.

It makes my heart feel very sad, makes it cry, that my Comanche friends have got into trouble, and I want my friends the Kiowas and Apaches to not get into trouble. My heart is very warm towards you, and I want you to listen to what I say, — not throw my talk away, — and I will keep you on a good road. I have given the Apaches their goods, blankets, and other things, and have the Kiowas' here to give to them, whenever they come after them; now, I want you to listen to this talk, and not forget I am your friend, and will do everything for you I can, to help you keep on the good road. Your friend,

J. M. HAWORTH.

We got a late start for the camps, and went as far as the mountain, near the head of Sulphur Creek, when, as it was very dark, and we feared we might miss the camp if we proceeded in the night, we camped out, spread our blankets on the ground, and were soon asleep. But in the course of the night a "norther" arose, with sleet and snow. The weather became very cold, and our blankets, having become wet, soon froze, so that the latter part of the night was not very comfortably spent. About four o'clock A. M., I arose, and finding a recess in a rock on the lee side of a cliff, built up a fire, and sat by it until daylight, when we made some coffee, broke fast, and proceeded on our way.

3*d.*—We arrived at Kicking Bird's camp a little past nine o'clock A. M.; found that all the chiefs except Quo-i-sau-be-at (Wolf-bow-case) were absent on their buffalo hunt. He, with what men there were about camp, soon came in, and I delivered the agent's message to them, and requested a guide to the other Kiowa camps; one was promised for the next day, but not being furnished, we were compelled to lie over another day.

In answer to their numerous questions, I gave them in substance the following reply: "There is no new road made for you. The commissioner told you, at the council, that the Comanches had got off the good road, which Washington had given them and you, and had gone back to the old bad road of raiding and killing people. He told them how they might get back on the good road again; that was, to stop raiding, and give him five of those raiding men. They have not got back, and now, if they do not get back in eight days, there may be trouble between them and the soldiers. I cannot tell.

"The Kiowas and Apaches have not left the good road; the agent has your annuities ready for you, and wants you to come close by, so as to get them, and be where he can take care of you."

5th. — Trotting Wolf coming in last evening, I read the agent's message to him, and gave him much the same talk I had given the others, when he set to work, and soon reported a guide to be in readiness this morning, to conduct us to Lone Wolf's camp. Accordingly, we were under way in good time, crossed several streams, tributary to the Washita, in deep channels, cut down in the red sandstone, also a number of ridges of variegated gypsum. Saw one or two herds of buffalo, with which our guide had to have a race, but his pony not having been trained for running buffalo, the race amounted to nothing more than the wild sport. Arrived at Lone Wolf's camp late in the afternoon. In the evening read the agent's message to Lone Wolf and three other chiefs, with several of the principal men of the encampment. Lone Wolf said, "The agent speaks of trouble between the soldiers and the Comanches, and wants us to come in close; there is a reason for all this which I do not understand. What trouble is it?

The following is my answer: —

"Lone Wolf may remember that, last fall, when he was in Washington, he was told that the Quahada Comanches, by constantly raiding in Texas, had made the Great Father's heart hard, and that he had sent his soldiers after them; that they would hear of it in a few days after getting home. This they did hear before getting home, and also that the soldiers had captured many of their women and children.

"Then, as you know, the Comanches came in, gave up all their captives, stolen horses and mules, and promised that they would be true friends of the white people if they would but give them back their women and children. They gave them back; but the Comanches went into Texas right away after their women and children were restored to them, broke their promise made to the agent, and returned to the old bad road of raiding, and killing people in Texas. This was very bad. Washington's heart had again become hard towards the Comanches, and he had given them ten days to bring in five of the raiders. There now remain but six days in which to do it. If they do not comply, they may have trouble with the soldiers. But Washington's heart is soft and warm towards the Kiowas and Apaches. He wants you to keep on the good road, and he will take care of you, and not let his soldiers trouble you. He has now told the agent to give you your annuities, and they are now ready for you. The agent wants you to come in, near by and all near together, so that he can keep the soldiers from disturbing you."

They listened attentively to what I said; then Lone Wolf replied that this was a subject of great importance, and would require much thought; he would give me his talk in the morning, and I must write it down and take it to the agent.

He then introduced conversation on different subjects; among other things told of the Osages having been among them, who called a "big council" of the Comanches, Cheyennes, Arapahoes, Kiowas, and Apaches.

He did not attend it, but learned that the Osages wanted, since they all had one mother (all the Indians regard the earth as their mother), that they should have but one fire (council), and all be one people. Afterwards some of the Osage chiefs visited him at his camp, and wanted to know what those white men (the surveyors) were doing in his country, — what he let them mark it all up for, — why he did not kill them. To which Lone Wolf replied, "They are my friends. I do not know what they are doing this for, — I do not understand it; but they are my friends, and I will not hurt them." The Osages replied, "They are our enemies;

they kill our buffalo; and we will kill *them* whenever we meet them on our land."

Before retiring, Lone Wolf very devoutly made medicine. He cleaned off a small space of the ground near the fire, between the fire and his bed; carefully brushed it; his wife brought him a couple of sacks containing cedar leaves and wild wormwood. Taking some coals from the fire, he laid them upon the clean earth, and, taking a handful of the cedar leaves, sprinkled them upon the living coals; likewise a small quantity of the wild wormwood; which made a dense smoke, with which the upper part of the lodge was soon filled. He then, passing his hands through the rising wreaths of smoke, rubbed his face and naked body with it, held it up to the Great Spirit, rubbed it upon the ground, &c. This ceremony ended, we retired for rest, and enjoyed a good night's repose in his lodge.

6th. — Received and wrote down Lone Wolf's reply to the agent's message as follows, namely: —

My Friend Simpoquodle (Kiowa name for the agent): You belong to the President at Washington. If the whites do anything wrong, I want you to take the good road.

I want you to go to the officers at the fort, and tell them to throw away their bad words, so that my people will not be made angry. I want to live friendly with everybody. I do not want to see any more war.

If any young men of the Comanches, Cheyennes, Arapahoes, Kiowas, or Apaches, go over into Texas and get killed, I think that is all right. If they kill any white people there, I do not want the whites to come upon us here, for this is a country of peace. Catch them there; kill them there.

My friend, I want you to tell my father at Washington that I do not want any war here in this country of peace that he gave to us, that I and my people may live in and hunt the buffalo. I do not want the soldiers to molest us in it. I want you to write to Washington that I am friendly to all these red people, and do not want to see any trouble among them.

I wish Washington would let it pass. If those foolish young men have killed any of the people of Texas, they are dead. Some of those young men have been killed: they are dead. Let it all pass; do not let it make trouble among the living.

I never hear any bad news from any other direction; but from Texas I hear very often somebody is killed. I know nothing about it — only what I hear.

I want you to sit still, and by and by I will come and see you. We have killed a great many buffalo, have many hides and much meat, are loaded heavy, and must come in slowly.

My friend Simpoquodle, I do not want you to get excited, and act in a hurry. If you hear bad news, do not be excited, but sit still. You must not believe the Comanches when they say the Kiowas have been raiding in *Texas*, for it is not true; they have not been *there*.

Big Tree was very sick. We made medicine for him, and he is now well, and running buffalo up above here on the river.

I want you to send this talk to my father at Washington.

Your friend, LONE WOLF.

On our return, about four o'clock P. M., we perceived a party of Indians driving ponies at a distance. Though they were at least two miles out of our course, our guide insisted on going to them, and in fact was determined to do so.

As we were comparatively unacquainted with the country, and knowing that we could not get into camp until long after night, we had no alternative but to go with him.

They proved to be a party of seven young Kiowa warriors returning from a raid into Mexico, upon which they entered just after my leaving them last summer.

Two of them were own brothers of our guide. They stated that they were very successful at the first, getting a good many ponies and mules, two scalps, and several Mexican blankets. They were afterwards pursued by a party of Mexican soldiers, who recovered most of their ponies and mules, so that the trophies of the expedition were two scalps, two or three blankets, and a few miserable-looking Mexican mules and ponies.

They left their stock upon a creek where there was plenty of good growing grass, and accompanied us to camp. Several of them knew me, for they shouted my name upon our meeting.

The night being very dark, the guide missed the way by several miles; but, reaching the Washita near the mouth of Rainy Mountain Creek, he discovered our locality, and by changing our course and following up the creek several miles, we arrived at Kicking Bird's camps late in the evening.

On approaching the camp, the returning braves arranged themselves under their leader in marching order, and brought in, elevated upon long canes, the scalps they had taken in Mexico. These had been trimmed, and stretched, while fresh, over small circular hoops; each was carried by the brave who had taken it. Then, after placing the interpreter and myself in front, they struck up the "Song of Triumph," accompanied at intervals by the war-whoop and the discharge of their fire-arms. This last is a signal that they had killed some of their enemies. They continued to ride slowly, their shrill, clear voices ringing out in the still air of night. Soon responsive shouts of triumph arose from the camp, as the women and maidens came out, with singing and dancing, to meet them. Peal after peal of laughter greeted our ears when they drew near enough to discover that the leaders of this band of returning heroes were Thomas and Caboon, the peace commissioners sent out by the agent. At first they felt chagrined; but, recognizing some of the voices of the returning braves, the singing and dancing were resumed, and the braves conducted to the camp, amid the continued shouts of joy and the report of fire-arms.

We found, on arriving in camp, that Stumbling Bear, Sun Boy, and others who went out on the hunt, had returned, leaving Kicking Bird on the road coming in.

The next day was rainy, and we waited for the arrival of Kicking Bird, which was not until evening.

Soon after, the chiefs and principal men assembled at the lodge where we were, and I read the agent's message.

Kicking Bird said that when he was at the Agency, he wanted his annuities; but the agent would not let him have them, and he did not know but that would be the way now.

I told him the reason the agent would not let him have them then was, that the annuities for the Kiowas and Comanches came packed together, and had not been separated. The goods for the Apaches came by themselves, separate from the others, so that the agent could give them theirs at once. Now the goods of the Kiowas and Comanches are separated, and you can get them whenever you go for them. He then said, "Last fall, Washington told us to come in close and sit down by the agent. We did so, and got no robes to trade with, and it made us poor all the year. I now want to know, if these five chiefs camped here with me were to go in, would we get our goods?" I answered, "I do not know. It would be better for all the chiefs to go in together, and then they could see that a fair distribution was made; there would be no ground for one chief to complain that he had not got his just apportionment. But I do not have that to do, and cannot answer for the agent."

He then turned to the subject of the Comanche trouble, and made the following speech: —

"This country from the Arkansas to the Red River was given by Washington to his red children — the Kiowas, Comanches, Osages, Wichitas, Cheyennes, Arapahoes, Apaches, and Caddoes. It was a country of peace. I now see white men in it making lines, setting up stones and sticks with marks on them. We do not know what it means, but are afraid it is not for our good.

"The commissioner by making one bad talk has set all this country on fire. He has required a hard thing, which was not in the road our fathers travelled. It is a new road to us, and the Comanches cannot travel it: they cannot bring in the five men. If they attempt it, many women and children will be killed, and many men must die.

"It all rests on the commissioner.

"This trouble will not affect the Comanches alone: it will spread through all these tribes, and become general. It is a new road to all the Indians of this country, and they will be affected by it.

"I have taken the white people by the hand; they are my friends. The Comanches are my brothers. By and by, when I am riding on these prairies, and see the bones of the Comanches, or the skull of a white man, lying on the ground, my heart will feel very sad, and I shall say, Why is this? It is because *Mone-kome-haint* * made a road the Indians could not travel.

"If Washington would put his soldiers all along on the frontiers, and kill every young man who goes across the line, we would cry for them; but it would be right. When they cross the line they take the chances of war.

"I do not want to see trouble in this land of peace; but I fear blood must flow, and my heart is sad.

"The white man is strong, but he cannot destroy us all in one year; it will take him two or three, may be four years; and then the world will turn to water, or burn up. It is our mother, and cannot live when the Indians are all dead."

I replied, "Do you think that the Comanches did right to go raiding into Texas, after promising the agent that they would do just as he wanted them to do, if he would only give them back their women and children? They often told him, in my presence, — I heard it myself, and you heard it, — 'There is but one thing we want: give us our women and children, and we will settle down, make corn, and do just what Washington wants us to do.' The agent worked hard, got their women and children; and then they went right into Texas, stealing horses and killing people.

"Washington has two kinds of children. He loves them both, and does not want them to quarrel and kill each other: that is the road they used to travel.

* *Mone-kome-haint*, the Kiowa name for the commissioner, meaning "without a pointing finger;" he having lost the forefinger of his right hand.

"Our Great Father has been trying to make a good road for all his children, — broad enough for them all, — if they would not quarrel and fight. But Comanches go into Texas, steal horses and kill people; Texans come here and steal ponies; but they have not killed any Indians *here*. Washington steps between them, takes both by the arm, holds them apart, talks to them, tells them they must stop quarrelling. He says, 'I shall put my soldiers between you; then, if you fight, you fight me. Your quarrelling must be stopped.'

"Now, the Kiowas have nothing to do with this trouble: it is between Washington and the Comanches. Washington gave you back your chiefs Satanta and Big Tree; his heart is warm towards you — the Kiowas and Apaches. He has told the agent to give you your annuities; they are now ready for you, and I think you will not be sorry if you go in and get them.

"It is because the agent loves you that he sent you this message; it is because I love you that I brought it; and I now want you to listen to my talk, and the message of the agent, and come in quickly.

"If you love the Comanches — who, by getting on the bad road after Washington gave them back their women and children, made it such very hard work for you and your friends to get back Satanta and Big Tree — better than you love your wives and children, and so stay out and miss getting your annuities, the loss will be yours, and you cannot blame the agent for it.

"The road you used to travel was a bad road — you

killing white people, and white people in return killing Indians. It is because Washington wanted a better road made that he has sent you better agents.

"Your agents used to get drunk, act foolish, carry pistols to fight with, &c. Now you have better agents, who do not get drunk or act foolishly, but do all they can to keep the Indians on the good road."

A great change in appearance came over Kicking Bird, who had been among the Cheyennes and Comanches, and had evidently been laboring under a wrong impression, and was quite angry at first. He now rested in a thoughtful position for some minutes, and then, in a calm and subdued tone, said, "I know the Comanches have been raiding in Texas, and that they have done badly; and now I want to ask you two one question. I want to know what you both think. Had we better go in and get our annuities, or stay out?" This was a soft way of putting the question of peace or war, — as going to the Agency would, under present circumstances, show that they were determined in their friendship towards the whites; while remaining out would be no less indicative of their sympathies with the Comanches.

The interpreter, without explaining the question to me, said he was no chief; he only interpreted what others said, and should not give them any advice. If they wanted to stay out, do so; if they wanted to go in, do that. I saw that they were not pleased, and had him explain the question and his answer to me. I then said, "Washington's heart is soft and warm towards the Kiowas and Apaches; the Apaches have got their annuities, and yours are there waiting for you. The agent will not bring them to your camps; he tells you, you can have them by coming after them, and I think you had better go and get them.

"The agent's heart is warm; he does not want any trouble to arise; but he is alone. Perhaps, if his Kiowa and Apache friends come in, they can help him to stop this trouble, even after it is begun, so that it will not amount to much."

A murmur of satisfaction spread through the lodge, with the expression, "Guit-är-kē tŏ'-zănt Thomis-sy," or, in English, "Thomas's talk is good;" and Kicking Bird replied, "Good! as that is your advice, we will go in to the Agency, and I will make my camp and sit down where the agent tells me."

The cloud which had been lowering over the camp since my first arrival was lifted, and cheerfulness restored.

The next day we returned to the Agency.

We learned, by several Indians we met on the way, that several war parties of Comanches had started for Texas since our going out to the camps, as they looked upon the commissioner's renewed demand for the five men, after they had complied with their agreement, as a determination for war on the part of government.

It was late in the evening when we arrived at the Agency, where we found that the agent had received another telegram, not exactly annulling the former, but ordering a continuation of rations until further orders.

It appears that the prompt action of the Washington branch of the executive committee, who hastened to Washington immediately on being informed of the previous telegram, had opportunities with the proper officers there, and labored to show up the probable results arising from the conditional release of Satanta and Big Tree, after a full and perfect release had been promised, — the still further aggravation upon the south-western tribes by the renewal of this demand, after, as they supposed, a compromise had been effected with which they had complied, — has been instrumental in causing this present change.

This course, by continuing a state of suspense, though preferable to the prospect of immediate war, is far from pleasant.

After reconsidering the situation, government ordered the continuation of rations to the Comanches, and three fourths of their annuities, upon condition that they bring in all the stolen stock — almost the precise conditions of the offer made by them to the commissioner at the time of the council, and by him utterly refused.

This vacillating on the part of the government cannot have a very salutary effect on the minds of the Indians. Making a positive demand, refusing any other consideration, and then retreating from it, after threats of extreme measures, when it is seen they will not comply, is construed by them into an act of fear or weakness on the part of government. It is, however, undoubtedly better to retreat from a bad position, even though it have not the best effect, than to adhere to it; yet it would have been far better not to have taken it at all.

Had the commissioner— who evidently has the welfare of the Indian at heart, and is very desirous of promoting it — but seen it right at the time to have modified the proposition of the Comanches to the present form, I have no doubt but it would have prevented much raiding in Texas the incoming winter, and perhaps saved the nation the expense of an "Indian war."

It may have been a correct view and motive to endeavor to exalt the authority and power of the state of Texas in the eyes of the Indian, but to do this at the expense of the dignity and authority of the general government is weakening the hands of all who are laboring in the work of civilizing this people, by destroying their respect for the government, and rendering its efforts and influence almost, if not wholly, nugatory.

CHAPTER XIV.

VISIT TO THE KICKAPOO CAMP. — CAMP AMONG THE MOUNTAINS. — KICKAPOOS. — RETURN TO KIOWA CAMP. — WHITE WOLF. — NEPHEW OF KICKING BIRD SHOT AT BY WHITE MEN. — TEXAN DESPERADOES. — BREAKFAST WITH AN OLD KIOWA WARRIOR. — MULES STOLEN BY COMANCHES, AND RECOVERED BY KICKING BIRD. — DEATH OF STUMBLING BEAR'S GRANDSON. — LONE WOLF'S SON KILLED IN MEXICO.

12*th Month*, 17*th*. — Having been furnished with an ambulance, comfortably fitted up for sojourning in camp as well as travelling from place to place, I left the Agency for the Kiowa camp on the 13th, the day after Kicking Bird, and the chiefs encamped with him, had received their annuities. The journey occupied two days, most of the way, I suppose, where a wagon never before had gone.

A part of the distance was exceedingly rough, especially through the "gap in the mountains," a wild, rocky pass, nearly two miles in length, between high, rocky bluffs. After remaining in camp until this afternoon, a party of perhaps a dozen of us started for the Kickapoo camps, in company with the Kickapoo chief and one or two others, who had been for a day or two guests at our camp, and had received several tokens of friendship in the form of blankets, coats, &c.

We travelled in a direction nearly south, passing several miles east of Rainy Mountain. This is a low, smooth, round-topped mound, nothing more than a hill; but standing alone on the plains, entirely isolated from other mountains, though not remote from them, it becomes a conspicuous object.

After crossing a wide plain between different ridges of mountains, we ascended to an elevated plateau surrounded by high, rocky peaks, among which the East Fork of Rainy Mount Creek — a fine stream of clear, pure water — has its origin. Here we encamped for the night.

Nothing, in the way of purely land scenery, could be more picturesque than this elevated prairie, surrounded by huge rocks, pile upon pile, with here and there a stinted cedar, struggling for life and a scanty foothold in the fissures by which they are rifted. These, rising as they do several hundred feet above us, in every conceivable form of serrated crags, present an outline against the clear vault of heaven equally striking with the most fanciful sketch the pencil ever traced.

Several fires were soon blazing on the bank of the clear stream, whose waters, lower down, had on several former occasions cooled my thirst and refreshed my drooping spirits, after days and weeks of sojourn on the plains, where no draught but turbid, sickening, alkaline water could be had, and many times an insufficiency even of that.

After the ponies and mules had been taken care of for the night, we gathered around these fires in the open air, and our evening meal was prepared.

Coffee was soon ready, with plenty of dried buffalo meat, and bread made after the most primitive style of art, — mixed with water, without salt, and baked upon the coals.

One woman, out of regard for my more civilized taste, plaited the twigs and small branches of a green bush together so as to form a network of twigs, spread a cake of dough upon it, and held it over the hot embers, turning it from time to time until thoroughly baked.

Meanwhile the rest of the group were in the enjoyment of great glee in anticipation of the account which they appeared to have no doubt I would put down to be read by the world of "white paper talkers," and the way the "white squaws would laugh about the good Kiowa woman, who baked Thomises bread on sticks to keep the ashes from sticking to it."

18*th.* — Early in the morning we were up and stirring, but, on account of the dilatory habits of the Indians, and the weather being cool and frosty, we did not get started until past eight o'clock. Crossing the stream, we followed its course for a mile or two farther, where it has its source among these wild, rocky mountains.

Our way for several miles lay over an elevated plateau,

stony in places, but mostly sufficiently smooth to permit of my trotting briskly along, although near at hand were masses of huge boulders, rising with the grandeur of mountain scenes, but rougher and more serrated in outline than any mountains I had elsewhere seen.

Indeed the Wichitas — formed as they are of bare rocks apparently rent and shivered by some awful convulsion of nature, lying and standing in every conceivable position and angle — excel the mountains of the east in the rough, notched, and cragged appearance which they nearly everywhere present, as much as they may fall short in real magnitude.

Medicine Bluff Creek — on which Fort Sill is situated, and which through its whole course winds about among rocks and mountains, sometimes cutting its way hundreds of feet deep in its rock-bound course — has its origin in the same beautiful plateau with the East Fork of Rainy Mountain Creek, emphatically a stream of the plains, flowing silently over treacherous quicksands and beds of red and yellow clay. We followed down the valley of the former stream several miles to the camp of the Kickapoos, which is situated in a wild, rocky glen, on both sides of the stream. Here we found a team from the Agency, which had been sent out with provisions for them by A. Williams, their agent.

The Kickapoos have recently arrived from Mexico, where they have been for several years past, at times raiding and committing depredations in Texas. In the early part of last summer, a party of them, in company with some Apaches residing among the mountains west of the Pecos River, were pursued from that state by United States troops, who followed them across the Rio Grande to their encampment, and captured fifty or sixty of their women and children. These captives have not yet been returned to them, but promised on condition of their coming and settling down on a reservation on the south-west side of the Arkansas River. This reservation was granted them in part payment for land once occupied by them in Kansas. Their agent, Andrew Williams, has been for some time waiting at the Kiowa Agency for the commissioners,(who prevailed upon them to leave Mexico, one of whom has gone to Washington), to deliver them into his hands. They have now been five or six weeks on this reservation, and still do not go to the Agency. The commissioner, who is getting a heavy salary, with expenses borne, is sitting quietly at Fort Sill, making no very vigorous exertion towards getting such a source of revenue off his hands, by bringing them in and turning them over to their agent. The latter is anxiously awaiting that event, in order to conduct them to their reservation, so as to be able to provide for their winter quarters. Their women and children, who were captured in the early part of summer, are already on their reservation, awaiting their arrival.

The object of the Kiowas in making this visit is the renewal of friendship, by exchanging presents, and to trade for some Mexican blankets, which, being waterproof, are more highly esteemed by the Indians than the

Big Tree (Addo Eta), Kiowa Chief.

Mackinaw blankets sold to them by the licensed traders, and issued as part of their annuities.

21*st.* — After leaving the Kickapoo camp on the 19th, Kicking Bird, his wife, and myself went to the Agency, where we remained one night, and returned yesterday and to-day to camp. A storm of snow much impeded our progress by balling upon the feet of the mules, and causing the ambulance to slide down the steep sides of the gulches we had to cross. Though I could lock the wheels, yet the snow and wet clay would allow the whole weight of the ambulance to press upon the mules, and slip down the steep banks in a manner rather more rapid than was pleasant or safe. Several bolts in the coupling finally broke, and the king-bolt bent so that the forward axletree turned over; and in this manner we entered camp, with the ambulance in rather a dilapidated condition.

On arriving, I found White Wolf, one of the Comanche chiefs who had not discouraged his young men from raiding in Texas, with his wife, occupying the lodge, where I have made my camp home this fall and winter. In the evening, Dangerous Eagle, his brother Big Tree, and their people arrived, and of course a "big smoke" and talk must of necessity follow. As they collected in the lodge, I was asked if I had not a looking-glass in my trunk. Replying in the affirmative, I was desired to take it out and have it carried out of the lodge, as not being good medicine to some of the party, particularly White Wolf. Not knowing how much more of the contents of my trunk might require removing on similar grounds, I thought best to remove it wholly, and so rid the lodge of all obnoxious medicine at once. This being done, rather than remain for some hours enveloped in clouds of tobacco smoke, I retired to the ambulance, and betook myself to sleep.

22*d.* — Repaired my ambulance by straightening the bent bolts, and tying the parts together with raw hide where the bolts were broken, so that, with proper care, I think I can get to the Agency with it.

To-day, while the young man who looks after Kicking Bird's ponies and mules, being his nephew, was looking for some missing ponies, after having taken my mules to the herd, he saw three white men, — probably hunters, as they proved not to be surveyors; one of them, for some purpose known only to himself, shot at him. The ball passed through his shirt and blanket, but fortunately missed his body, and he escaped unharmed.

The Kiowas are much excited about it this evening, and had he been killed, in all probability the earth would have drunk other blood than his ere the sun of another day had risen. That little party, if no more, might have looked upon the setting sun this day for the last time.

The free press of our country would have been flooded with inflammatory articles against the Indians, with horrible and soul-stirring accounts of "Indian barbarities," "three men killed by the Kiowas," &c., &c., while there might have been no one to have given one word of explanation to the world. It is high time that the injuries received, and the aggravating circumstances, which excite the uncultivated minds of these savages to acts of retaliation and barbarity, were beginning to be understood, and, if possible, stopped.

We hear abundance about Indian depredations in Texas, but rarely of the robberies committed by white people from that state against them. These are not seldom nor small. Over two hundred head of ponies and mules have been stolen from the Indians of this reservation alone, since the council, in the 10th month last, and the affiliated bands of the Wichita Agency have suffered about the same. Yet Governor Davis, at the council at Fort Sill, made the public declaration, "My people have committed no depredations against you," in the face of hundreds of Indians and many white people who knew to the contrary.

It is a well-known fact that there is a gang of desperadoes, having their headquarters about Red River Station, Jacksboro', and Waco, in Texas, who make a regular business of horse-stealing and other desperate deeds. These are furnished, as I have been informed from reliable sources,* with false hair, masks, and other Indian

* On one occasion the sheriff of one of the north-western counties of Texas informed me, that twice in his official capacity he had called out a portion of the militia to put down Indian depredators in his county, and in the ensuing skirmish one or two had been killed. The individuals killed on both these occasions proved to be white men, so thoroughly disguised with false hair, masks, and Indian equipage, as to readily be mistaken for Indians.

disguises, so as to pass readily for Indians when it suits their convenience to do so; and I have no doubt, while it must be admitted that Indians have done, and are still doing, more or less raiding in that state, that a large amount of the so-called Indian depredations and barbarities, even of the darkest dye, are committed by these savages with white skins.

A still darker shade, if possible, is given to their crimes by attributing to others what they themselves have done. This they do by furnishing telegrams and newspaper paragraphs, — anonymous, of course, but giving the authority of Major or Captain Someone, who has lately arrived from such a place and reports so and so, — giving the details of their own deeds. Sometimes the Indians thus reported on the war-path have been sick in their own lodges, on their own reservations, or running buffalo hundreds of miles from the scene of the reported depredation.

This has lately been the case with Satanta and Big Tree, whose doings in Texas since their release have furnished hundreds of paragraphs for the newspapers, while to my certain knowledge the latter was at home, sick in his lodge, and the former enjoying — after two years' confinement in prison — the pleasures of the buffalo chase, on territory assigned for the purpose.

23*d.* — Breakfasted with an old Kiowa warrior, an uncle of Kicking Bird, who had a Mexican wife. I was directed to sit on the side opposite the entrance, at the right hand of Kicking Bird, under what is commonly suspended from the lodge pole as the medicine sack. Of this I took no notice on sitting down, but presently, on turning my head, felt something softly brushing my ears, which proved to be a quantity of hair.

This had once covered the heads of the victims of the old man's prowess. After I had finished my breakfast, I reclined back in a position to notice more particularly this peculiar institution of the American savage.

The scalps had been trimmed and stretched, while fresh, upon small hoops, about four inches in diameter, and strung upon sticks, by running a stick like an arrow, only larger and about two feet in length, through them, near one edge. There were three of these sticks, each of which contained a dozen or more of these sickening trophies of his former bravery, the long hair of which hung down, and was partially concealed by a blanket. The sight was as ghastly and sickening as civilized eyes ever beheld, but to the savage mind a trophy attesting the bravery and strength of the possessor, as it is not presumable that the original proprietors of these locks yielded them up without a struggle.

I had often before partaken of the hospitality of this old man and his wife, but always in warm weather, when the meal was served in the open air, under an awning, and had never before been inside of their lodge. The wife is a fine-looking little woman, who was undoubtedly captured by him while young; and it would not be at all surprising were the scalps of her parents hanging in her lodge as evidence of her husband's valor.

They have a very pretty little girl, probably about eight years of age, and I could but hope that the time may soon roll around, when such a spectacle as her father's lodge affords may be done away forever, and remembered even by Kiowas only with disgust and abhorrence. Truly this would be a very great change from their present state of feeling; but knowing that there is One who can change the hearts of men, as a man turns a watercourse in his field, such a thing not only is not impossible, but through the efficacy of divine grace, is probable.

30*th.* — Having removed to the Washita River, above the mouth of Rainy Mountain Creek, on the 25th instant, our mules and ponies were turned upon new pasturage, and last evening the young man to whom their keeping is intrusted reported several head as missing, — mine among the number. This morning Kicking Bird set out himself to look for them. He soon found the tracks of my mules, — which he knew by their shoe-prints, — accompanied by those of a single unshod pony; whence he was led to believe they were stolen by an Indian.

He accordingly pressed rapidly forward, following the trail for many miles, until it at length brought up in a Comanche camp, where he found the mules lariated, thus proving the correctness of his supposition. I need scarcely add, that he was in no very pleasant humor about it, and it was in all probability well for the Comanche that he had reached camp before being overtaken. He returned late this evening, with my mules, without having found his own stock.

1*st Month*, 11*th*, 1874.—Last night an infant son of Ko-yone-mo, Stumbling Bear's daughter, died. I was awakened in the night by the death-wail in the lodge, but a few steps from my ambulance, in which I slept. This morning the body was buried, at some distance from camp, being borne to its last resting-place by the mother. The child had been sick for nearly two weeks, and its death expected for some days.

As there is so much superstition among them, I did not press the matter of seeing the burial, or the jugglery of the medicine-man. But I heard the passionate cries of the mother, whose face and arms were smeared in blood, from gashes of her own inflicting. The wailings of the family and near relatives, as they left the lodge for the burial, burst upon the ear in a prolonged, dismal cry, which gradually died away in the woods as the distance increased and the party approached the grave. I heard also the groanings, singing, and unearthly noises made by the medicine-man in his attempts to drive away the evil spirits which were the cause of the child's sickness and death, repeated from time to time after it was considered dangerously sick; but all was of no avail. The child is dead.

In connection with this account I should mention a circumstance in which I was particularly implicated, as corroborating a superstitious notion of this people. It appears that in their doctrine of signs and omens, it is considered an omen of death to a child for any one to step over it. Some few days before this child was taken sick, I was in the lodge, which I consider my camp-home, belonging to Stumbling Bear. Sun Boy came in, and sat down upon one of the mats, which are used as lounges by day and as beds at night. It is a part of his medicine that no person must pass between him and the fire. Ko-yone-mo came in, with her infant, in its cradle, upon her back, and seating herself by Sun Boy, laid her babe back behind her, so that it extended across the mats, from the side of the lodge to the place where she sat. Other women came in, and seated themselves around the lodge, while the side opposite to Sun Boy was occupied by the cooks, with kettles of meat, coffee, bread, bake-kettle, dishes, &c. The passage on that side of the lodge, from where I was seated to its entrance, was completely obstructed. At this juncture my name was called by some one outside the lodge. I at once arose to go out, but one glance around the lodge convinced me that the only way of egress was behind Sun Boy and those sitting by him. Without hesitating, I passed behind him, when this babe lay across my way; and not being aware of the dangerous omen of stepping over it, nor yet well enough versed in Kiowa politeness to wait for the mother to lift it out of my path, I stepped over it. A smothered groan was uttered by every woman in the lodge, with the hand laid upon the mouth, in token of bad medicine. It being too late to recall the act, I went out of the lodge. I had stepped over a living child as over a grave; that child would surely die; and, unhappily, in less than three weeks its grave could be walked over.

13*th.*—This is a day of wailing in our camp. News arrived this morning of the death of two Kiowa braves—the one a son of Lone Wolf, the other of Red Otter, Lone Wolf's brother. They were killed while on a raid in Mexico. Lone Wolf's son was wounded in the knee, a year ago last summer, while raiding in Texas, and came near losing his life. This, it seems, did not satisfy his thirst for blood, and the Kiowas determining to raid no more in Texas, he, the past autumn, went into Mexico, where it appears he has been killed. The camp resounded with the death-wail,—the song of mourning for the unreturning braves,—mingled with the war-whoop. This was revived at stated intervals for several days.

CHAPTER XV.

RELIGIOUS FEELINGS. — AN INSTANCE OF THE OVERRULING OF PROVIDENCE. — SINGULAR WEATHER. — CAPTAIN BLACK BEAVER'S SPEECH. — VISIT TO THE WICHITA AGENCY. — STEREOSCOPIC VIEWS IN KIOWA CAMP. — MURDER OF A SURVEYOR. — TRADING FOR AMMUNITION.— SULPHUR SPRING.

My mind has been of late much impressed with a sense of divine goodness and mercy, far beyond the utterance of words, in which I was favored to see the futility and utter insignificance of words, as between the soul and its Maker and Redeemer, who sees the very secrets of the heart, and knows the intents and motives thereof.

As the husk is valueless, except as enclosing the precious kernel, so words of themselves are powerless, except as they contain the precious seed of life. As a groan may be more powerful in giving an idea of intense suffering than the best set form of words, so there is an exercise and travail of spirit too deep for words to express, or the carnal mind to comprehend.

Words can no more convey to the understanding of

him who is dead in sin the peace which the world knows not, — the beauty, the glory there is in holiness, or the soul-satisfying enjoyment of being filled with the love of God, which passeth understanding, — than the colors of the bow in the cloud can be conveyed to the conception of one born blind.

Even true prayer and communion between God and the soul of man may exist without words. We read that "Elias was a man subject to like passions as we are, and he prayed earnestly that it might not rain; and it rained not on the earth by the space of three years and six months. And he prayed again, and the heavens gave rain." Of this last prayer no word is uttered, but after the people of Israel had been brought to confess, "The Lord he is the God," and the "Law" vindicated by the slaying of the prophets of Baal, "Elijah went up to the top of Carmel; and he cast himself down upon the earth, and put his face between his knees," but spoke not except to bid his servant "seven times to look towards the sea." Here was an exercise of spirit before the Majesty on high, not manifested in words, but answered with power, not only in the sending of a great rain, but in the renewal of the strength of the prophet, so that he even outran the chariot of Ahab.

Though I have written very little in these pages relative to my spiritual exercises and conflicts, it has not been because I have been exempted from trials, temptations, and many discouraging besetments of the enemy, or that in all cases I have escaped without wounds.

But, seeing there are many who run without being sent, — who talk much of their experiences of God, of Christ, and a spiritual life, who have not borne the fruits which become a life of holiness, — I have felt averse to writing respecting these things; lest, like some spoken of by a prophet, who, in declaring, "'The Lord liveth,' swear falsely," not having experienced the verification thereof for themselves, by testifying to things too deep for me, I may appear to arrogate to myself more than is becoming the low state of humility in which I desire to live. Yet I now feel to record, as the experience of my soul, "Hitherto hath the Lord sustained" and supported me, else I must have fainted and given out by the way.

Truly I may say, in all humility and abasedness of spirit, — "knowing that in me, that is, in my flesh, dwelleth no good thing," — whether fruit be borne, yea or nay, that I have been among this people with much sorrow and many tears; under discouragements and heavy burdens; in heat and in cold; in hunger, in thirst, and in weariness; in sickness, in weakness of the flesh, and weakness of the spirit; in perils, in privations, and in cruel besetments of the enemy; alone as to the outward, and a stranger among a strange people; having home, wife, and children, in a manner as though I had them not. Yet hath the Lord supported, and by the right arm of his power, notwithstanding my many slips by the way, sustained and upheld in all and through all; may his name be magnified.

Even at times, when his gracious presence has been,

or seemed to be, withdrawn, his hand has been underneath, to bear up, and keep me from falling, to make a way where man could make no way, and to overrule the counsels of the heathen, and machinations of evil and designing men; so that I have not only been preserved alive through dangers seen and unseen, but even the enemies of truth, and those who know not God, have been made to entreat me well. "This is the Lord's doing, and it is marvellous in my eyes."

As an instance of the overruling power of Providence in making use of the bitterness and envy of man to accomplish his own purpose, as well as by his own secret power to preserve those who put their trust in the arm of his might, I will mention the following circumstances: —

At the time I was sent for to come out to camp, just previous to the Great Medicine Dance, I was impressed with a belief that it was the design of the tribe to retain me in camp until Satanta should be released; or, in case government should fail to keep faith with them, to take my life as the first act of hostility. I found the agent had the same impressions, and as a consequence withdrew all requirement, on his part, of my going out; thus leaving me entirely at liberty to act in accordance with my own feelings, or as I might be best satisfied in doing. On fully weighing the subject, according to the best of my ability, I believed it to be my duty to go with them.

Subsequent occurrences, and information received,

proved beyond a question these impressions to have been correct. But behold the marvellous ways of God in turning that which was designed for evil to good account. Some person, or persons, probably, to cause an unendurable disappointment, and provoke the Kiowas to acts of hostilities, sent them word, in the name of the agent, that Satanta and Big Tree were already at the Agency, and for them to come in immediately in order to take them to camp. They accordingly mustered all the warriors of the tribe, in order to make them a grand reception, and came in, bringing me with them, after an absence from the Agency of four weeks. Two days out, I was taken very sick, and continued getting worse, which occasioned their bringing me directly to the agent's house, before learning that Satanta had not been released. Continuing very sick, I was taken to the doctor's office, where I remained in a weak state, daily visited by Kiowas until they left. They departed from the Agency under feelings of very great disappointment.

After getting out north of Mount Scott, about twelve miles from the Agency, they stopped and held a council as to what they should then do. An Apache woman, who understands the Kiowa language, overhearing a remark made by some one of the tribe, indicating the character of the proposed council, informed her husband (Apache John), near whose camp the council was to be held. He immediately sent her, with another woman, to secrete themselves near the council lodge. As it was held at night, they easily did this, and distinctly heard what was said, and the decision arrived at.

In this council it was decided that five of their most daring and brave men — men to be relied upon for their powers of cunning and strategy — should be selected to return to the Agency, seize the agent and myself, and rush with us to the plains, beyond the reach of the soldiers, whither they were to be joined by the tribe, and where we were to be held as hostages until Satanta and Big Tree should be released. The five men were selected, of whom the notable White Horse was one; another was Running Wolf, than whom the tribe possess no more vile or treacherous character.

Having obtained all the information deemed essential, the women retired from their place of concealment, and reported to John, who immediately mounted his pony, came in, and notified the agent of the intentions of the Kiowas.

Two nights after this, the five men arrived at the Agency just after dark, occasioning some surprise among the employees, as the Kiowas had left but three days before, and the agent had prudently kept the plot a secret, except from his wife, son, and one other young man. White Horse, on entering the house, not knowing what information the agent had received, and wishing not to raise any suspicion, took off his revolver and gave it to the agent's wife, and sitting down in an arm-chair in the private office, one of the arms so lifted his blanket as to disclose another beneath it, of which the agent spoke to him, much to his confusion and embarrassment.

They were treated with the utmost kindness, supper provided, and conversation carried on, in which the agent betrayed no indication of his knowing the object or design of their visit. They were evidently confused and disconcerted, and not accomplishing their designs at first, they waited until the next night, still not being being able to carry the plot into execution, and the following morning returned to camp, the agent giving them beef, sugar, and coffee, for their journey.

They reported to the tribe that our "medicine was too strong, and they could not touch us."

Thus, through the watchful care and all-sufficient protecting power of Him who never slumbers nor sleeps, was way made for my return, and our deliverance from this deeply-laid plot for our capture and detention.

Here we see five of the most desperate characters, men whose hands were "swift to shed blood," selected by one of the most fierce tribes of North American Indians, turned from their purposes without any visible agency. As there was no outward manifestation by which this work was wrought, and yet a secret power, as they acknowledged, so "strong that they could not touch us," may the Lord alone, who works in secret, and to whom the most hidden things are known, have all the honor and praise.

17*th.*—Last night the ponies and mules were brought in, in order to have an early start for the Agency in the morning. Although there was nothing to prevent an early start, we could not, from the habitual slowness of the Indians, get under way until eleven o'clock. Soon after noon the wind arose, and the weather grew cold, with a dense fog, at a little elevation from the ground, which, singularly enough, froze in the tree-tops, until ice was formed on the twigs a half an inch thick, while the grass on the ground was dry. The women became so chilled that some of them cried like children.

After a little search, a comparatively sheltered place was found, and we went into camp early. Kicking Bird, having had a nice robe prepared for my wife, brought it, just at leaving camp, for me to take for her. By adding this to my bed I slept very warm and comfortably.

31*st.* — Captain Black Beaver, a Delaware, who had come to this Agency in order to talk to the Indians of this reservation, to-day made a speech in the office to such of the chiefs and principal men of the Kiowas and Comanches as were present, in which he labored honestly and faithfully to induce them to stop raiding, send their children to school, settle down, and do as their friends the Quakers wanted them to do.

"The Quakers," he said, "are your friends; they made a treaty with the Indians more than two hundred years ago, in which both parties had bound themselves, and their children after them, to be friends to each other forever. This treaty has never been broken. The Indians have never taken any Quaker's blood, and the Quakers have always been true friends to the Indians.

"Our grandfather at Washington knew this, and for this reason had sent the Quakers among us. He knew that they would do right by his red grandchildren. He sent two of them among us to build us a school; they made us a good school, and we know that they are good men, love the Indians, and will take good care of the Indians' children.

"He has now proved them, and has taken them away from us, and sent them to you. One of them — Mr. Thomas — has been with you a long time, and you know he is a good man. Mr. Alfred (A. J. Standing) is also a good man; and when you are ready to send your children to school, you will find that they will be kind and good to them.

"The stone school-house to which we (Delawares and Caddoes) send our children is yours. We know it is yours, and will give it up at any time when you want it. We only use it because you do not, and we have not room enough in our own school-house."

He further said that he had attended the great council at Okmulgee, in which fifteen Indian nations were represented; and they wanted all the Indians of this territory to be united, to become one people, and to have one common cause. The raiding of the young Kiowas and Comanches worked against the progress, and to the injury of all Indians.

2d Month, 20th. — Having been back and forth between the Kiowa camp and the Agency, and feeling much depressed with illness, I concluded to remain in at the Agency for a while, and try the effect of better diet. On the 16th inst. I went to the Wichita Agency, and spent a few days there, during which I rode out to several Caddo settlements, also to the Pawnee, Wichita, and Comanche camps.

The Caddoes are rapidly improving. When I first became acquainted with them there were but two or three farms among them, and their houses, though of pretty good size, were of the most miserable description, being close, dark, smoky, and filthy. Now they have about two thousand acres broken for crops, over one hundred good frontier houses, with windows of glass, doors and chimneys, with some household furniture — tables, chairs, bedsteads, and the like. The houses have been mostly built by themselves. They have also quite a quantity of stock, besides ponies. The school is in a flourishing condition, having about sixty scholars, and a prospect of twelve or fifteen more in a few days.

On a little tour around among the camps, with Dr. F. Grinnell, we found the Pawnees indulging in an athletic sport requiring the exercise of some skill, as well as practice, to perform.

Two of them, grown men, had a ring of some flexible material, about four inches in diameter, and each of them a straight wooden rod, about four feet in length, with a small knob or button at one end and a double hook at the other, similar to the flukes of an anchor on a small scale. Starting off at a full run, one of them would throw the ring with all his might ahead of them, which, striking the ground, and rolling rapidly from them, presented only the rim; each poised his rod above his head, and hurled it at the ring, the knobbed end foremost, with such dexterity as that one or the other of them would seldom fail to catch the ring upon the hooks at the end of the rod.

We saw some other games played by the Wacoes and Towackonies, but were more interested, on approaching a Caddo settlement, in observing the men and boys engaged in another kind of exercise, which required some strength, as well as skill and taste in its execution. While some boys were drawing rails with a wagon, a couple of men were laying out the worm, and putting up a fence. I think I never saw a fence laid up more plumb at the corners, or that deviated less from a straight line; and I could but think that the fine taste manifested by the agent in all his work was being copied by his Indians. The Caddoes, like the other Indians, are averse to labor, and are easily diverted from it by discouraging circumstances. Still, they are rapidly rising in the scale of civilization, and I think, with proper encouragement, will soon become a self-supporting people. Some of their young men are learning the trades of carpenter and blacksmith. The Wichitas, though far behind the Caddoes, have made some improvement, especially in the dress of the women, since my coming among them. They have fifteen or twenty children at school; beyond this they are not advancing very fast.

3d Month, 5th.—I came out to camp day before yesterday, alone, and meeting a band of Comanches, while talking with them they took it upon them, by way of making themselves agreeable, to relieve me of both my lariats.

Yesterday and to-day I have been busy showing the "Alphabetical Object Teacher," Kaleidoscope, and Stereoscopic Views. I have been much surprised, as well as amused, at the effect produced by the exhibition of the latter. As a body, the Indians of this country who have never been east, and, as a consequence, have seen but few white people, are disposed to disbelieve the accounts they receive respecting their numbers, the magnitude of their towns and cities, and the extent of the country they occupy. They believe that their own people who have been east have been duped by some kind of sorcery, or, as they would say, "medicine." They also think it is impossible to make an imaginary picture. Hence a picture is to them "proof positive" of the existence of an original. Consequently, my exhibiting towns, buildings, rural scenes, and soldiers, has had a most convincing effect. This was much heightened by having some mountain scenes from Colorado, familiar to them, and which they recognized at once. This was, in fact, the strongest adducible evidence that the accounts they had received were so far from being exaggerations that the half had not been told them

One middle-aged man, who has always treated these reports with the utmost scepticism, was particularly struck with them. He could not sufficiently express his surprise, but beat upon his mouth in utter astonishment. Sun Boy, who had often told him what he saw in the east, would say to him in Kiowa, "What you think now? You think all lie now? You think all chiefs who have been to Washington fools now?" Again and again would he look them over, with his hand upon his mouth, dumb with amazement. After he had looked them over several times, being a war-chief, he called in his warriors, and exhibited the pictures to them, talking to them all the time. I could understand but a part, yet would gather such expressions as these: "Look! see what a mighty powerful people they are!" — meaning white people. — "We are fools! We don't know anything! We just like wolves running wild on the plains." Such an effect on the war-chiefs and warriors cannot but be very salutary, and must conduce much towards deterring them from going on the war-path against such a "mighty powerful people." I could but wish that a good stereoscope, with suitable pictures, could be exhibited in every Indian camp in the land, and properly explained to the people.

13*th.* — Last evening, in coming in to the Agency, I got some distance in advance of the Kiowas, who were coming in for rations, in consequence of their taking several hours for a nooning. Though I drove very slowly, to permit them to overtake me, they did not; so

I encamped by myself, at the head of Cache Creek. Just at dusk, on returning from a little stroll among the rocks near by, what was my surprise to find my ambulance taken possession of by an Indian, who was sitting in it, revolver in hand, ready to defend his position! On my approach I recognized him as a Comanche chief by the name of Wild Horse. I went up to him, wanting an explanation of his proceedings. He said that coming to the place with some of his people, intending to encamp there for the night, he saw my ambulance, and, coming to it to have a talk, he found no one with it, and placed himself there to keep his people from stealing anything from it in my absence. I expressed my gratitude to him for his kind attention, at the same time would greatly have preferred entire solitude, but felt no uneasiness for my personal safety, and gave as little opportunity for the exercise of their pilfering propensities as circumstances would permit.

While I was in camp this time, a German belonging to Hackbush's surveying party was murdered by an Indian. This was, as usual, attributed to Kiowas. I endeavored to investigate the matter, and am entirely satisfied that it was not done by any of that tribe. Otter Belt, a young Comanche, says he was encamped near the surveyor's, and saw a party of nine Cheyennes go to their camp. Under the impression that they had gone there for no good purpose, he went to the camp himself. The Cheyennes inquired what he came there for; he replied, "To see you. What for you come?"

To which they replied, "To get hair." He talked to them some time, endeavoring to dissuade them from their purpose, and finally invited them to his camp. They went with him, and told him that a son of their chief Little Robe had been killed by whites, and they were seeking an opportunity to revenge his death; but at last talked of going into Texas, and killing some one there. A day or two after, as Cheyennes continued about, he moved his camp away to avoid getting into trouble in case the Cheyennes should kill some of the party, which he believed they intended to do, and now believes they did the deed. The surveyors belonging to Colonel Denman's party also believe it to have been done by Cheyennes, who were about the camp a great deal, passing back and forth, between it and the Kiowa camp.

The Kiowas deny all knowledge of the deed until after it was committed. Subsequently the impression was conveyed by one of the party to individuals at the Wichita Agency, that the Indian was not the first aggressor in the case. It has been the practice of the Cheyennes, and also the Comanches, to shift their crimes upon the shoulders of the Kiowas, who have enough of their own to bear; but all their talking to the whites being done through the Cheyenne or Comanche language, they have much the disadvantage as regards clearing themselves of those charges.

Since traders have been permitted to have a post in our camp, I have noticed that Indians come to trade, bringing large quantities of robes to sell, for which they want ammunition; but as the traders have no license for selling arms and ammunition to Indians, they cannot sell to them, or keep them for that purpose. As a consequence, they take their robes away, saying they can get pistols and ammunition of the Cheyenne traders, who are located above here on the river. Many loads of robes have been taken away from here on that account, much to the detriment of the Kiowa and Comanche traders. The Indians in a few days return, having revolvers and cartridges which they have purchased. This has a tendency to create dissatisfaction on the part of our Indians towards their agent, and sometimes they get considerably excited over it. It is also drawing a large amount of trade from the regular licensed traders of this Agency, into channels over which our agent can have no control. From the amount of ammunition purchased by some of the Comanches, I fear they are providing it for a wrong use. As their regular hunting operations are largely carried on with the bow and arrows, they cannot have a legitimate use for such quantities as they are purchasing.

24th. — In coming to the Agency to-day, after crossing Sulphur Creek, having been informed that there was a "bad medicine" spring near where we crossed, I stopped and searched for it. Taking my olfactory nerves for guide, I soon found a strong spring of sulphur water. It is beautifully clear, of a warm temperature, probably not far from one hundred degrees

Fahrenheit, strongly impregnated with sulphur and other mineral substances, which incrusted the stones, small sticks, leaves, and grass, which dipped into the water, with a cream-colored crust, while a slimy sediment of a deep scarlet adhered to the stones at the bottom. This spring is at the base of a rocky mound, several hundred feet in height, and is a strong body of water, affecting the whole creek into which it flows with a strong sulphurous smell, through its whole subsequent course to the Washita River.

CHAPTER XVI.

VISIT OF THE EXECUTIVE COMMITTEE. — COUNCIL AT THE WICHITA AGENCY. — THOMAS WISTAR'S SPEECH. — J. E. RHOADS' SPEECH. — OTHER SPEECHES. — SIMILAR COUNCIL AT THE CHEYENNE AGENCY, AND AT THAT OF THE KIOWAS AND COMANCHES. — START FOR CADDO. — ADVENTURE AT THE WASHITA, AND RETURN.

THOUGH the Comanches — with the exception of parties of young warriors, who continued to raid in Texas — kept pretty quiet through the winter, it became very evident, towards spring, that they, with the Cheyennes, meant more than an ordinary season of raiding. The season for procuring robes had been unusually prosperous, and large quantities, amounting in the way of trade to thousands of dollars, were expended in the latest improved revolvers, cartridges, and other ammunition.

Members of Congress, in the mean time, were discussing the propriety of turning the whole Indian work over to the military department, when a portion of the Executive Committee of Friends met at Washington, and proposed that some of them should visit the Indians of the south-western Agencies, and hold councils with the different tribes, before that measure be resorted to.

Accordingly, Thomas Wistar and James E. Rhoads, of the committee, and M. C. Cope, all of Philadelphia, came out for that purpose, accompanied by Cyrus Beede, of the superintendent's office, and William Pickerel, of Iowa. A council was held, at the Wichita Agency, with the Indians of that reservation, and the Comanches and Apaches. Afterwards, a part of the committee had a council with the Cheyennes and Arapahoes, at their own Agency, while the remaining part came to the Kiowa Agency, and held a council with the Kiowas.

As a clearer idea of the labors of these Friends can be gained from their speeches, than without them, I have taken the liberty of introducing them in these pages, having first submitted them to the Friends who delivered them, for correction.

The council was opened on the 5th day of the 4th month, 1874, by Cyrus Beede introducing the Philadelphia Friends, stating that they came representing a society who never fight either Indians or other people, who have the recommendation of the agents to Washington before they are appointed and sent among them; they are true friends of the Indians, and should their talk appear as though trouble might possibly arise, it is not because their hearts are not right; but, having been to see our father at Washington, they will speak as true friends, and tell you what Washington has to say.

Thomas Wistar then arose and said, —

"Brothers: For some time past I have felt much for you, believing that danger and trouble are fast gathering around you; and, as your old friend, it was my duty to leave my home, now in my old age, once more to take you by the hand, and see you face to face, — to show you what your present danger is, how you may avoid it, and preserve peace and happiness, not only for yourselves, but for your children.

"Brothers: I believe you have been greatly injured in many ways by bad white men, and my heart is sorry for you; but I must tell you that you yourselves are in part to blame. These white men, by entering into your country, have, by so doing, disobeyed your great father, who has made a law, intended for your protection, that no white man shall enter the Indian Territory, without first obtaining his permission.

"Brothers: Have you not, over and over again, let these men come near to your camps, traded with them, and thus encouraged them in violating the command of Washington? I believe I speak the truth when I say that no good white man will be found in your country without first having obtained the consent of your great father; and when you find such men, you should inform your agent, that he may remove them.

"Those men who come in violation of law are not your friends, — although they [may] appear to be so, — but they are your enemies, and they have caused, and will cause, trouble, so long as they are with you. Their object is to take some advantage over you, and enrich themselves at your expense.

"Brothers, let us turn our eyes on the other side, and see what has been done in that direction. Some of you have been so regardless of the wishes of your great father, as, at different times, to leave your homes, to plunder, steal, and murder some of Washington's white children. Their cry has gone up to his ears, and he is now offended, because he has been endeavoring to make a good road for you, but is now discouraged about you; and he is offended with his red children for their bad work. But we have gone again to his house, and asked him to wait a little longer; for we believed you would do better. For a short time you gave him no trouble, but afterwards he again heard the cry of his white children, that you had stolen again, and murdered again.

"Then Washington lost hope, and called some of his big captains, and asked them what he should do with you. They said, 'There is no use in waiting any longer,' and advised him to send your agents and friends home, and put soldiers in their places. Now, your friends, out of love for you, and pity for your women and children, have begged Washington not to order your friends to go home just now, for when he commands us to leave you we shall have to obey him.

"Brothers, let me entreat you to think seriously of what will then be your distressed condition. Instead of your good agent and his friends, with his door open to welcome you, — with his schools for the instruction of your children; with his mill, and ploughs, and wagons, — you will be turned over to the soldiers, with their swords, guns, and drums. My heart grows sick, when I think of such a change, well knowing how it has always been with the Indians when the soldiers have [had] the charge over them; that sooner or later they have been harassed and destroyed; and, as your true friend, I fear this will be your sad experience.

"Brothers, although it is growing dark, yet there is a little light left. Washington's door is not quite closed. You still may become a happy people. All I can now do, — all that your friends can now do, — is to look up to the great and good Spirit, who made both you and us, and beg him that he will change your hearts, and incline you to live in peace with your Indian brethren and the white people. We know — and I am persuaded some of you also know — that stealing and murder are exceedingly displeasing to the Great Spirit; and he has promised to reward all men according to their deeds. To all those who love him, and do those things which please him, he has promised happiness, not only in this life, but in that beyond the grave; but to the wicked, whether they be white or red, sorrow, pain, and death."

Dr, J. E. Rhoads then addressed them as follows: —

"Brothers: Four years ago I was at a council with all the Indians of this region, held on the North Fork of Canadian River, where the Cheyenne Agency now is; Asa Habbit was the only Comanche chief present, but we saw several Kiowa and Comanche chiefs afterwards, at the Agency at Fort Sill. We told you then that the Great Spirit had taught us to walk in the peace road, — that we always walked in it, — and we asked you to walk in the same road. We told you if you did we would try to do you all the good we could. Since then our people have built these houses for the Indians, have helped them to make farms, have given you many wagons, have opened schools for your children, and have tried to teach you the white man's road.

"We found that Washington did not send you good sugar and rations. We asked him to send better food to you, and he did so. We heard that you did not listen to our peace talk, but went on raids into Texas. Then Satanta and Big Tree were taken prisoners, and we asked Washington that they should not be killed; and after a while we asked him to let them go if you would promise not to raid into Texas. Some of Washington's people laughed at us, and said you would not stop raiding till you were killed. When we heard that Satanta and Big Tree were released, we were glad, hoping now the Kiowas and Comanches would keep their promise, and live at peace. Soon we heard that though the Kiowas did not raid in Texas, the Comanches did. Then we felt sad. Washington's Texas children cried to him, and asked him to protect them; and many of his chiefs said you must be put under the charge of the soldiers. We went to Washington, and asked him not to be angry with you, and we would come and ask you to stop all raiding.

WHITE BEAR (SE-TI-TAH, SATANTA), KIOWA CHIEF.

"We know it is only some of your young men who raid, but we know that if they do not stop, Washington will send our peace people home, and send the soldiers to compel you to stop raiding. Already the soldiers have killed a good many of your young men who were raiding. We know that these young men were doing what the Great Spirit did not want them to do, for he wants all his children to live as brothers.

"Now, we ask you to promise again that all your people will stop raiding. Then your agents will stay, and we will do you all the good we can. We find but few rations in the commissaries, but this is not your agent's fault. It may be that Washington is discouraged by your continuing to commit depredations on his Texas children.

"We know that Washington has [some] bad [white] children, who sometimes steal your horses; but you had better bear this, and wait till Washington stops his Texas children from robbing you, than to go on raiding. If you stop raiding, none of Washington's people can say anything against you, and we can get him to do more to protect you, and send you good rations. If you let bad white people come among you, and you buy whiskey of them, they will steal your ponies; for only bad white men will sell you whiskey. We are glad to find so many Indians on this reservation (Wichita and Caddo) who farm, raise cattle, and hogs. We want you all to raise cattle and hogs, and send your children to school. These Indians who farm and raise cattle are doing what

Washington wants them to do, and they can have plenty of corn to eat, and can raise plenty of cattle, after a while, to eat too. You should not kill their cattle, nor let your people eat up their crops. If you want corn, or cattle, or hogs, you should raise them yourselves. If you will really stop raiding, — throw it away altogether, and stop your young men from it, — then everything will go on well; Washington will do all he can to protect you. We will now read what he says, viz.: 'Promise them that if they will stay on their reservations, and not go off them, they shall be protected.'"

After a short speech from M. C. Cope, C. Beede followed with a strong speech, reviewing his labors among them, — the agreement he made with the Kiowas and Comanches one year ago; the great labor of the agent, himself, and their friends, in procuring the release of Satanta, Big Tree, and the Comanche women and children; the pledge of the Kiowas and Comanches that they would never more raid in Texas if the prisoners were released, — telling them that the Comanches had violated that pledge; and Washington's heart had become hard. Now they would have to quit raiding, or their peace friends would be taken from them, so that they could do no more for them. They would be turned over to the soldiers, and would find that Washington's hand is as heavy as his heart is kind. He called upon them now to speak, that these their friends might carry their words to Washington, so that he might know what to do.

After short talks from the two agents, Richards and Haworth, several of the chiefs replied, one after another, stating in substance that they had heard the good talk their friends had given them, — that they thoroughly understood it; that they were sorry Washington's heart gets tired so quick; they did not get tired of trying to keep their foolish young men from raiding; that they had not entirely succeeded, but they did not raid nearly so much as formerly; they were encouraged to continue trying. They thought Washington ought to be more patient, and not let his heart get tired so quick. Nearly every one wanted something done for him, as he was a friend to Washington, trying to walk in the white man's road, and was very poor indeed, &c.

Nearly the same talk was made to the Cheyennes, Arapahoes, and Kiowas, at their Agencies. At the Kiowa Agency a few Comanche chiefs came into the office, followed by some of their young men, one of whom, addressing the Friends, said that it mattered not what the chiefs said in council with the whites; they, the young men, were the warriors, and should not listen to them or any one else; they should do as they pleased. Washington might be a big chief among white people, but he was not their chief, and had nothing to do with them, and that they should not be controlled by him. Dr. Rhoads made some remarks to his chief, White Wolf, which he could not gainsay, but still there was very little softening down immediately; and yet the young man, when he left, did not carry himself so tauntingly as at the outset. It may very likely have been a device, on the part of the chiefs, to convey the impression, that though they were anxious to travel in the white man's road, the young men had the power, and if they saw fit to raid, they could not restrain them.

For a time it really appeared that the Comanches and Cheyennes would be more quiet, but they mutually encouraged and strengthened each other in that which will ultimately result in injury to themselves. They smoked the war-pipe together, and brought it to the Kiowa camps; but, with the exception of a single chief, it was rejected by them. The Arapahoes also refused to smoke with them, so that the effect of the council may not be entirely lost, though many of them may have occasion to remember the faithful warnings of these their true friends, after a realizing experience of the chastisements which their own stubborn folly has brought upon them.

17*th.* — As my health was not considered sufficient to justify me in going out to camp immediately after the council, the agent proposed my taking the Friends to Caddo, in order for them to take the cars at that place. Accordingly, we set out on the 13th instant, and travelled as far as the Washita River, at Cherokee Town, in a little over two days. On arriving at the river we found it high, notwithstanding teams had been crossing the day before.

Not being able to get satisfactory information respecting our getting across, — as the town was on the opposite side of the river, — I took out one of the mules, and rode into the water. I soon found the current too strong to admit of my turning around, and so I was obliged to cross over. The mule, which was a large one, swam some distance before making the shore at a point much lower down the stream than where I entered it. The water ran over the mule's back, and of course I got pretty thoroughly wet, and not being able to recross without much more danger than I had as yet experienced, on account of the direction and strength of the current, and the steepness of the bank where I should be compelled to land, I went up into town, and got a man to take me back in a skiff. It being impracticable to get the ambulance across, arrangements were made for the Friends and their luggage to be taken over in a skiff, which was successfully accomplished, Dr. J. Shirley engaging to take them to Caddo in his ambulance. I then took my mule farther up the stream, and with the aid of a skiff, happily succeeded in getting him back, and started on my return.

Last night encamped entirely alone on Beaver Creek, about fifteen miles from the Agency. After lariating out my mules, and partaking of some supper, I retired to my ambulance to sleep. Notwithstanding my lonely situation, being, in all probability, many miles from any other human being, I was favored to feel sensible of the Divine Presence, before betaking myself to sleep, and thankfulness was the clothing of my spirit, not only for the many preservations I have experienced in my wanderings in this wild and solitary land, but that I am not left comfortless in the wilderness.

After a very comfortable night's repose, I started early, and arrived at the Agency about ten o'clock, A. M. On the road this morning, access was obtained to the ever-wakeful ear of the Great Master, whom I desire to serve, far beyond what it is often my lot to experience; and I was enabled to pour forth the petitions of my heart in words, not only on my own behalf, but on behalf of my most precious family, as they individually came before the view of my mind, while the people among whom I live were also remembered, in a manner surprising even to myself. Tears of gratitude and love flowed unrestrained. This season of favor was succeeded by a comfortable calmness, in which my peace flowed as a river.

"Praise the Lord, O my soul! and all that is within me, bless His holy name."

CHAPTER XVII.

JOURNEY TO KIOWA CAMP. — NIGHT AT WHITE WOLF'S CAMP. — COMANCHES STEAL KICKING BIRD'S HORSES. — TOUR WITH THREE KIOWA BRAVES. — KILLING BUFFALO. — BREAKING THE WILD HORSE. — MOUNTAINS. — SOIL. — MESQUITE TIMBER. — RETURN TO CAMP. — COMANCHES. — WILD BEES.

4th Month, 27th. — I started alone for Kicking Bird's camp. Getting a late start, and the mules being poor and fatigued by use, I found I could not reach camp; and seeing an Indian camp a mile or two out of my course, though I knew not to what tribe it belonged, I found that I must of necessity spend the night not far from it. Knowing, however, that even were they hostile I should fare better as a guest than as a neighbor, I feared to be found occupying the latter position, as most likely I should be before morning, if I attempted it; since lariated mules are not accustomed to keep silent. I resolved to throw myself upon their hospitality. This I effected without being observed by any of them, until rising out of the cañon through which the creek flows, I drove directly into camp, apparently to the surprise of the Indians.

On driving into camp, I beckoned to a man, who was sitting with others, to come to me, at the same time stopping my mules. He approached, accompanied by a young man and a woman ; when, who should it be but White Wolf, one of the most determined of the hostile Comanche chiefs, accompanied by the same young man who had told us, in the agent's office, they would not listen to their chiefs, nor yet to Washington. This band has been continually committing depredations in Texas, and, with their chiefs, are averse to being controlled, and are particularly unfriendly to my being in the Kiowa camp. Yet now I was wholly in their power, — had, as it were, voluntarily placed myself in their hands. In answer to their direct questions, I told them I was alone, and was unarmed. After a few moments' consultation, White Wolf said to me, "The sun will soon go away; will you sit down by me, and sleep?" I answered, "My mules are tired, and I came to your camp for that purpose." He replied, "That is good; when the sun comes back, you may go on your road." Then he bade me follow the woman, who was still standing near. She conducted me to his lodge, where I unharnessed my mules, which were taken care of by the women.

Supper was soon announced, and I partook of the rude cheer of a hostile chief, rendered propitious by his ideas of the sacred rights of hospitality. After this I retired to my ambulance, by the side of his lodge, and betook myself to sleep, free from anxiety, though knowing well that I was surrounded, if not by actual foes, by an unfriendly band of people.

28*th.* — After breakfast in White Wolf's lodge, I was soon *en route* for the camp of my destination, accompanied by the wife and little daughter of "mine host," who went with me several miles, in order to answer the challenges of the several Comanche pony herders whom I would have to pass. Afterwards they pointed out Kicking Bird's camp to me, and left me to pursue my journey alone.

What a lesson is here for civilized man! A rude chief of an unfriendly tribe of savages, whose hand is skilled in the shedding of blood, manifesting such a sense of the sacredness of the rights of hospitality, as not only to receive and entertain one whom he regarded as an enemy, but, after having done this, set him on his right road in peace. Surely, if he knew not from the Scripture, the law, "Be not forgetful to entertain strangers," the same finger which wrote the commandments upon the flinty rocks on Mount Sinai had engraved it upon his heart, and he obeyed the writing.

When I arrived at camp, I found Kicking Bird in a fearful state of exasperation against the Comanches. They had, from time to time, stolen horses from his herd, until he could endure but little more of this kind of treatment. He found, on returning from the Agency, that they had stolen two of his best horses, also one belonging to his daughter. Stumbling Bear had followed their trail for twenty miles or more to the southward, but being sick he had to turn back. After writing a letter to the agent for Kicking Bird, and eating a second breakfast, I was desired to accompany three young Kiowas on a search for the stolen ponies, endeavor to follow the trail, see if they had been left behind, and if so to bring them back. The object of *my* going was to explain their business, in case of falling in with soldiers, so that they might search the country as far as Red River. Without waiting to give the subject sufficient thought, I started with them, Kicking Bird furnishing me with a good young horse, and equipments for the trip. Stumbling Bear rode on ahead, and climbed a mountain, in order to point out to us the place where he left the trail. We then travelled briskly forward, making only a short tarry for dinner about four o'clock, until after sundown, when we alighted and took off our saddles, preparatory to spending the night. My ears caught the feeble tinkling of a bell in the distance, to which I called the attention of my companions. They immediately sprang upon their unsaddled ponies, and were off like the wind in the direction of the sound, leaving me in charge of their saddles and blankets. They returned in half an hour or so, driving a couple of beautiful ponies, which bore no mark of ever having been handled, except the wearing of the bell. One was a pure milk-white, and the other a beautiful gray. They had strayed far away from any herds, and had been so long in these solitudes as to have become entirely wild.

As my companions failed to lasso them, and knowing one of them would not leave our horses to go away alone, they selected the gray one for preservation, and sent an arrow through the other. Portions of the latter were soon broiling on the coals of our camp-fire for supper.

Though I had often eaten horse-flesh before, being tired, not having felt well for some hours, and, withal, having partaken of a hearty dinner about four o'clock, I declined sharing the repast, prepared my bed, and retired for the night, leaving them in the enjoyment of their meal.

Our route to-day was, first, over a plain covered with mesquite timber, and bounded by isolated mountains, among which we wended our way until, after getting entirely past them, we came upon a richer soil, as indicated by the more luxuriant grass, especially in the valley of Otter Creek.

29th. — We continued on nearly south, until about noon, when, being in the midst of many thousands of buffalo, which were occupied, some in leisurely grazing, some in wallowing and rolling in the dust, some in fighting, but most in a wild, impetuous flight, the trail we had been following was completely obliterated by the vast numbers of buffalo tracks, and we gave up the attempt to follow it farther. The timber skirting Red River was discernible in the south, perhaps six or eight miles distant. We now turned westward, and were soon running the buffalo, though I, being encumbered with a heavy Spencer carbine, which I had taken in order to lighten an Indian for the chase, and feeling weak, did not attempt to join in it any farther than to keep near enough to see the wild sport of the Kiowas.

Two calves, one cow, and one bull, were soon rolling in the dust, pierced by the well-directed arrows of my companions. One other cow was fatally wounded, which we did not attempt to recover. I could but notice that the bow and arrow, in the hands of the Indians, were more effective than their fire-arms, of which they had a supply.

After loading ourselves with meat from the slaughtered animals, — many choice bits being eaten raw by my friends, — we turned our course towards the north, and arrived at Otter Creek in the middle of the afternoon, where we cooked some meat, and took supper.

Here one of the men succeeded in throwing the noose of his lasso over the head of the wild pony, which, after losing his mate, had followed us all day. Notwithstanding his rearing and plunging, kicking, lashing, and biting, he was soon made fast to a tree, and gradually drawn up to it, until he had but very little play room, but used what he had to the greatest possible advantage. He manifested his wildness and strength by the most furious striking and kicking, whenever approached. An old blanket was repeatedly thrown upon him, which would soon be under his feet, while he continued the most violent exertions, lashing out in every possible direction, as far as the shortness of the rope with which he was tied would permit.

Though foiled and brought up on every occasion, he would not give up, while his merciless tormentors took a barbarous delight in punching him with poles, and striking him with long sticks. After continuing this cruel sport for about an hour, during which time, in his mad plungings, he had thrown himself several times upon the ground, he at length fell exhausted, and lay quiet and docile as a lamb. Thereupon, after some patting and manifestations of kindness, the lariat was removed, we saddled up, and started on ; the pony, rendered manageable by exhaustion, was driven by one of the party. We reached the mountains, and finding a convenient stream of pure water, about dark, encamped for the night.

The Wichita Mountains present from the south a much more bold and striking outline than from any other point, no doubt from the lower level of the plains from which they are viewed. Mount Scott and Mount Sheridan were distinctly visible most of the day in the far north-east, while the more south-western peaks of the group, being near by, arose from the level grassy plains in sublime grandeur.

The almost entire absence of timber on these mountains gives them a peculiarly sharp and rugged outline in the distance, while a nearer approach but increases the roughness of the general contour. Huge rocks, lifting their heads far above their fellows, and standing out in bold relief, — deep, cavernous spaces and yawning chasms, — give a jagged roughness to the face of the mountain, from bottom to top. This gives rise to endless varieties of lights and shadows, which absorb the attention, and engross the mind from the contemplation of other and inferior objects.

30*th.* — Our partially tamed pony, having had sufficient experience of the sweets of domestic life among Kiowas, and not seeing the advantage of more education in that way, took the easier way of securing his independence by leaving us in the night.

After travelling rapidly, we had passed the mountains, but stopped for dinner at the base of Mount Webster, where we found some pure sweet water issuing from its rocky base. I had long been anxious to ascend this, the most elevated of the western Wichitas, but was now too much fatigued and worn out with travel to make the attempt, and was but too glad to arrive at Kicking Bird's camp, which we did about the middle of the afternoon.

Our journey to-day, like most of our first day's travel, lay through barren plains, between broken and isolated mountains, among a growth of the dreary, dead-like mesquite. This tree is naturally very late in putting on its spring garments, at best; but now, like its kindred tree, the locust, is suffering from the attacks of the borer. This gives a sombre aspect to the country, presenting as it does miles and miles of half-dead, broken-down trees. We passed through very many miles of it, which had this dead-like appearance above ground; but the root, remaining alive, continues to send up briery sprouts, to be in turn cut down by the destroyer.

This tree bears a bean-like seed, in large, long pods, which is much sought after in their season, by the natives, as an article of food. They prepare it by pounding it into a coarse meal, put sugar with it, and mix it with water; then let it slightly ferment, and dry it. They undoubtedly have other methods of preparation, but this gives it a pleasant vinous taste, not disagreeable to the palate. They sometimes break these small cakes, reducing them to meal, and boil in the water in which meat is cooked, making a kind of mush.

The soil south of the mountains is very thin for many miles, when it assumes a better aspect, being richer and covered with good grass. In some places, as we passed, it reached our horses' knees.

It is very noticeable that where the soil is thin and poor the prairie-dog abounds, all through this country, while the better qualities are equally alive with the pocket gopher. Neither of these animals appears in any degree disposed to encroach upon the natural rights of the other.

Game of all kinds is more plentiful south of the mountains than north of them, probably from the fact that the Indians seldom, if ever, encamp there, on account of their fear of being in too close proximity to their Texas neighbors for the safety of their pony herds. We saw many antelopes, some deer, and a great many wolves.

The elk, though formerly very numerous, are becoming scarce, but are still to be met with in the grassy vales, among the mountains.

I found, on returning to camp, which is situated on Yellow Paint, or the west branch of Rainy Mountain Creek, that Kicking Bird had talked so sharply to the Comanches that they had brought in two of his best horses, but left one unaccounted for.

Uncle Joe, as he is called, the old Kiowa whom Kicking Bird sent to the agent with his letter, returned to-day with a letter from the agent, which I read and explained to them. Being very tired and stiff from my long horseback journey, I retired to my ambulance.

Soon Kicking Bird came in, and sat down for a talk. The Comanches continue to harass him, by following and camping near him, so that their immense herds of ponies soon eat up the grass, and he is compelled to move; again they follow him, and at every opportunity steal his horses and mules. The Pĕn′-ha-tĕth′-kas, No-ko-nies (Bands of Comanches), and the Apaches are upon the best land, near the Agency, except on the east, where he would be particularly exposed to the Texas horse-thieves and whiskey-dealers, so that he is at a loss to know what course to take, or what to do.

The Comanche chiefs are now using their best endeavors to get the Kiowas to take the pipe and go with them into Texas, to revenge the death of the Comanche young men who were killed last winter, while raiding in that state. He says there are four Comanche chiefs who

Kiowa Girls.

are opposed to this course, while the Cheyennes are ready to go with them. This antipathy to the people of Texas arises from the wrong treatment they received in being forcibly driven from their lands in that state, for which they have never received any compensation. The Comanches claim to be descended from some of the ancient Mexican tribes, with whom the Spaniards made war and drove to the northward. They crossed the Rio Grande, into the northern part of Texas and the adjoining portions of New Mexico, where they remained, and continued to raid upon the Spanish settlements in Mexico, taking many of their women and children prisoners. Afterwards they took part with the people of Texas in the revolution by which the republic of Texas acquired her independence. A treaty was then made, while Sam Houston was president of the republic, by which a tract of country was set apart to the Indians, and guaranteed to them forever.

The conditions of this treaty were observed by both parties until the annexation of Texas to the United States, when a tide of immigration set in from the southern states. This was composed of people who did not regard the treaty, or the rights of the Indians, and settled upon their lands as well as in other places. This, as might have been expected, led into hostilities, which resulted in their expulsion from their lands, where many of them had begun to make farms and to live by agricultural pursuits. They were finally driven across the Red River, into the country they now occupy, and still continue to hold unfriendly and revengeful feelings against the people of that state. These are in no wise lessened by the frequent raids upon their stock by parties residing in Texas.

5th Month, 6th. — Since my last entry I have been in camp until this time. There being two or three Comanche camps near ours a part of the time, I had frequent opportunities of observing their pony herds. Many large American horses, fully shod and branded, are among them, as well as mules with mane and hair worn off by the collar and trace, showing that they have been worked this spring in the harness. This confirms the truth of what the Kiowas have often told me, that parties of Comanches are raiding in Texas most of the time. One day, White Wolf came to our camp, and in his talk with Kicking Bird stated that several of their young men had been killed in Texas the past winter, and they intended to revenge their death by raiding and killing people there. He and the young man who was with him rode horses with shoes on, and which were branded with Texas brands.

Kicking Bird, as well as other chiefs, have repeatedly informed me that the Comanches and Cheyennes have smoked the war-pipe together, but as yet have got but one Kiowa chief to smoke with them. There are undoubtedly young men among the Kiowas foolish enough to join them, if they are not restrained.

Came in to the Agency, travelling most of the day alone.

The Comanches, being desirous of making it appear that the Kiowas have been raiding in Texas, and thereby to place them in an attitude in which they would be included with themselves in any act government might enter upon to suppress their raiding, have reported the Kiowas as participants in those raids; in proof of which they state that the sons of Lone Wolf and Red Otter were killed in Texas. It can easily be seen that, if they could make it appear that the Kiowas are equally guilty with themselves, and succeed in arraying government against the Kiowas, they would be driven to unite with them in their hostile intentions, to the strengthening of their own hands.

In order to ascertain the truth, and if they were not guilty, which they steadily affirm, while they admit going into Mexico, I have been the more watchful, and have endeavored to investigate the circumstances of the death of those young Kiowas. The Caddoes and Apaches, who get their information from both Comanches and Kiowas, have no hesitation in declaring that they were killed in Mexico. Finally, in conversation with a Comanche chief, he stated that he restrained his young men from raiding in Texas, but allowed them to go into Mexico. Lone Wolf's son, with a few other young Kiowas, went with them.

They went into Mexico, and the Comanches took a Mexican boy as captive. The Kiowas disapproved of taking captives, and remonstrated with them against it; and finally made their night camp at a little distance from theirs. They were pursued by the Mexican soldiers, and the two young Kiowas were killed; the other Kiowa young men left, and did not rejoin them. The Comanches crossed the Rio Grande, and commenced a system of depredations in Texas on the Nueces River. They were there attacked by soldiers, and several of the party were killed. The remnant of the party started for their own country; but meeting another party of Comanches, they turned about, went back, and were again attacked by the soldiers, and several of them killed; making on both occasions twenty-two of their people killed; that the Kiowas left them after Lone Wolf's son was killed, and before recrossing the Rio Grande into Texas.

By this testimony it does not appear that the Kiowas have been violating their pledge by raiding in that state. Since ascertaining that they raided in Mexico, I have made a little progress in their minds against it, not so much because it is wrong, as by asserting Mexico to be Washington's brother, and that Washington would not permit them to raid upon his brother's children any more than his own. The idea that Mexico is Washington's brother seems to take hold of their minds, as they talk much about it in their camps.

16*th.* — On taking my daily walk out from camp, I was joined by three Kiowa boys, and we bent our steps towards the mountain north of us. They stated that there was Ah-pean-ha (tree-sugar, that is, honey) in a certain ravine, to which we directed our course, as I knew that honey is sometimes found in the ravines among the mountains. After going some distance, perhaps two miles, from camp, we came to a clump of cedars which fairly roared with a large kind of bee, of which the trees and bushes of the ravine appeared to be full. I watched them, and saw that some of them were loaded with pollen. They were much larger than the common honey-bee — about the size of an Italian drone, but destitute of the rings around the abdomen, which was of a shining black, while the shoulders were yellow. Their motions resembled that of the honey-bee mustering. They were collected more about four dead cedars than anywhere else. On going near, I saw that they were passing in and out of holes in the trees.

Though I knew they were not the common honey-bee, I did not know but that they might store some honey in their nests. I mentioned the circumstance to some of the Indians, by way of inquiry. They, not thoroughly understanding me, as Kicking Bird was not in camp, insisted on my going and showing them to some women.

Accordingly horses were brought in, and I led the way to the place; a tree was cut down, and, though there were bees in the tree, there was no indication of honey or brood. I apprehend that they are a kind of borer that deposit their eggs in the dead wood of the cedar, and that the growing grub cuts out large holes in the body of the tree, admitting air and water, and thus hastening the decay of this almost imperishable timber.

CHAPTER XVIII.

KICKING BIRD'S INTERVIEW WITH THE AGENT IN HIS PRIVATE OFFICE. — WOMAN'S HEART'S STORMY VISIT. — KIOWA COUNCIL. — KICKING BIRD DEJECTED. — INTERVIEW WITH KICKING BIRD AT THE TRADING-HOUSE. — THE MATRON AND SEAMSTRESS LEAVE THE SCHOOL, ETC.

5th Month, 22d. — Last evening Kicking Bird, according to his usual practice, came into the agent's private office to have a little social talk. Running Wolf came slyly into an adjoining room, and stood by the door to listen to what was said.

The agent remarked that he was sorry that so many of the Kiowa chiefs were angry at him because of the shortness of their rations, as he had tried every way in his power to have a sufficient supply in readiness for the occasion, but had failed.

Kicking Bird replied that the Kiowa chiefs were not all mad. His heart felt good that the Comanches had brought in the stolen stock (as will be explained on another page). He did not smoke the [war-]pipe with the Comanches, and now he understood that several of the

Comanche chiefs were tired of it themselves. He was a humble man himself, wanted to do right, and to have the Kiowas do right. He had brought his daughter up to love the white man, and taught her that the white man's road was the right way to travel, and he intended to bring up his son Little John in the same way, that when they grow up they would take hold of the white man's hand and walk in his road.

The agent asked him what he thought of the Comanches. He replied that he had no doubt but that there were some, perhaps many, of the Comanche chiefs who like himself were humble men, anxious to do right, and to have their people do right, but that there were many of their young men who would not be controlled. He thought that the class who wished to do right would increase among them.

This was the substance of what was said, as nearly as my memory retains it. Not one word was uttered derogatory to the character or standing of any Kiowa chief; yet this cowardly Running Wolf went to camp, and informed the Kiowas that Kicking Bird was in the office of the agent, filling his ears with lies against all the Kiowa chiefs.

Woman's Heart, who had accepted the Comanche pipe, was particularly angry, and came with Running Wolf and another young Kiowa to the Agency in a state of mind bordering on frenzy. He charged Kicking Bird and myself with misrepresenting the Kiowa chiefs to the agent; that they were not, as we had represented to him, bad men; that, in consequence of Kicking Bird's lying about other Kiowa chiefs, they and the young men had thrown him away. The agent tried to pour oil upon what he supposed to be the troubled waters; but it being fire instead of water, the flame but increased. Finally, without giving us their hands according to their usual practice, they went away in a rage to sow their wildfire in camp.

This morning, word came early that the Kiowas were coming to the office to talk matters over. As it was necessary that I should go away in order to make arrangements for going to camp, and was detained longer than I expected to have been, I missed being at the council, and must rely for my account of it upon information received from others, who were present and may be relied upon as truthful.

When the Kiowas began to enter the office, and until it was filled, every one as he came in strung his bow, placed it where it could be instantly seized for action, put his quiver of arrows in the most convenient position, also placing three or four arrows across his lap, uncovered the handle of his revolver, turned it in the right direction for correct grasping, while many of them trembled with excitement. After the others had entered, Kicking Bird, accompanied by Trotting Wolf and his own brother Couguet, rode up calmly and coolly, as though they knew nothing of what might be going on.

After securing their ponies, they entered the office, Kicking Bird in advance of the others, who, pleasantly looking around the room so as to comprehend the situation, seated himself, and with stoical coolness he and his companions proceeded to place their bows, arrows, and revolvers in the same position for convenience, should their use become necessary.

With this manifestation of a willingness to use the weapons of death, should circumstances develop in that direction, on the part of all the Indians in the room, Kicking Bird addressed the agent, informing him of the charges preferred against him (K. B.), and calling upon him to keep nothing back that he had told him, but tell his people his whole talk. This the agent was enabled to do through the freshening influence upon his memory occasioned by the stormy visit of Woman's Heart last evening. This was followed by talks from Kicking Bird and the agent, as well as some others.

Notwithstanding the agent in his talk gave Kicking Bird credit for having done more for his tribe than any other chief, yet as he had previously said that he regarded Big Bow's talk as a good talk, and received it as the words of the whole tribe, and made it the base of his report to Washington (it being made in council), while he simply received Kicking Bird's (not made in council) as his own individual, friendly talk, not as the voice of the tribe, Kicking Bird, not fully comprehending the difference between a public speech and a private talk, thought that the agent, as well as his own people, had cast him away, and left in very bitterness of heart. He bade the interpreter "tell Thomissy I will take him to camp because I promised that I would; but I think he had better not go until this matter is settled," and left without my seeing him.

I expressed regret to the agent that Kicking Bird had gone away without my seeing him. The agent after dinner proposed that I should ride up to the store and see him, if I felt like it. As that accorded with my feelings, — although I had little hope of seeing him, as he had told the interpreter that he should go to his camp without stopping, — I went, and was very agreeably surprised to find him, his wife and daughter, still there. I went in, engaged an interpreter, and had an opportunity with him in a private apartment. I found he thought himself rejected by the agent, as well as by his own people, and was feeling very badly.

I told him that I had not come to make a talk to him, but as I understood that his people had thrown him away, since he and I were brothers and walked in the same road, when they threw him away, they threw me away also.

We were one and travelled one road, and the Kiowas could not throw him away without throwing me away with him. I had lived with him and his people a long time, and had learned to love them, to regard them as my people, and, as he knew, had worked hard with him for their good. But since they had thrown us away, I had no further business in this country, and should probably return to my home, and be with my wife and children. I could not bear to go away, and not see him and take hold of his hand again before I left. And now I had one word to say to him. I wanted that word to sink down to his heart; I did not want him to throw it away. That is, even though his people had thrown him away, to go straight forward in the road he had been travelling, not turn aside either on the one hand or the other, and he would find that the Kiowas would soon come back hunting for Kicking Bird, and saying, "We want Kicking Bird to come and go to our agent, and talk for us." The agent had not thrown him away, and he will say to the Kiowas, "If you want to talk to me, bring me Kicking Bird." If he would but keep straight forward on the same road he had travelled so long, the Kiowas would yet hunt him up, and say to the agent, "Kicking Bird is our chief." Now remember this my last talk.

Kicking Bird replied, "I long ago took the white man by the hand; I have never let it go; I have held it with a firm and strong grasp. I have worked hard to bring my people on to the white man's road. Sometimes I have been compelled to work with my back towards the white people, so that they have not seen my face, and may have thought I was working against them; but I have worked with one heart and one object. I have looked ahead to the future, and have worked for the children of my people, to bring them into a position, that, when they become men and women, they will take up with the white road. I have but two children of my own, but have worked for the children of my people as though they had *all* been mine. Five years have I striven for this thing, and all these years Big Bow has worked against me to keep my people on the old bad road. When I have brought in and delivered up white captives to the agent, Big Bow has taken more. Now for a little while *he* has come on to the good road. The agent has taken him by the hand, and thrown me away after my many years' labor.

"I am as a stone, broken and thrown away, — one part thrown this way, and one part thrown that way.* I am chief no more; but that is not what grieves me, — I am grieved at the ruin of my people: they will go back to the old road, and I must follow them; they will not let me go and live with the white people. But I shall not go away on the gallop; I shall go to my camp, and after a while I shall go a little farther, and then a little farther, until I get as far away as it is possible for me. When they show me the "big chief" they select, I shall follow him wherever he leads. When you take hold of my hand to-day, you have taken it for the last time; when you see me ride away to-day, you will see Kicking Bird no more: I shall never come back to this place."

Being exceedingly anxious to impress on his mind the

* His meaning was, that he had been rejected both by the agent and the Kiowas for very different reasons: the former, as thinking he did not use his influence sufficiently in behalf of civilization; and the latter, because of his earnestness to leave their old customs, and adopt those of the whites.

necessity of his continuing on the good road, I again expressed to him the concern of my mind that he forsake not the road he had travelled, and knew to be a good one free from stones, and the Kiowas would yet be glad to hunt him up to lead them back to it.

We went down stairs; his wife, daughter, and the babe were there. He looked upon his infant son, and then upon his daughter, and turning to me, said, "I have taught my daughter to love the white man and his way, so that she may grow up in it and love it. I expected to have led my son up in the same road, that, when grown, it would be easy to him, and he would travel in it; but to-day it is all cut off: they will know the white man's good and smooth road no more." He then started his wife and children off to camp. I did not know what he was doing until I saw they had mounted, and I parted with them in the saddle. Kicking Bird himself returned, and seated himself in an obscure corner of the store in apparent dejection. One and another of the white people about the store gathered about him.

Though they knew not to the full extent the force of the storm that was bowing him to the ground, yet it was easy to see that he was in deep trouble. I saw that every one of them sympathized with him, and respected him as a good man.

I stepped forward and said to them that they all knew Kicking Bird, and why his people had rejected him. It was because he had proved himself their true friend by laboring to bring them into friendly relations with the white people and the way of being civilized. They were fully aware of his worth and services to his people, and also to the whites; and now, in this time of his great trouble, I proposed that we manifest our respect and sympathy for him by uniting in making him some present that he might have to look upon, if he should not come in for a long time, and be reminded that he still had friends among the whites. The proposition met with a hearty response, and he was called upon to go around and select the articles which he wished. This being done, I bought a woven coverlet, and gave it to him as my individual present.

He then said, "You have done this to show your good feelings and friendship towards me; now, what can I do to manifest my friendship and regard for you?"

I replied, "That which would give us the greatest proof of his friendship towards us was to continue hereafter on the same road he had been travelling,—not turn from it in any direction, and he would find that it would be eventually for his own good."

A voice from some one of the company said, "Kicking Bird, you have not thrown Thomas away?"

He quickly answered, "No; he is my brother."

"Why, then, do you not take him with you to camp?"

He replied, "I will take him with me if he wants to go now."

I said to him, "Last night, Woman's Heart came to the agent's house very angry, and told the agent that Thomas and Kicking Bird told lies about all the Kiowa chiefs, which is not true. I talk straight talk to the agent about all the Kiowas; and now the warriors, through listening to the misrepresentations of Running Wolf and Woman's Heart, had thrown him away, and his life was in danger. My going out with him would but make harder work for him, and perhaps bring him, in the present excited condition of their warriors, into greater danger. Perhaps I had better not go with him just now, but I did not throw him nor his people away."

He replied, "That is good; that is the way I feel. You go and sit down by the agent, and not go home. In thirteen days I will come for you. I now know why Thomissy has not talked, and why I have had to keep silence. When my heart has been full, and I have gone to the agent to talk, when I would get there I was kept still, I could not talk. We have been secretly watched; I see it all now. I will now go to my camp, collect my band of people, and when I come again, you will know who is chief of the Kiowas."

Thus the second time have I, poor and weak though I am, been made the humble instrument in an Almighty Hand of turning this strong man's heart towards the right way. This indeed affords a little ray of comfortable hope that I am in the place of divine allotment.

24*th.*—Yesterday the matron and seamstress at the school left for their homes in Kansas. Trotting Wolf—a Kiowa chief—had repeatedly informed them that they were in danger of being carried away captives by the Comanches; and a few days since, taking both of them by the hand and looking them seriously in the eye, said, "By and by you see the red man kill buffalo on the plains. Comanche no good." The same day another Kiowa told them that the fourth sleep from that time was fixed upon as the time to carry the design into execution; saying to them, "You better go away."

This information, with other circumstances of which they had personal knowledge, led them to believe there was a plot laid against them, and prudence dictated that they should leave. They therefore, after putting the school-children's clothes in the usual order for vacation, making the girls' dresses, and arranging the affairs of the department over which they were placed in such order as that nothing could possibly suffer from their leaving a week before vacation, left yesterday morning — the morning before the "fourth sleep" spoken of by the Kiowa.

Subsequent events tended to prove the correctness of their suspicions, and that their departure was none too soon. Last night it is certainly known that Indians were prowling about near the school-house, and noises were distinctly heard at the window of their room, indicating an attempt to gain access thereto. Both the superintendent and his wife heard these noises; the former arose, and going to a window, saw a dark figure going rapidly away, pursued by a dog belonging to one of the employees at the school-house. Others in the building heard footsteps about the premises. The superintendent could not say positively that what he saw was an Indian, as, the moon having gone down, it was dark; but just before the moon set, the carpenter, being disturbed, looked out of the window, and saw three Indians on horseback so near the house that he could distinctly distinguish the colors of their horses and blankets. A mule and pony were stolen from near the carpenter's shop, afterwards found to have been done by Comanches, and an attack made upon a pony herd about a quarter of a mile from the school-house; but the herder being awake, and using his revolver rather freely, they left without accomplishing their purpose.

Whether there really was any design against those young women or not, circumstances certainly indicated it, and at all events they had left, and were removed beyond the reach of danger.

CHAPTER XIX.

THE COMANCHE MEDICINE MAN. — DEPREDATION ON AGENCY STOCK. — DISCOURAGEMENT OF THE KIOWAS. — INTERVIEW WITH KICKING BIRD. — PEN-HA-TETH-KAH'S AND QUIRTSQUIP'S BAND RETURN. — THEY REPORT OTHER COMANCHES AND CHEYENNES ON THE WAR-PATH.

AFTER leaving the Agency on the 8th inst., the Comanches, at the call of a young medicine man belonging to the Quahada band, went out to make medicine not far from the junction of Pecon Creek and the North Fork of Red River. This is a new thing with the Comanches, they, according to the Kiowas, never having before made medicine as a tribe, which corresponds with the statements of white people who have known them for many years.

This young medicine man makes bold pretensions. He claims that he has raised the dead to life. He is reported to have raised from his stomach nearly a wagon-load of cartridges at one time, in the presence of several Comanches. He then swallowed them again, informing the Comanches that they need not fear the expenditure of ammunition in carrying on a war against the whites, as he can supply all their needs in that line. He can make medicine which will render it impossible for a Comanche to be killed, even though he stand just before the muzzles of the white man's guns. He ascends above the clouds far beyond the sun — the home of the Great Spirit, with whom he has often conversed.

He has done these things in open daylight, in the presence of many Comanches, remaining in the sky over night, and coming back next day; he has been known to do this four times. In short, he has power to control the elements, to send wind, lightning, thunder, rain, and hail upon his enemies, and in no respect is he inferior to the Great Spirit.

The main body of the Comanches believe all this, and are afraid to disobey him for fear of his medicine if they offend him.* Horseback, who has hitherto been friendly, has brought in and left his ambulance with the agent,

* How this bold pretender succeeds in deluding the minds of this people may be understood from the following. It is given out that at a certain time he will visit the sun, the dwelling-place of the Great Spirit. A number of prominent persons are in attendance as witnesses. He withdraws himself a short distance from them, charging them to look directly at the sun until he speaks to them, then to let their eyes slowly fall to the place where he is standing; as they do this, they will see dark bodies descend to receive him, with which he will ascend. His directions being complied with, the dark objects descend to him, and, being blinded by their continued gazing upon the orb of light, he bids them slowly raise their eyes, and the dark objects arise, while he conveys himself away, and keeps himself concealed until the time appointed for his return. These men, thoroughly deluded, believe and report that they saw him ascend to the sun.

and gone to the great medicine council. Some few are bold enough to brave his medicine, and remain near the Agency. What the result will be it is impossible to forecast; but in all probability the Comanches will be led by him wheresoever he sees fit. It is seriously to be feared that he will lead them to destruction, in which many others may become involved.

On the morning of the 10th inst. it was found that the mules used at the school-house, also a pair of mules and a pony belonging to parties residing at the Wichita Agency, who were here on a visit to their children, had been stolen during the previous night. It was soon ascertained that other ponies and mules were stolen from a neighboring herd.

A Caddo, whose pony was stolen, followed the trail to the Comanche camp, and recovered his with little difficulty; but they were exceedingly unwilling to give up the mules belonging to the Agency. He, however, succeeded in getting them, but returned without securing the stock stolen from the herd. The night following his return forty-one head of ponies were run off from the Agency and Măden herds.

The Caddo and George Chisholm were sent to follow the trail. On the 21st inst. some of the Comanche chiefs brought in twenty-two head, but it was observable that it was the most worthless stock that had been returned, the best having been retained by them.

On the 23d, G. Chisholm and the Caddo returned, bringing three head more and the following night their pony and mule were stolen from near the carpenter's shop, as heretofore related.

The agent despatched Honowēah, a friendly Comanche chief, to their camp with a message to them. He returned on the 2d of the 6th month, with a message from the medicine man and chiefs with him, that they should not return the stock they now have in their possession, but should keep it to make peace with when they come back in the fall.

They also state that they have decided to commit no further depredations about the Agency, provided the soldiers are kept from molesting them; but they want it distinctly understood, and send this as a fair warning, that, if the soldiers come upon them, they shall come in and kill whomsoever comes in their way.

They propose, in short, doing as they please, and, like a more civilized portion of our republic a few years since, desire to be let alone, promising on their honor that they will not do as much harm as they will if they are interfered with.

Honoweah says there are no Kiowas with them; but the Cheyennes are in league with them; and confirms the report of their having abundance of whiskey in their camps, which they procure from traders in the Young Territory of Texas usually denominated the Pan Handle of Texas, and from Mexicans.

The Pen-ha-teth-kahs and Quirlsquip's band, he reports, are not with the others, but are remaining faithful to their pledges of loyalty to the government.

Horseback, having been again attacked with bleeding at the lungs, had been left, and is coming back with his family as fast as the condition of his health will permit, while his people are going away.

The Kiowas on Pecon Creek, becoming discouraged by the long-continued shortness of their rations, made up their mind to come in to the Agency just this once, and if the sugar, coffee, flour, &c., had not yet come, they should conclude that the talk of its coming was all lie, and they should, after all, be obliged to go to the plains for subsistence, where they would be under the necessity of joining hands with the Comanches and Cheyennes, and throw Washington away, or subject themselves to being plundered by them. But just the evening before the day for issuing, a supply came to hand sufficient for the issue. This had the effect to allay the discontent of the Kiowas for the present.

On the 6th day of the 6th month, Kicking Bird and Big Bow came in, together with their people, for rations, after the other Indians had gone out to camp. Kicking Bird informed me that he wanted a talk with me alone, and requested me to meet him at the trading-house the next day, where he had engaged a young man, in whom he had confidence, to interpret for him. Accordingly, although it was the first day of the week, I went to the store, and we had an interview in a private apartment. He stated that the Cheyennes and Comanches had not given up their foolish notions, and were still hovering about the place where the Kiowas intended to make their medicine camp. He apprehended that they meant mischief by so doing. He also stated that Lone Wolf (who has returned from Mexico, where he had gone to bury the body of his son), when he found his son's body lying on the ground, kneeled down over it, and vowed by the Great Spirit that on that ground where his son was killed he would take the life of some white man. Now, in order to kill a white man on that ground, he would have to catch one and take him there. Since his return he had been much in the Cheyenne and Comanche camps, but he (K. B.) did not know as he had taken the pipe with them. In view of these things, he thought I had better remain at the Agency for the present, and he would go to the camps of the Cheyennes and Comanches, have a talk with them, also with Lone Wolf; and if it were safe for me to come to camp, he would come after me, and if not, he would send and let me know. I had a very satisfactory interview with him, again urging him to continue on the road in which he had been travelling for several years, not be drawn away by others; and though it might seem rough and hard for a time, it would become smoother and better, and would lead to great good to himself, and through him to his people.

In the afternoon of the same day, some of the Pen-ha-teth-kahs came to the Agency. They had, after a severe struggle on their part, broken away from the main body of the Comanches, and come back. They, with Quirlsquip, who with his people had also escaped and come back in order to avoid the consequences of going with them, report the Cheyennes and the other Comanches to be on the war-path, and determined on the shedding of blood. It appears that, after getting all the Comanches out to the medicine council, the hostile portion of the tribe undertook to hold those who were disposed to be friendly, and force them into their hostile measures. Many of these are breaking away and returning to the Agency, thus weakening the hands of the hostile element of the tribe, which may become so weakened as to cause them to give up their intentions altogether.

They state that it was Lone Wolf and his party who, on their return from Mexico, captured the cavalry horses at Fort Concho, in Texas.

Putting all facts and reliable information together, it appears evident that hostile demonstrations are intended by those tribes. These are hanging around the place where the Kiowa medicine dance will occur, in order to draw some of their young men into the measure, and so involve the Kiowas equally with themselves in the trouble consequent thereon.

CHAPTER XX.

LEAVE THE WORK ON ACCOUNT OF POOR HEALTH. — CAPTURE OF THE SUPPLY TRAIN, AND MURDER OF THE MEN. — ADOBE WALLS. — KIOWAS NOT ENGAGED IN THESE DEPREDATIONS. — THEY REGISTER THEIR NAMES. — MEETING WITH THE CADDOES. — ATTEMPT OF CHEYENNES ON THE WICHITA HERDS. — MURDER OF THE WOOD-CUTTER AT FORT SILL. — LONE WOLF AND HIS BAND BECOME HOSTILE. — CONCLUSION.

My health continuing very poor, I have been obliged to leave the work in which I have been for so long a time engaged, although there has never been a time, since my being among the Kiowas, when there was more need for a restraining influence being exercised among them than at the present. Many of their old associates among the Cheyennes and Comanches are becoming hostile, yet, as I am not able for the task, I am compelled to leave the field for others. Accordingly, on the 2d day of the 7th month, I proceeded to the Wichita Agency, with the expectation of going from thence to Wichita, in Kansas, on a train that was expected there about that time, loaded with supplies for these agencies.

This train, composed of three wagons accompanied by four men, never arrived, being attacked on the 3d, near Buffalo Springs, by about forty Indians. The men were killed and scalped, the mules run off, and the wagons burned. Appearances indicate that three of the men were killed instantly, while the fourth was probably subjected to death by torture and slow burning, while tied to the wheels of his wagon, over a fire of corn and oats, which formed part of his load. The bodies of the three men killed in the onset were removed and buried by a ranche-man, whose ranche was but five or six miles from the place, and who had warned them of their danger, and endeavored to dissuade them from proceeding farther when they passed his ranche an hour or two previous. As the Indians continued hovering about, the remains of the burned man could not be moved away, and they daring not remain at the place long enough to dig a grave, it was unburied until Agent Miles passed on the 5th. He and the party with him gave it a burial.

Many murders have been committed in the frontiers of Kansas, reported to have been done by Indians; yét it is thought that some have been done by white desperadoes in Indian disguises. Of this I cannot testify, but from what I know of the character of some of these desperate men, they would not be obliged to stoop in order to perpetrate any species of crime. A company of these characters, we are told, have been formed in Kansas, and make their headquarters in the Pan Handle of Texas. south of the Canadian River. These they have partially fortified, and are known as the Adobe Walls, from the material used in their construction. According to the best information I can obtain, the object in establishing this outpost appears to have been to build up an illicit trading-post, where whiskey, arms, and ammunition may be exchanged with Indians for their stolen stock. This place, according to Indian reports, was recently attacked by the Indians, who were at first repulsed with some loss to themselves; but afterwards gaining access to the interior of the walls, they report having killed all the men within.

Other depredations having been committed in the south-western parts of Kansas, the people there are much alarmed, and are leaving their claims in some of the more remote and exposed settlements. These depredations occurring at or just before the holding of the great medicine dance of the Kiowas, and it being their superstitious idea that any of their men who neglect the attendance of that, the great yearly assembling of the tribe, will not live until the return of the anniversary, they are supposed to be all present. Hence the reports of Kiowas being engaged in any of these depredations are not entitled to credence. Not but that a portion of the tribe might have engaged in hostilities immediately after the close of the medicine dance. This took place the 3d of the 7th month; after which that portion of the Kiowa tribe with which I had been so long associated came in to their Agency, registered their names as friendly Indians, and submitted to the roll-call in order that it might be known where they are; being desirous of remaining at peace with the whites. The other portion of the tribe, with Lone Wolf at its head, joined the hostile Indians. It is now no small satisfaction to me, in looking back upon the privations and hardships endured while wandering with this people, notwithstanding my utter failure in accomplishing that for which I went among them, — that of gathering their children into a school, — that those with whom I was most intimately connected, and with whom I made my camp-home, have steadfastly refused to join the hostile element, and are now manifesting their allegiance and friendly attitude towards the government.

The roads to Wichita being closed, or rendered unsafe for travel except by an armed force, I was obliged to remain at the Wichita Agency for over two weeks, most of the time very feeble.

While here, a party of Cheyennes made an attempt to run off the stock belonging to the Wichitas; but as they were on the watch, the attacking party were driven away, with the loss of a war-bonnet, whereby the tribe of the attacking party was exposed.

An attack was also made upon a man who was herding cattle belonging to the wood contractors engaged in supplying Fort Sill with wood, killed him and run off fifty-three head of cattle; but a company of soldiers, starting immediately in pursuit, recovered the cattle, without seeing the Indians who had run them off. While the wilder tribes were thus opening hostilities the more quiet, if not more civilized, Caddoes were anxious to learn more of a better and higher mode of life. At a religious meeting held with Guadelupe's band of Caddoes, which I attended, some of the simple truths of Christianity were communicated to this poor people. They were very attentive to what was said to them, and at its close expressed an anxiety that meetings for their religious instruction should be continued among them, stating that some of the things which had been told them were new to them, yet they might be true. They knew that something told them in their hearts that it was wrong to lie, to steal, to get drunk, and to murder; but they did not know it was the Great Spirit that was telling them, in this way, the path they ought to travel. If this was really true, as had been told them, — and they were inclined to believe it was, — it was high time they were paying more attention to it, and they wanted meetings for their instruction continued among them. They wished the agent to be informed that they desired more instruction in this direction. It has long been my opinion, that to present the sublime doctrines of the gospel to these untutored people, without a preliminary work of preparation having been first accomplished, might be comparable to casting "pearls before swine," or sowing good seed on the "stony ground;" it would not be likely to be productive of the best results.

But with these Caddoes I believe the preliminary work to have sufficiently progressed to warrant the beginning of a deeper work, even the committing to them of the good seed of the kingdom.

As in nature the rough ground must be grubbed, the soil broken up — cleared of stones, and, perhaps, left to the mellowing effects of the rigorous frosts of winter — to insure the successful cultivation of that grain which is outwardly, as the staff of life, contributing to the nourishment and growth of these bodies, so I believe there is a preliminary work to be done among this people, before their minds, enslaved and enchained by superstition, can so receive the seed of the word of life as to insure its growth.

Not but that they may be, and are, heirs of salvation, and that a manifestation of the "grace of God which brings salvation" has in some measure appeared unto them; but that while their secret enmity, their superstitions, and ignorance prevail, a prior work is needed before presenting the sublime truths of the gospel. After the soil is properly prepared for its reception, a wise husbandman must know the times when to commit the seed to the ground, and the best method of sowing it. Otherwise, not only all previous labor may be lost, no grain produced, but by thus preparing the soil for usefulness, and then neglecting to commit the seed thereto, it is but rendered more susceptible of producing a greater growth of weeds. In like manner, after the preliminary work is — as appears to be the case with these Caddoes — sufficiently advanced, a new class of laborers should be introduced to the field, — even sowers of the seed, — instructed and furnished by the Lord of the field, lest previous labor be worse than lost, by leaving the prepared ground to grow up with the weeds of vice, many of which may be of foreign seed.

In taking this view of the work among this people, I can but desire that the eyes of the agents, and others concerned, may be opened, and turned towards the great Husbandman, looking to Him that spiritual-minded laborers may be sent into the field, as they may be needed to accomplish His designs, whose the work is, and to whom the glory of their redemption must belong.

Although the following occurrences took place after my leaving the Wichita Agency, I thought it would not be improper to insert an account of them, according to information received from persons residing there at the time. About the time of my leaving there, the hostile Indians belonging to the Kiowa, Comanche, and Cheyennes Agencies, were turned over to the military department, and all who remained out from the Agencies were considered hostile. A month or so afterwards, two bands of Comanches, who had not been able to come in sooner, and not being satisfied to remain out with the hostile element of the tribe, in an unfriendly attitude, broke away, and came to the friendly Comanche camp on the Washita River near the Wichita Agency. A small company of soldiers had been located at that Agency for some time previous, and General Davidson, with more soldiers, proceeded to that place, to give conditions to the Comanches who had but just arrived, upon which they might come in. At first, not knowing that it was the military arm with which they must deal, they treated his proposition with contempt, but when better informed, agreed to the terms, and proceeded to surrender their arms. They gave up their guns and pistols, but a question arising about the bows and arrows, which had not been required of any band who had heretofore come in, it was referred to the general for decision, and a messenger despatched to him by the officer in charge.

The chief, desirous of a little council with another chief, mounted his pony, giving a loud whoop, to call the attention of the chief with whom he wished to speak. This was misunderstood by the soldiers to be the war-whoop, and he was fired at by the guard. Lone Wolf, with his party, being near, returned the fire; thus a battle was commenced, which resulted in the death of several citizens, the burning of several Caddo and Delaware houses, also the Wichita school-house, the sacking of Shirley's trading-house, with other outrages. The Comanches deny any hostile intention, and the fact of their surrendering arms before its commencement argues strongly in their favor, as it does not look reasonable that they would surrender arms on the eve of an intended battle.

The Kiowas, Apaches, and those Comanches who came in and registered their names as friendly to the government, though placed some two miles from the fort, where they were peculiarly exposed to Texas

Kiowa Woman, Big Tree's Sister.

horse-thieves, — who stole upwards of one thousand nine hundred head of their stock within a year thereafter, — and although they were kept almost in a state of starvation, from the failure of the contractor to supply their rations, continued loyal to the government through all, and started as many of their children to school the following winter as the building would accommodate. One of their chiefs, — "Dangerous Eagle," brother of the notorious "Big Tree," — went into the school, and rendered valuable assistance, by explaining to the children the wishes of the teacher, and assisting in bringing them under easy control.

The teacher, A. J. Standing, — my colleague in the Caddo school, at the Wichita Agency, — reports the children as quiet, affectionate, obedient, apt in learning, neat and cleanly in their habits, and in all respects pleasant and agreeable in their manners. Their parents manifested great interest in the school, furnishing the boys with velvet vests, and the girls with nice shawls, from their limited means.

Kicking Bird continued to use his influence for good to the time of his death, which occurred the 3d of 5th month, 1875. Being aware of his approaching end, he told his people "he was dying; he had taken the white man's road, and now he was not sorry for it; that he was dying holding fast the white man's hand." Whilst advising his people to keep in the white man's road, he passed away. His people have followed his advice, and, for the first time, have attempted to raise some crops, cultivating, this year, about two hundred acres of land.

Having now brought to a close this account of my life among the Indians, it remains only for me to say that I left the Wichita Agency on the evening of the 18th of the 7th month, for home, by the way of Caddo, and was favored to make the journey in nine days, reaching there on the 27th, where I found my family well, and we mutually rejoiced in being thus favored to meet again.

My story is told. My faith in the efficacy of a true peace policy in treating with the Indians is unabated. While it may be urged that it has proved a failure, the preceding pages will sufficiently show that the peace policy has not in all cases been carried out in the true spirit of peace, from the fact that our nation has not had sufficient faith in it to give it a perfect trial, but, while offering peace with one hand, has grasped the sword with the other.

Interested parties have not been wanting to keep the public mind in agitation against the Indians, by reporting deeds they have never committed; and, on the other hand, spreading among them stories of bad designs and intentions, on the part of government, towards them, which were never entertained. Until the pure principles of love and peace are recognized as the essential elements for Christianizing and civilizing men, a pure peace policy will not be likely to be inaugurated by the government, or sustained by the people.

APPENDIX.

SOCIAL LIFE AND RELATIONS OF THE INDIANS.

It may be thought that, in a work of this kind, more light might have been thrown upon the social life of the Indians than has been done in the foregoing pages; but it should be borne in mind that the writer was almost entirely ignorant of the different features of Indian life when first going among them, and the little knowledge he may have gained since was incidentally picked up, from time to time, as circumstances brought them to view. These, so far as related to the foregoing narrative, have been mentioned as the work progressed. It should also be borne in mind that the work was not designed as a dissertation on Indian manners and customs, but a simple narrative of the life of the writer among them. Yet, as something more particularly relating to these subjects may be generally interesting, a few pages here, in conclusion, will be devoted thereto, — premising this, that my observations apply only to the Indians of the southwestern Indian Territory, and more particularly to the Kiowas, Comanches, and Apaches.

Man, in whatever position he may be found, whether in savage, barbarous, or civilized nations, is pre-eminently a social being. He finds that associated action gives power and leads to success, where individual exertion would be expended for nought. Hence he gathers into clans, tribes, or nations, according to the degree of civilization or associative power attained. Every clan, tribe, or nation, having its own ends in view, whatever jealousies may exist towards others, must of necessity act in concert in all important matters relating to other tribes or nations.

The Indian is no exception to this rule. However savage he may appear to others, among his own people he is a man. The same qualities, to a very great extent, which constitute a *man* with us, make a *man* with the Indian. He stands in the estimation of his people in exact accordance with his manifestation of these qualities. He must be brave and courageous in war, wise in council, cool and fearless in the midst of danger, ardent in his friendship, hospitable to strangers, and enthusiastic in his patriotism and devotion to the welfare of his tribe.

With the chief, the affairs of his tribe become personal matters — actually his own. An affront offered to any of his people is offered to himself. Since for a friend to suffer for his misdeeds or want of wisdom is more keenly felt than if he alone suffered the consequence; revenge is more fully glutted upon a friend than upon the actual perpetrator of a deed calling for it. Hence, in his administration of justice, he takes but little pains to inflict punishment upon the perpetrator of crime, except through a friend or a relative. Though he may be barbarous in the extreme, no stranger seeking repose or refreshment in his lodge will be turned away unsheltered or unfed. In his lodge an enemy is a brother, warmed by his fire and sharing his food, and for whose defence even his own life would be risked. I myself have sought and found refuge in the lodge of a hostile chief whom I would have feared to meet alone on the plains.

Ready to supply the wants of a friend, they hesitate not to ask favors from others. Though we call it begging, with them it is not so. It is the right and privilege of friendship. As nothing is too valuable to give, so nothing is too much to ask of a friend, or appropriate in his absence. This with him is not theft. His friend would have given it. The writer, on one occasion, after buying articles at the trading-house for an Indian, had twelve dollars left, which another Indian wanted, but was refused; he then applied to the agent, who directed it to be given him. On going to camp, and explaining the transaction to the Kiowa to whom the money belonged, he exclaimed, "Ugh! All right; give it to him, he my brother."

They undertake long journeys, visit distant tribes, to renew their friendship. Such visits are received with ceremonious feasting, and valuable presents are exchanged. A horse and riding equipage, of such value in the eyes of the owner that money could not purchase them, are cheerfully given to a friend, upon an expression of admiration.

The people belonging to the same chief encamp together, and sometimes several chiefs belonging to the same tribe, with their people, dwell in the same camp. Good feeling prevails among them: no disputes; no quarrelling. They love company, and visit much from lodge to lodge. It not unfrequently occurs that the people of several lodges eat together. They go to one to eat meat, to another for bread and coffee, and so around. No one in camp is deficient in food while another has it. The manner of partaking is worthy, perhaps, of description. The company is seated, or squatted, rather, around on the matting that forms the beds at night, their feet gathered under them. Short boards or thick pieces of hide are placed before each one; the meat is taken out of the kettle by the fingers of the woman who officiates as cook, and apportioned to each one, and placed before him; bread is apportioned out, and cups for the coffee furnished to each. The party is some time in partaking of the meal, which is enlivened by much conversation, amusing tales, and laughter, while the meat is torn to pieces by the teeth and fingers, sometimes with the assistance of a knife. On the arrival of a visitor, no matter what his business or of what tribe, food is set before him, and after he has rested and refreshed himself he may explain his business.

Their taste being, in some respects, rather obtuse, the flesh of which they partake is not objected to, even though it be too long since it was killed, or even whether it was killed at all. Many a buffalo calf, dying with its mother, is thus served up. They have no idea of being filthy in their habits, as who has? What if they did not wash their hands before mixing the bread, or taking up the meat? Meat is meat, and, therefore, clean. No matter if it has been carried thirty or fifty miles, swinging and flopping upon the sides of a mule, until covered with dust, sweat, and hair; it needs no washing, or at least gets none, before being put into the camp-kettle. If the hair, boiled into strings and served up with the beef, is unpalatable, it is quietly taken out of the mouth, and thrown away. Hair is clean, dust is clean. If dirt is, as has been defined, matter out of place, there is none in an Indian camp; for what can be out of place where nothing has a place?

As might be expected of a people whose subsistence depends upon the chase, they are not particular as to the kind of meat used, unless proscribed by "medicine." The buffalo, antelope, or deer, has the preference; if these cannot be obtained, a pony or mule, a dog or a wolf, supplies the deficiency; and even the poor little land tortoise does not come amiss. To the latter I became somewhat partial, from the fact that, being thrown into the fire alive, and roasted with his shell on, there could none of their filth be introduced. Do not consider this act cruel. A tortoise thrown into a hot fire, with his back down, never struggles, or gives any indication of pain, but is apparently dead immediately, while he would live for hours with his head severed from his body. The Kiowas and Comanches do not eat birds or fish, neither does the Kiowa eat the flesh of the bear. They are forbidden, in the code of *laws*, as unclean — tabooed — or, in plain Indian, "bad medicine." Hence with them the wild turkey is valuable only for its feathers, which they use to wing their arrows.

After a meal, water is always offered to all who have partaken of it, to rinse the mouth and wash the hands. After this the pipe may be in order, but not necessarily. If it be introduced, the women withdraw, and some important subject is discussed. The pipe is always circulated from one to another, from the right towards the left.

The chiefs and principal men in a camp always have a smoke in the evening, in which every one observes his "medicine," or religious vows, made upon some occasion of sickness, danger, or enterprise, in which spiritual aid was invoked, and a vow made if successful. A medicine-man belonging in the camp prepares the pipe, and lights it, often burying a pinch of tobacco, taken from the bowl of the pipe, in the ground, as an offering to their mother, the earth, and after lighting the pipe, blows a whiff or two of the smoke upwards, to the Great Spirit, and another towards the earth, and passes it to the one at his left hand, who performs some peculiar ceremony in accordance with his "medicine," and passes it on; each in turn takes the pipe, until it reaches the one nearest the entrance of the lodge, when it returns, passes the medicine-man to the extreme right, whence it commences another round. Plans for the next day are agreed upon, and other matters relating to the tribe are talked over, while the pipe is circulating. Social conversation, tales, &c., are in order between the times of smoking, or after each pipeful has been exhausted. Thus the evening is spent with the old men. In the morning, an old man walks out in front of his lodge, and, in deep, stentorian tones, announces the plans for the day, as agreed upon the evening before.

In the matter of dress, though apparently cumbrous and disgusting to civilized eyes, it is pretty well adapted to their mode of life. Their out-of-door life is chiefly spent on horseback, and while the mornings and evenings are cool, the middle of the day may be hot; the blanket is easily dropped from the shoulders when too warm, and brought up again when cooler. It is also better adapted to camping out at night than any garment cut to fit the body, allowing of greater ease and freedom of motion, besides making a softer and warmer bed, without an extra outfit. Their ornaments are heavy, cumbrous, costly, and, many times, inconvenient, especially those of the warriors.

They wear a profusion of rings on their fingers and in their ears, from the latter of which hang small brass chains, terminated by small pieces of tin, or German silver, cut in fanciful forms. They also wear a heavy ornament upon the breast, made of sea-shells, turned into the form of pencils, and drilled or bored through from end to end, and known to traders as hair-pipe. Many of these are strung on leather, and suspended from the neck, so as to spread over the breast. These pipes being costly, such an ornament often costs from sixty to one hundred and twenty dollars. Their moccasons and leggings are usually ornamented with beads and fringes, which are differently made by the different tribes, so as to indicate the tribe of the wearer. Hence a moccason, a war-bonnet, or an arrow lost by a raiding-party, and found, leads to the discovery of the tribe of the depredators. Small bells are often worn on the fringes of the leggings, making a tinkling as they move about. The women wear brass wire upon their arms as bracelets. These are cut of the right length to reach around the wrists, one a little larger than another, and reach one third of the way to the elbows.

The scalp-lock of the men is worn in a long, heavy braid, hanging down upon the back, while the side-locks are carefully wrapped in fur, or strips of cloth of different colors, and hang down in front of the shoulders. One or both of these side-locks are severed in mourning, and burned or buried with the dead — the only occasion of cutting the hair. They scarify their faces, breasts, and arms, and smear themselves with their own blood, on the loss of near friends, and sometimes cut off a joint of a finger: this last is practised by the Cheyennes and the Kiowa women. During the season of mourning all ornaments are put away, as well as all gayly-colored clothing. These are usually burned or buried with the dead. The mourner wanders alone, in solitary places, giving utterance to the most dismal wailing. However they may have felt towards an individual while living, when dead he is always spoken of with praise, though his name is seldom uttered by them. They are animated in conversation, and sometimes imaginative. Exploits of former chiefs form a large portion of the evening entertainment, and are greedily listened to by the young, who, through the natural vividness with which youth receive exciting events, in telling them in after life are apt to get them exaggerated. Hence the deeds of former times far exceed those of the present degenerate days. Traditions are also told over to the young by night, some tribes refusing to tell them in the daytime.

The young men and warriors have many games of chance, which they play, accompanied by singing and sometimes drumming; these are often continued throughout the entire night. Indeed, in large camps of from one hundred to two hundred lodges, seldom a night passes without hearing the sound of the drum, continued until long after sunrise.

The girls and young women are not without sports, different, it is true, from those of the young men, but equally exhilarating. The children, of both sexes, have their evening dancing fires, where they exercise until late in the evening. Night, indeed, is the season for mirth, revelry, and voluptuous enjoyment in an Indian camp, and there is usually more noise then than in the daytime. Day sports with the men consist of horseracing, and exercising with the bows and arrows; with the women, of ball playing. Most of their sports, except the last, and their dancing, are a species of gambling, in which horses, blankets, robes, bows and arrows, in short every article of value, are wagered, won, and lost. Perhaps I ought not to have excepted from the latter class of sports the young women's game of ball, as here many a heart is smitten by the blind god and lost. A little past the middle of the afternoon of a pleasant day, the work having been accomplished, except the preparations for the evening meal, all the belles of the encampment, in their best and most showy attire, and highly decorated with paint and ornaments, armed with a crooked club, assemble on the ball-ground. This is a level piece of ground just outside of the camp, which has been freed from brush and other impediments to the coming conflict. Several old women, having charge of young children, gather in groups around. Stakes are set twenty rods apart, preliminaries arranged, the party divided, and the game commences. This is a violent contest, by each party, to drive the other to its home stakes, by scrambling, running, kicking, and knocking the ball from the ground with their clubs. Some of them acquire such expertness as to send it half way to the stake with a single blow.

As the game goes on, the ground becomes surrounded by spectators of the other sex, who watch, with excited eagerness, the activity of the fair (?) combatants. Some of the latter, by their clumsy gait, awkward and ill-directed efforts, secure to themselves various appropriate epithets, of no over-pleasing character, from the old women, while the graceful figure and movements of others, with their well-timed blows, raising the ball high in the air, far above the reach of the opposite contestants, towards the goal of victory, — whose gay colors always show at the right place, at the right moment,— win for themselves more pleasing and equally appropriate encomiums from them.

The young men are silent witnesses of the contest, which ends abruptly on the setting of the sun. Their ears were also open to the remarks of the old women. If the heart of any one of them is touched with the tender passion, he seeks acquaintance and cultivates a friendship with a brother or other near relative of the maiden, tells him of his love, and by the gift of a pony, or some valued present, procures his good offices as a friend, to intercede in his behalf, not only with the object of his affection, but with her parents. *He* magnifies the bravery, strength, courage, success in the chase, and other good qualities of his friend to his parents, conveys to his sister some present from him to herself, with information of his love and the number of ponies he possesses, and finally gives *him* an invitation to the lodge. If a favorable impression has been made, he is met at the entrance of the lodge by the object of his love, who takes his horse, unsaddles it, and lariats it out, while he is invited into the lodge by the father or brother. If she is not duly impressed with a sense of his worth and tender affection, she is not seen. Should the course of love run smooth, eventually, perhaps not for weeks, a contract is made; her value is extolled by her mother, while her father, anxious to drive as good a bargain as possible, fixes her price in ponies, blankets, or other articles of value. Terms agreed upon with the parents, he at length offers to give her all the ponies she wishes, and she names two, four, six, or eight, as she happens to fancy; he promises to buy calico, beads, paint, &c., for her, whenever she wants them, and she finally becomes his wife, without other ceremony, and they go off to the plains after buffalo.

A quantity of meat and a number of skins secured, they return to her father's lodge, where she dresses and prepares the skins for a lodge. Eventually a new lodge appears in camp, and the tribe numbers one more family. Of course, in such matters there must necessarily be a great variety of proceedings; but the description above given shows the general practice of those tribes with which I have been most acquainted.

Sometimes a young man is poor, not able to give any ponies, and if his love is reciprocated, he elopes with her, and his friends have to settle the matter with her family, by conciliating their ire, for his having dishonorably stolen their daughter, with ponies and other valuable gifts. After this he is in no danger, and may reside in the camp of her people.

When a man takes a wife belonging to another tribe, he goes and lives with her, as his own tribe hold him thereafter in light esteem. Among most of the tribes a man may have more than one wife, and in some instances as many as six; usually each wife has a separate lodge, in which she and her children reside, while the lord of the family is at home in any one of them, and occupies them at his pleasure.

Among the Comanches frequent instances of desertion occur, but it is of more seldom occurrence with the Kiowas and Apaches. Parental affection is very strong, and more strongly manifested towards the boys; both parents are proud of a son — a young warrior — who may become a great man in his tribe, while in a daughter they see only the advantage of the servile assistance in the household. As a consequence, the girls are brought up to labor, while the boys, furnished with bows and arrows, are allowed unrestrained liberty, and are very seldom, if ever, corrected. They may tyrannize over the girls, and, as the future lords of the tribe, are seldom chided in any respect. If any one of them, however, becomes unbearably insolent, on some occasion when the principal men are together, and he is present, he becomes the subject of cutting sarcasm, to which he cannot utter a word, and from which he may not withdraw; he must endure until he most heartily abhors himself. Eventually he learns to conduct himself with more becoming dignity and decorum.

A young man withholds his opinion in the presence of his seniors. At length, after having sat in the councils of the chiefs, and been urged to give his opinion, he answers, "I am a young man: I have not wisdom to speak before wise men; yet I think," so and so.

In their arrangements and general economy they have no system or method, but are governed according to the dictates of the moment, or as the occasion may demand.

Their ideas of religion are vague and unsatisfactory. They believe in a multitude of good and evil spirits, each class having a great chief, by whom they are controlled. These spirits rule the affairs and destinies of men. The Great Good Spirit brings about all that is good or beneficial to men, as health, peace, plenty, and happiness, through the medium of inferior good spirits.

All good and useful animals were made by him for their use, while such animals as the panther, venomous serpents, and reptiles were made for the injury of men, by the bad spirits. The flesh of such animals is not fit for food, hence is proscribed by their "medicine." All the evils to which they are subject, as sickness, war, hunger, and distress, are brought upon them through the influence of evil spirits. Hence their system of religion involves no particular duties further than that the aid of the Good Spirit is to be invoked, and the wrath and enmity of the evil must be appeased. They believe in a future existence, but I could never ascertain that they have any idea of accountability. Their religious observances and superstitions are denominated "medicine," and are "made" by all, in some form or other; but the medicine-man or sorcerer is expected to conduct all important "medicine making" for the tribe. The medicine-man is not only the physician, but the priest of the tribe, and takes much pains to lock the whole system in mystery. They powwow over the sick, make medicine for rain, for success in the chase, raiding, and for the protection of their warriors. This is done by some mysterious process, by which the enmity of the evil spirit is appeased, and the protection of the good secured. A charm is worn, by which the individual may be recognized by his protecting spirit; nearly every person, old or young, wears something of this kind, and attaches them to his war-horse.

Their system of medicine involves a belief in witchcraft, sorcery, and supernatural agency. Almost every object in nature is the dwelling-place of a spirit. Animals know this, and make medicine for their protection before engaging in any conflict with each other. The buffalo chief, while leading his herd, meets another. Each bellows forth his defiance, stops, tears up the earth with his horns, gets down upon his knees, rubs his shoulders in the dirt thus loosened, with his fore feet paws it over his body, filling his hair with dust and dirt. This is his war medicine. He then rushes to the combat. Sometimes both are killed, sometimes one ; oftener one gives up conquered, and slowly limps away, while the conqueror triumphantly leads away both herds. The Kiowa learns his war medicine from the buffalo. After discovering his enemy, he stops, re-covers his body with war-paint, which he carries about his person, and which he has not bought from a trader, but dug from the earth.

The earth is the mother, not only of men, but of animals. The mother is the natural protector of the young. The buffalo, by loosening the dirt with his horns, and the Kiowa by digging his war-paint, calls the attention of his mother to her child; and, by covering himself with some of her elements, clothes himself for the battle with her spirit and power. Such is the regard of the Kiowa for the earth, that, as they have repeatedly told me, no one of them will kill a person while he is digging in it. He will attract his attention in some manner, and having made his own medicine, cause him to cease digging and to look up. When he looks up his medicine is made, and they are on even footing for the contest.

A round ball is sometimes found in the stomach of a buffalo, which, after being removed, becomes hard, and resembles, except in weight, a smooth round stone: this, whatever its origin, is regarded by the Indians as his medicine of life. Their idea is, that it renders it very difficult, if not entirely impossible, to kill him. A buffalo is sometimes pierced through and through with arrows or bullets, and still has strength to fight furiously in his own defence. If, however, he is overcome and vanquished, his stomach is searched thoroughly for this remarkable stone, as they call it, which the Indians suppose he has swallowed. If one is found, it is taken possession of, not only to attest the power of the man who has it, but also to render him invincible in battle. I have seen these medicine stones three inches in diameter.

The Comanches regard the wolf as a brother, who many times evinces the warmth of his brotherly affection by warning them of impending evil. In their journeys, should a wolf spring up before them, look at them, and bark, or howl, as he sometimes does, they will turn their course, and travel no farther in that direction on that day. The wolf has warned them of danger, and they must heed the warning. As it was not my design to make a treatise of their superstitions, perhaps what has been written in this respect will be sufficient to render intelligible their ideas of religion, and what is meant by the use of the word "medicine."

The Indian has been described as being grave and brave, possessing a lofty independence of character, and a stoical insensibility to pain. Without here speaking of the other qualities of his nature, so far as my acquaintance and observation extend, the Indians of the southwest, while they may be grave in important councils, are sociable, lively, and even jovial in conversation, and as much enjoy a joke as any class of people I was ever among, provided it does not cut their pride too closely, and are as capable of turning their wit to their own account. While I do not intend to reproduce much that has passed before me in proof of this position, I propose to introduce a few anecdotes illustrative of their superstitious notions, and the peculiar humorousness of their character.

ANECDOTES.

THE SIGNAL STATION AS A WEATHER FACTORY.

THE Cherokees, though perhaps the most advanced in the arts of civilization of any tribe in the Indian Territory, are still very superstitious, and firm believers in the power of "medicine," as the following will illustrate: —

When the signal station was being built at Fort Gibson, in their country, some one, in a joke, told the Indians it was designed for a weather factory, and when it should be completed and in working order, the white people would be able to control the weather for the whole Indian country. A few days after its completion and equipment, a tremendous storm set in, accompanied by a heavy rain-fall of some weeks' continuance. The Indians attributed so unusual a storm to the strong "medicine" of the sergeant who had charge of the station, and determined on putting a stop to such proceedings by killing him and destroying his Weather Factory. Accordingly they assembled in large numbers, and were prevented from the execution of their object only by the firmness of the commander at the fort. Though the object of the station and its appendages was fully explained to them, many of the Indians still look upon it with suspicion, and regard the sergeant with great awe, as being a most powerful "medicine-man," capable of bringing another deluge, and drowning the entire nation.

BAD MEDICINE IN QUIRTSQUIP'S CORNFIELD.

At the council held at Fort Sill, in the fall of 1873, Quirtsquip, a Comanche chief, made complaint to Commissioner Smith, that Washington, while he was there, made promise to him that the agent should make him a house and a cornfield, and he would like to see something of it. The commissioner inquired of him if his agent had done nothing for him. He replied that the agent did make him a little field, and he came and sat down by it. There immediately arose the most terrific thunder-storm he ever knew, right over that field. He looked about, and it was all clear everywhere else; but just over his field and lodge the clouds whirled, and the lightning and thunder were awful. When he saw that it was clear all around, he concluded there was "bad medicine" in the field, decamped, and had not been back to it since.

Caddo George on the White Man's Road.

In the summer of 1871, Caddo George, having had a field made, raised some corn to sell. He accordingly went to Shirley, the trader, and contracted his corn, and was furnished with a corn-sheller to shell it, and sacks to put it in. In due time the corn was delivered, which, from some cause, weighed unusually heavy. George, however, was paid in goods, at a heavy price, corresponding with the weight of the corn.

When the sacks were emptied, — which was not done for some days, — a large stone was found in the middle of each sack, fully accounting for the greater weight of the corn. George was called to an account by the trader, when he acknowledged to putting the stones in the sacks. He stated that, having started on the white man's road, he thought it was a pretty good road, and was anxious to follow it up. He accordingly watched the white men, in order to learn it well. The trader had cheated him a great deal, and he thought it was part of the white man's road, and he would try and cheat him just a little. The logic was good, and as George had been paid, the trader could recover nothing, and had to consider the explanation satisfactory.

WHAT BECAME OF THE CATTLE.

At the time of the council held at Old Fort Cobb, on the Washita River, in the summer of 1872, rations ran short, and a small party of Comanches were sent into the Wichita Agency for a supply of beef. The acting agent turned out eleven head of cattle to them. On their way out, passing a Caddo farm, they saw a quantity of watermelons, of which the wild Indians are passionately fond. The sight of this luscious fruit was too strong a temptation to the Indian, to whom the cattle had been intrusted, and he immediately struck up a bargain for what melons he and his companions could eat, giving five steers for them. While engaged in eating the melons, another got away, and they saw no more of him; so that they went on to the council with only five, instead of eleven beeves. The paper he brought from the acting agent giving a greater number than they delivered, led to an investigation of the subject. The leader of the party explained the transaction, pleading as a palliation for the offence that he did not make the trade so much because he wanted the melons, as to encourage the poor Caddo to keep on in the white man's road, which he was working and struggling to follow. He was surprised that the white chief should call him to account for doing what appeared to him to be a meritorious deed. Ten Bears, the head chief of that band of the Comanches to which the party belonged, then took the subject up, and said he was surprised that a "big fuss" should be made for what appeared to him to be a praiseworthy act. He thought the deed in itself indicated an advancement in the white man's road beyond what he had an idea any of his people had attained. If he had been following the old Comanche road, he would have stolen the melons, instead of paying liberally for them. This was putting the case before the commissioner in a new light, and as nothing more could be done, the Indian was fully exonerated.

Why they Cried.

Several years ago a delegation of wild Indians were induced to go to Washington. On their way, as usual, they stopped a short time at Philadelphia. A worthy Friend of that city, anxious to cultivate good feelings with them, invited a couple of the prominent chiefs, with an interpreter, to dine with him. Upon the table was some horseradish served in vinegar. One of the chiefs, at the suggestion of the interpreter, who wished to see some sport, helped himself to this rather largely, and taking a mouthful by way of tasting it, it proved rather pungent, and brought the tears to his eyes, accompanied by some contortions of physiognomy, which attracted the attention of the other, who asked what he was crying about. He replied he was crying about his father, who was killed some time before. The other thought he would try the horseradish, and it having the same effect upon him as upon the first, he was asked, "What for you cry?" "O, me so sorry," he replied, "you no die when your father did."

White Man's Medicine Biggest.

One of the chiefs who went with the delegation tc Washington, in the fall of 1872, told Agent Tatum, on his return, while narrating the wonders of the trip, that the white man's medicine was far ahead of Indian medicine. He said that when he was in Washington, a nice suit of clothes and many other nice things were given him, and a fine trunk was furnished him to put them in. He thought a great deal of them, and anticipated having a fine time exhibiting them to his people, when he got home. When he went to get into the cars, a couple of men jerked it away from him, gave him a little piece of brass money, and threw the trunk on to a kind of cart with two wheels, and ran off with it, and he saw them throw it into a little house on the other side of the platform; at the same time he was hurried into the car, which started off without his truuk. He felt very badly, and kept thinking what a strange people these white folks are, to give him nice things and then steal them away from him. He still kept that little piece of brass money, but just before getting to Kansas City a man came around gathering up all these little pieces; the interpreter told him to give him his; he did so, and received a little piece of paper, which could be of no use to anybody, as it was not big enough to make a cigarette of. The cars stopped, and he was taken to a hotel. There were great piles of trunks, and among them was the very trunk that was stolen from him and thrown into that little house in Washington. How it ever got there he could not tell, but was certain of one thing, "There was the biggest medicine in that he ever saw in anything."

One Place where White Man cannot go.

A number of years ago an Arapaho chief asked a commissioner, who had been sent to the Cheyennes and Arapahoes, what the white people thought of a future state. He replied that those who were good, — loved the Great Spirit, did not murder, lie, steal, or cheat, — when they died, would go to a good place, where there would be no sorrow or pain, and would always remain happy; but those who murder, get drunk, lie, and cheat, when they die will always be miserable. The chief, who had never seen a white man who did not answer the latter description, burst into loud laughter, at the same time clapping his hands with delight. The astonished commissioner inquired what he was laughing about. "O, me so glad!" he replied; "one good place where white man no come."